MW00629331

of CABBAGES
& KIMCHI

of CABBAGES
& KIMCHI

A Practical Guide to the World of Fermented Food

James Read

Illustrations by Marija Tiurina

PARTICULAR BOOKS

It Starts with a Fizz...

SITTING IN MY KITCHEN, I can just hear the occasional muted bubble pushing its way out of a kimchi pot airlock. It's barely noticeable, a faint background burp escaping a couple of times a minute, like a tiny, slumbering drunk uncle. This hushed sound represents a hive of activity taking place inside, as raw cabbage, chilli flakes and garlic turn into a sour, savoury, fizzy jar of joy. It's the sound of fermentation, of living food, of an unpaid microbial army getting to work.

We usually see food as something that once was living and growing, that we harvest, stabilize and stick in the fridge. Fermentation, however, flips this, breathing new life into inert ingredients, rejuvenating and transforming them into something effervescent and alive. It is culinary alchemy.

The satisfaction of cooking and sharing food is a wonderful thing, and part of that is giving the gift of your time. All fermentation takes time, whether a few hours for yogurt, or many months for soy sauce – and so it offers the sense of delayed gratification otherwise found making sloe gin or Christmas cake. But more than this, there's another sense of achievement, one more familiar to gardeners than cooks, which is that of having grown something yourself. The prickle of contentment when doing a morning check on your sauerkraut or hot sauce and hearing the little 'phut' as you open the jar which heralds the beginnings of fermentation is a bit like seeing the first hints of fruit bursting out of the flower of a tomato plant.

If you prefer to think of fermentation as a weird, folksy relic of the past, from a time of larders instead of fridges, when food was either tinned or entombed in aspic, I'm afraid to break it to you that the practice is still very much at large. In fact, I can almost guarantee that you've eaten or drunk something fermented today, whether it's bread, chocolate, cheese, salami, olives, wine or coffee. It can be simple, it can be complex, but it is completely basic to almost every food culture on Earth.

While it's true that fermented foods continue to be integral to our cuisine, so many of them have been dried, pasteurized and essentially neutered by industrial processes and the demands of global supply chains. The ones that have survived and thrived are predominantly those which can be brought to the heel of mass manufacturing and chained to the yoke of shelf stability – typically products in which microbes naturally die, as the yeast in bread does when it is baked, or otherwise meet a more abrupt end via pasteurization, like vinegar. The foods that most interest me are the ones that arrive at our lips still brimming with life, effervescent and vital – and I'm far from alone, as chefs increasingly exploit microbes to wring exciting new flavours out of ingredients. Unlike restaurant techniques such as sous vide, however, fermentation is something anyone can do at home with little to no equipment. If you've never encouraged bacteria to grow on your food before, I'm excited for you! There's magic in the transmutation of a jar of raw cabbage into sparkling sauerkraut, and the way it continues to evolve even when we put our protean snack away in the fridge.

Our very first contact with fermentation didn't require our active involvement – it was, quite literally, a part of us. Bacteria inside our very bodies have co-evolved with us to break down otherwise inaccessible nutrients – our large intestines are full of a complex microbiome which ferments the parts of our food that we can't digest ourselves. It wasn't long before we sought external sources of fermentation too. Even as we were beginning to poke our hairy heads above the parapet of sentience, we discovered that certain fizzy, overripe fruit made us feel good, and promptly fell back down. Archaeological records show we've been intentionally employing microbes in drink preparation for at least eight thousand years, from a time when Neolithic villagers were fermenting hawthorn and chrysanthemum rice wine in central China – pickling ourselves before we figured pickles out – and not long after that we were putting bacteria to work making all sorts of other things. Since then it's become entangled in some pretty incredible bits of history, lore and legend. From Gene Simmons terrifying Russian children in order to advertise kvass, to kimchi diplomacy in the Vietnam War and kombucha aboard the International Space Station, fizzy food really gets about.

Our fascination with fermentation has led us down all manner of unexpected paths, from simply combining the discarded core and skin of pineapple with sugar water to make tepache, to cooking down grape juice, fermenting it into wine and then fermenting it again while transferring it between a series of ever-shrinking oak barrels over twenty-five years to make balsamic vinegar.

The range of fizzy flavours runs from the unmistakable funk of kimchi through to the gentle tang of Greek yogurt. While the techniques behind different fermented foods and drinks vary considerably, as you fill up a corner of your kitchen with various bubbling jars and bottles you'll find there's plenty of common ground between them too.

Fermenting can be quite an addictive habit. Like many hobbies, it will reshape how you view the world – or at least your kitchen. Suddenly tropical fruits become laden with potential for hot sauce, hardy vegetables yearn to be kimchi'd, those odd teas left in the back of the cupboard demand to be turned into kombucha, long-forgotten boozes become vinegars-in-waiting, and the jars . . . Oh the jars. You will gradually accumulate a terrible hoard of them, until you are sleeping atop a bed of variously sized glass vessels in search of fermentation projects, like Smaug jealously guarding a makeshift recycling centre. First it will be a shelf, then a cupboard, then a shed, as you collect ever more glass containers of exactly the right size or shape for this, that or the other. (I apologize in advance to anyone with whom you cohabit.)

To mitigate this inevitable hoarding, be fussy. You want big jars, of course – anything under 15cm tall will have limited potential. I mention height in particular, as the shape is important – tall and narrow is generally what you

The path to fermenting nirvana is paved with reused jars – any that are allowed to reach the recycling are, in a sense, an admission of failure.

want, because the vast majority of ferments thrive with limited access to oxygen, so the less exposed surface the better. What's more, skinny jars with shoulders allow you to wedge larger pieces of fruit or veg in the top to keep them and their more finely chopped brethren submerged in liquid, further reducing the exposed surface area, which will prevent nasties from growing. The exceptions to this are vinegar, which loves oxygen (so in this case squat, wide jars are good), and drinks like kombucha, kvass, tepache, lemonade and ginger beer, which will only carbonate when really limited air space forces the gas back into bubbles (so in this case flip-top bottles are best). You needn't limit yourself to glass though – a lot of ferments like sauerkraut and kimchi are traditionally made in glazed stoneware pots or crocks, which being designed for the purpose often also incorporate a small moat that acts as an airlock (allowing air out to release pressure, without letting any back in), which saves you from 'burping' jars.

There are few feelings more satisfying than seeing the first bubbles of life in a fresh ferment.

Sometimes the shape of your container won't alone keep boisterous bits of fruit or veg from floating to the surface to escape their fizzy fate; in this case, some weights to keep everything submerged under liquid will help. You can definitely get creative. A small plate or saucer will do the job, as will a shot glass jammed under the lid, a smaller glass jar or Ziploc bag filled with water (double-bagged in case of leaks), a glass votive candle holder, those little mesh elevator things you get in cornichon jars and even a large wedged sacrificial cabbage leaf. I wouldn't use anything made out of metal, though, as many will corrode with prolonged exposure to acid. The same applies to any pleasantly proportioned flat stones you've found at the beach (limestone, for example, will dissolve).

Whatever container and weights you use, make sure they're thoroughly clean – for the most part full sterilization (i.e. ensuring that every single microbe is eliminated) is not necessary for home fermentation, as other factors (such as salt or acidity) will prevent pathogens from growing. For this reason you should be very careful with adjusting the ratio of salt in the following recipes, as it's there to prevent mould growth, and if you're on a reduced salt diet, I'm afraid you'd do better to reduce your portion size. In recipes which include it, sugar is essential to fuel fermentation – a process which will largely consume it anyway – so please don't cut it out (or worse, replace it with substitutes), as your microbes will not thank you.

Any recipes which call for water, by the way, simply mean tap water. On the basis that it may contain microbe-killing chlorine, you'll sometimes see it recommended that you should only use bottled or filtered water for fermenting things. Thankfully chlorine is very low in UK tap water; but if your water is more highly chlorinated, simply leave it out in a jug overnight and this will allow any chlorine to evaporate off.

Once you've done all the prep work, you can largely kick back while our tiny friends get to work. Occasionally human intervention will be required to guard against explosions. I read somewhere that 'you're not a real fermenter until you've mopped your ceiling'. This, thankfully, isn't a risk with most of the recipes in this book, but a few of the drinks can get rather excitable in summer – in particular, kombucha and all the libations in the tepache chapter. Kvass tends to be lazier, but my next bottle may now spite me for writing this. For these, the violently fizzy stage occurs largely once they have been bottled, and is exacerbated by warmer temperatures, excess sugar (or fruit containing sugar) and minimal space at the top of the bottle. Of course, we do want *some* fizz, so to avoid losing all carbonation when checking your bottles, it's best to just loosen the lid slightly – over the sink – if using glass swing-top bottles, or simply look for swelling if using plastic. If they have become very effervescent, try to slowly relieve the pressure by opening and sealing the bottle repeatedly, and once it's calmed right down pop it into the fridge (and then repeat the procedure, if necessary, a few hours later). Of the foods, kimchi and sauerkraut are most susceptible to pressure overloads, but the way they tend to catch you out is by capturing gas beneath the cabbage leaves so that they all push upwards and try to escape the jar as you open it. Since a high degree of carbonation is not so necessary with these, it's better to leave more headroom (at least 5–10cm) at the top of your container, so they have room to expand, and to regularly 'burp' your jars by opening them and shoving everything back down with a fork.

The temperature at which you store your ferments has an enormous bearing on the speed of their metamorphosis, and sometimes even their very character (sauerkraut made at higher temperatures, for instance, will be less microbially diverse). This is very similar to the way that bread will rise faster in a warm kitchen than in a cool larder. The vast majority of these recipes will

Cleaning the ceiling is a fermenter's rite of passage.

perform best at room temperature (18–22°C), with soy sauce needing to be kept a little hotter for the first few days, and kimchi preferring something closer to a cellar temperature.

As your hot sauce, kvass or tepache approaches the finish line, the simplest way to check whether it's ready is with the carefully calibrated equipment in the middle of your face – after a few batches you'll recognize the scents of the volatile aroma compounds that declare it is done. This varies in different ferments, but with anything involving fruit or veg you'll often detect a smell that's somewhere between pear drops and ripe bananas, with a slight sour note. If you'd like to adopt a more scientific approach, a cheap electronic pH meter will let you know the exact moment to put your pickling pot into the fridge – for most things, pH 4.4 or below is the acidity you're after.

Sampling your creation will of course inform you of its progress – the taste of kimchi changes distinctively from raw to fizzy, whereas kefir follows a gentle gradient between tasting simply of milk and becoming slightly sour and grassy, while vinegar goes from tasting alcoholic to neutral and almost watery, before acidity kicks in to let you know it's ready.

After you've made any of these ferments once, you'll have a better idea of how long they should take to be ready in your particular environment, and for this reason you may like to keep a diary of previous batches. A roll of masking tape and a marker pen are useful for creating a tearable roll of quick labels to jot down what's in each jar and when it was started. This way you can tabulate your results for each batch with fermentation durations and tasting notes. It can't only be me that finds kimchi spreadsheets appealing?

I'm confident that the recipes in this book will help you make many delicious meals. I can't promise that they will cure your ailments or help you

They might get sleepy in the fridge, but they'll never stop fermenting.

live longer, though. One frustrating thing about fermented foods is the amount of misinformation around them. They're often seen as health tonics, and wherever such claims attach themselves to food, mythology and hyperbole are sure to follow. I've largely avoided offering information about the salutary effects of fermentation, as the science is still inconclusive – especially relating to the microbiome, where research is so cutting edge that anything I write will likely need updating as soon as this book is printed. Thus, I prefer to think of fermented foods as tasty, and probably good for me.

A few things are certain though. The microbes in fermented foods won't provide much benefit or fizz if they're killed via pasteurization – but it is easier to stock them commercially that way – so *caveat emptor* if you're buying them from a shop. Also, our gut microbiome is phenomenally complex – the human colon contains one of the highest microbial densities recorded in any habitat on Earth, and these bacteria affect everything from obesity to mental health. How they interact is not entirely clear, but we do know that they benefit from a broad and varied diet, which fermented foods (obviously) can play a delicious part of. Furthermore, the very act of fermenting certain foods can unlock more of the nutrients. This is because some plants contain compounds called 'antinutrients' which block absorption of vitamins and minerals; fermentation destroys some of these, however, allowing our bodies to access the good stuff. In summary, I believe we should all be fermenting more, but I think we should enjoy the fruits of our labour rather than take morning shots of them like bitter medicine.

As you expand your fermenting repertoire, you'll start to build up a useful little culinary arsenal that can be deployed in meals throughout the week. The secret to so much great food is time. (Often you'll hear this misattributed as love. It's not love, it's time, which you tend to invest only in people that you're fond of.) It takes time to make a batch of pineapple and garlic hot sauce or oatmeal stout vinegar, but it's time that can be bottled up and dispensed later to turn a quick dinner into something really special. Most of the living ferments I love, while delicious forked straight from the jar or swigged from the bottle, are also ingredients to enliven other things. Faced with the perennial problem of what to cook for dinner when time's tight, having pre-prepared, long-lasting ingredients to hand can be a godsend.

While vinegar and soy sauce run on a timeframe of weeks or months, other recipes (like yogurt and tepache) are very quick, and you'll probably end up making them on a weekly basis. It's not by my design, but the things that take longer to brew have correspondingly long shelf lives, so you can safely make them in larger quantities. Between these fast and slow routines, you can easily end up with elements which can be combined into the same meal – my dinner last night was a plate of kefir-fried chicken, kimchi and rice with a couple of hot sauces on the side and a glass of juniper beer.

These ferments are to be experimented with not only in their implementation, but also in their very making – if you can kimchi Chinese leaf, why not Brussels sprouts? If you can brew kombucha with peach, why not mango? If you can make kvass with honey, why not maple syrup? I've included my favourite iterations, and been mindful to try and demonstrate the huge range of possibilities, but this is by no means a conclusive tract on all that's fit to ferment. I have highlighted the important ratios and philosophies to which you should adhere, but experimenting with different flavours to see how they transmute over time is one of the joys of fermentation. I hope that once you've made the recipes I've included you'll be inspired to tinker and play, and find many, many more combinations using your favourite spices, seasonal gluts of fruit or unexpected online grocery substitutions.

James Read, Harringay, January 2023

Chapter one

Sauerkraut

SAUERKRAUT, OR 'SOUR CABBAGE', is the irreducible ideal of fermented food: it's as at home in a salad as a stew, it contains only two ingredients and it'll stop you getting scurvy. What finer place from which to begin surveying the landscape of fizzy foods?

It forms a key part of the German culinary identity. Tinsel is nicknamed 'silver-plated sauerkraut' (a Christmas poem tells of how the ceremonial tree was saved from a lametta shortage by blow-drying and painting strands of sauerkraut, which is later recycled back into a New Year's Eve dinner); going for a winter's stroll to a country pub in northern Germany is called a *kohlfahrt* (which sounds like a later consequence, but means 'cabbage walk'); and farmers have developed cabbages famed for their sauerkraut, like the pointy, conical *Filderkraut* and the salt-lashed *Dithmarscherkohl* (the juice of which is also marketed by an enterprising 'krautmeister' as a shampoo, a shingles-relieving skin cream and a variety of schnapps, though this last item has regrettably been sold out since 2013).

While the name we've adopted in English positions it as a German dish, sauerkraut's true roots are less clear. The earliest mention I've found using the name is in a 1549 treatise by pharmacist, translator, architectural commentator and noted plagiarist Walther Ryff on food and drinks 'in daily use by us Germans'. Ryff mentions that sauerkraut, served as it is three or four times a day in Bavaria, makes for an unhealthy and even 'evil' diet, causing (and pardon my Middle High German here) 'coarse, thick, melancholy blood' – though maybe he wasn't much into preserved food, as he also suggests that salted dried flatfish should be 'banned by law'. Then there are those German writers who would have you believe that it's a totally Teutonic taste – 'Our noble sauerkraut / We should not omit to mention it / A German invented it / And thus it is a German food' declares the eighteenth-century poet Ludwig Uhland (while wiping away a cabbage-briny tear of pride). Meanwhile, modern German artists have made sauerkraut their muse too. In a 1969 Tokyo performance piece named *Sauerkrautpartitur* ('sauerkraut score'), Joseph Beuys placed a portion on a music stand, and proceeded to 'read'

music from it which he then conducted – the idea being, of course, that the fermented veg symbolizes improvisation and creative freedom.

Tracking its origin story further back, the primordial brine becomes murkier. At least one sauerkraut scholar proposes that it was Genghis Khan who brought the pickled cabbage to Europe during the thirteenth century, and this would follow from earlier mentions of fermented cabbage preparations in Chinese literature. However, evidence exists of non-fermented cabbage pickles in Europe from the second century BC – avowed cabbage enthusiast Cato the Elder writes so fervently about the restorative properties of dipping the stuff in vinegar that it begins to feel as if one is reading a Latin translation of Goop.

Whatever its true place of birth, sauerkraut's versatility allowed it to move across Europe with all the visa-free vim of a Schengen citizen; you'll find it on the *zakuski* snacking tables of rural Russia and in the brasseries of Paris, served up as *choucroute garnie*. It has been nurtured sufficiently in Germany (its spiritual homeland) to have evolved a couple of extra flavours – a scattering of juniper berries here, a handful of caraway seeds there – and, as it heads north, through the Baltic states, it has picked up some shredded carrots which accelerate the fermentation along a bit due to their sugar content. Maybe they were added to help the lactic acid bacteria to thrive in the chill of a Tallinn winter?

Downstream from Germany, at the eastern end of the Danube, you'll find cabbage heads fermented whole. Since this iteration is essentially a simplified sauerkraut minus the shredding, it's perfectly possible that this is the fermented cabbage progenitor. I often see these shrink-wrapped heads in Romanian, Turkish and Bulgarian grocers near where I live, and they are quite beautiful in their brassican integrity. If you want to try making it yourself, keep in mind that while this version requires less chopping, it involves more waiting, as the fermentation process takes much longer to proliferate through the dense, uncut vegetable. Indeed, versions of sauerkraut exist as far afield as Latin America – *curtido* is the Salvadoran take on fermented cabbage, bolstered with carrots, onion and oregano. Traditionally paired with corn flatbreads (*pupusas*) stuffed with cheese or refried beans, *curtido* embodies how simple, sour pickles make the perfect snack on a hot day.

Sauerkraut is generally made with the most ancient of cultivars, the simple green or white cabbage. The wild ancestor to cultivated cabbage was first found across the rocky coasts of northern Europe, as (like samphire) it is tolerant of salt – so you might say that in making sauerkraut we're reuniting the brassica with its briny birthplace. The family tree that descends from this wild cabbage has branches ranging from broccolini to Brussels sprouts, and includes the inimitable 'Jersey cabbage', which grows on stalks up to 10 feet tall. These were once immensely desirable for use as walking sticks, but as of writing only a single Jersey couple still makes the cabbage canes.

Few other ferments can claim to be such internationalists, and the reason behind sauerkraut's global appeal is, of course, that it's cheap, easy and endlessly flexible. The reasons for its popularity burden it with the same stigma borne by cabbage – it's seen as peasant food. The seeds of brassicaphobia were sown in many of our earliest memories, when Roald Dahl painted poor Charlie Bucket's pre-Wonka life as punctuated by 'thin, cabbagy meals three times a day'. By way of contrast, witness the rise of cousin kale. While one seductively curlicued cultivar has been promoted across food blogs, social media and restaurant kitchens as a smoothie-stuffing green princess, the ugly sisters Savoy and white cabbage remain markers of culinary poverty – the preserve of the frugal student, the wartime pastiche and the stew pot. Stigmatized by its raw ingredient, no one is going to get away with poshing up sauerkraut. All the better though – let's keep it uncool. Let sauerkraut be its own saviour, let cabbage be its own champion. I don't know about you, but I'm not going to let late-stage capitalism take a plate of Savoy sautéd with cumin and lemon away from me, nor this essential ferment from my fridge.

The Jersey cabbage stalk, used for fencing, rafters and walking sticks.

Though it may have somewhat fallen from grace of late, in the seventeenth century sauerkraut was very *à la mode* among French royalty. When Princess Liselotte von der Pfalz moved to Versailles after marrying the brother of the Sun King Louis XIV, she wrote to her sister in Germany, 'I have also made Westphalian-type raw hams fashionable here. Everyone eats them now, and they also eat many of our German foods – sauerkraut, and sugared cabbage (sweet and sour).' In the Grand Est of France, in Alsace, sauerkraut was thriving by now to such an extent that *surkrutschneiders* (sauerkraut 'cutters' or 'tailors') would create their own secret blends of cabbage and spices to vie for the appetites of their customers.

As well as tingling the tastebuds of jaded French nobility, the fermented veg was responsible for saving thousands of lives. In the 1750s, scurvy was becoming more of a threat at sea than piracy – during one voyage of circumnavigation, Commodore George Anson lost more than two-thirds of his 1,955 crew to the disease. This was a grim, slow demise, prefaced by the loosening of the teeth, nerve damage and the re-opening of long-healed wounds; as the body fails to produce collagen, cartilage begins to disappear and the chest collapses. Quite apart from the pain and suffering, this constant depletion of human resources was a major frustration for the British Navy, and they were desperate to come up with a cure.

A Scottish doctor, James Lind, conducted an experiment giving pairs of scurvy-ridden sailors one of six daily treatments – cider, 'vitriol' (sulphuric acid), vinegar, seawater, oranges and lemons, or a mix of seemingly random spices. Those on the citrus regime fared far better than their poor comrades, and even helped care for the other patients. Lind retired soon after to write *Treatise of the Scurvy*, which he published in 1753, and this could have been the end of the awful disease. Instead, though, he overlooked the importance of his own discovery, dedicating only five paragraphs (out of four hundred pages) to his revelatory experiment, and concluded that scurvy had multiple causes and so required a panoply of remedies. Once the book was done, he further obscured his discovery by 'refining' his results to create a boiled 'rob' of lemon juice (possibly at the behest of the Navy, as a concentrate would have been easier to transport). This elixir would have been entirely bereft of vitamin C, which is destroyed by heat.

When Captain James Cook was procuring supplies for his first global voyage on the *Endeavour* in the 1760s, he requested three tons of sauerkraut from the Admiralty in the name of scurvy research. The ship was loaded up from the Plymouth docks with provisions that also included malt (the favoured, cheapest treatment for scurvy) and Lind's lemon 'rob'. Sauerkraut's real boon was its longevity. Although it only contained half the vitamin C of fresh limes, it kept for months rather than weeks in a ship's hold.

Cook was pleased with his fermented cabbage, though among the rest of the ship's rations he hadn't fully appreciated its singular benefits. Thus, in the provisioning logs for his second voyage aboard the *Resolution*, he added a raft of items which he marked as potential 'antiscorbuticks' – 'salted cabbage, Portable broth, Saloup [a popular coffee alternative made from orchid roots], Mustard, Malt, and Mermelade of Carrots' – but also 'Sour Krout'. This he took in even more prodigious quantities than on his first voyage – on a single ship he packed nearly 8 ½ tons. He wrote, 'it is a very wholsome food and a very great antiscorbutick, a pound of it is served to each man each Beef day' (Tuesdays and Saturdays). Cook notes that sauerkraut will 'keep any length of time', which must have made a pleasant contrast to the salt beef, which was so heavily brined (in order to survive a couple of years in the hold) that it would routinely be towed behind the ship in nets for days to desalinate it.

The crew didn't take to this unfamiliar fare easily, so Cook hatched a scheme. By restricting it first to the officers' table he piqued the sailors' interest, and allowed their appetites to follow. Before long he notes, 'I found it necessary to put every one on board to an Allowance, for such are the tempers and disposissions of Seamen in general that . . . the Moment they see their Superiors set a value on [the ship's provisions], it becomes the finest stuff in the World and their inventer a damn'd honest fellow.'

Cook did not lose a single sailor to scurvy on either his first or second voyages, and, on his return to London, he made a thorough account of the methods employed to 'preserve the health of his crew'. He recognized the efficacy of sauerkraut, which would have provided the equivalent of at least 40mg/day of vitamin C – four times the minimum necessary to fend off scurvy – commenting in his report to the Victualling Board that 'Sour Krout . . . did so effectually preserve the people from a Scorbutic Taint that not one dangerous case hap'ned in that disorder during the whole Voyage'. The Royal Society awarded him the Copley Medal for his research.

In the 1780s, just as Cook's newly discovered continent was being absorbed into the British empire, the American colonies were breaking away. In Pennsylvania, where the German population was so high that the new Constitution was presented for discussion in their mother tongue, newly arrived migrants were turning to sauerkraut for a taste of home. Enterprising *Krauthobblers* ('cabbage shredders') began offering their services door-to-door to poor farmers without the equipment to process their harvest. As the industrial revolution arrived in Pennsylvania, one Henry J. Heinz began selling horseradish and sauerkraut from his wheelbarrow door-to-door, before hitting upon tomato ketchup. At the advent of the First World War, German imports and ideas fell from favour in America, and sauerkraut found itself briefly renamed 'liberty cabbage', while German measles became 'liberty measles', hamburgers 'liberty steaks', and Dachshunds 'liberty pups'. (If this sounds absurdly outdated, you may recall that Republicans, in 2003, tried to rename French fries 'freedom fries' in response to France's opposition to the US invasion of Iraq.) In spite of this culinary jingoism, fermented cabbage remained popular, and to this day it's customary in Pennsylvania to have a plate of sauerkraut for good luck on New Year's Day, while wishing your fellow diners as much fortune 'as there are strands of cabbage in the pot'.

Nowadays, cabbage is cheap, salt is cheap, water is cheap – therefore, sauerkraut is one of those rare products on which even the most frugal of manufacturers would struggle to scrimp. You should find a sauerkraut that's at least half-decent in most mid-sized supermarkets, and in any Eastern European shop worth its salt (I've listed the various names for it overleaf). The Hengstenberg brand, much loved in southern Germany for its Bavarian-style (meaning mild) sauerkraut, is also widely available in shops across Europe. Like most fermented foods, it can be tricky to find an unpasteurized version without making it yourself or venturing to a food market or health food shop; I tend to find that supermarket sauerkraut runs a little mild, so making your own will allow you to customize it to your own taste anyway.

So, sauerkraut is not exotic, rare or Instagrammable. On the other hand it's delicious, versatile and approachable. For anyone who finds kimchi a touch fiery, sauerkraut can be the fizzy slip road to the autobahn of fermented veg. Its simplicity also allows it to venture further than other fermented veg into the revivifying domain of comfort food.

British food doesn't traditionally shy away from stodge – our shepherd's pies, our toad-in-the-holes, our bangers and mash – but what we're not so good at is bright, sharp sides to cut through them. We do have our moments (e.g. vinegar-drenched fish and chips), but it's a culinary meme that's largely missing from traditional British food. It's notable that some of our favourite adopted dishes incorporate sour elements. Pita-wrapped *gyros* would not be complete without tzatziki and lemon, nor guacamole without a squeeze of lime – even the Big Mac is built upon a foundation of gherkins. Think of sauerkraut whenever you're making a big bowl of something rich and comforting – it has enormous elevating potential.

Indeed, such an array of roles exists for our fermented cabbage, that I must advise you to start making a new batch as soon as you put one in the fridge. It works as a superb sandwich-filler, performing double duty as both the sour

SOME MORE WORDS FOR SAUERKRAUT

Bulgarian	*kiselo zele*
Croatian-Serbian	*kiseli kupus*
Czech	*kysané zelí*
French	*choucroute*
Hungarian	*savanyú káposzta*
Latvian	*skābi kāposti*
Lithuanian	*rauginti kopūstai*
Polish	*kiszona kapusta*
Romanian	*varza murata*
Russian	*kvashenaya kapusta*
Slovak	*kyslá kapusta*
Slovenian	*kislo zelje*
Turkish	*lahana turşusu*

and the crunch; the Reuben (see page 33), crowning glory of the New York deli, is built around it. It's also very welcome stuffed into dumplings (arguably also a kind of sandwich), as well the pierogi houses of Poland know. Combined with raw cabbage, carrots and onion, it makes an excellent coleslaw. And soups, oh soups! I could dedicate an entire section to sauerkraut in soups – from Russian *shchi* (with mushrooms and beef, pork or lamb) to Polish *kapuśniak* (incorporating pork and *kiełbasa*) and Czech *zelňačka* (again with sausage but also paprika and caraway seeds) to Hungarian *székely goulash* (which switches the sausage for pork shoulder and doubles down on the paprika). Even *kimchi jjigae* is a Korean riff on the same theme. Wherever you stand on soups bulking up into stews, or stews thinning to soups, sauerkraut sits happily all along the continuum. Heated sauerkraut may initially seem somehow unheimlich but, once you've brooked its entrance to the pot, it will become clear that it's a classy companion for any occasion. Use it in a sauce with mussels, to fill pierogi (see page 34), or simply with pasta and bacon (as in the Austrian *krautfleckerl*). Not forgetting, of course, the redoubt of the fancy boxed bit of the brasserie menu, *choucroute garnie* (see page 36), presenting sausages and smoked meats upon a bed of sauerkraut and potatoes.

Unsurprisingly, Sauerkraut Shares a lot of its microbiology with kimchi. Both ferments are catalyst-free 'wild' ferments (though you'll find companies more than willing to sell you unnecessary starters – ignore them), and they harbour similar families of lactic acid bacteria. One of these, *Leuconostoc mesenteroides*, is the workhorse for the first 3–5 days of fermentation – this microbe is a 'heterofermenter', which means that it produces more than one thing, thus simultaneously reducing the pH with lactic acid and producing carbon dioxide (which pushes out oxygen, cutting the risk of contamination by nasties that need it). Then, once the red carpet of appropriate acidity has been rolled out, *Lactobacillus plantarum* reigns – it's a homofermenter, meaning it only makes one thing: more lactic acid. Sauerkraut which is made at higher temperatures or with more salt will see *Lactobacillus* dominate sooner, resulting in a less nuanced final product – various studies with panels of sauerkraut tasters have confirmed my suspicions to be true: that the best sauerkraut is fermented at 18–22°C using 2.0–2.5% salt. These conditions will allow complexity to develop from *L. mesenteroides* fermentation, without taking an interminably long time (as would result from a lower temperature). The last part of the process often (though not always, as is the nature of wild ferments) sees another Lactobacillus species arrive – *L. brevis* – which is another CO_2 producer, adding the last bit of fizz to your jar.

Compared to other vegetable ferments like cucumber pickles or kimchi, sauerkraut is traditionally fermented for quite a while – from one week to up to about six – so the Lactobacillus strains have much more time to work. This results in a finished product that's quite acidic – at pH 3.5 it's about seven to ten times as sour as kimchi or cucumber pickles would usually be (pH is a logarithmic scale, which means a pH of 3 is ten times more acidic than a pH of 4, and a pH of 3 is one hundred times more acidic than a pH of 5), but if you want a milder sauerkraut, sample it when it's still quite young. Once you're happy with how it tastes, putting your sauerkraut (or indeed any ferment) in the fridge will slow the souring process down to a crawl.

There are two ways to go about salting vegetables for fermentation – either you can add a larger amount of salt than you want in the end product and rinse it off once some has been absorbed (which is traditional for kimchi), or, as is the sauerkraut method, you simply add the final salt quantity at the beginning and leave it at that. As sauerkraut gained popularity in the sixteenth century, salt was still an incredibly valuable commodity, with lucrative trading routes like northern Germany's Old Salt Route being rife with bandits and tax officials (a 50% levy had caused such ire in 1451 that the Pope himself intervened), so krautmeisters would be rash to wash good money down the drain.

The desirable bacteria in sauerkraut have no need for air (they're 'anaerobic'), but there are plenty of less benign bacteria that will bully their way into your cabbage if given oxygen to breathe. So it's critical to get rid of all the air before fermentation begins – sauerkraut makes this particularly tricky, as the fine lattice of shredded cabbage creates myriad pockets to entrap little aerated oases for pathogens. This is why it's a harvest tradition in Germany to summon the children to stamp on the freshly salted leaves. While the idea of busying one's offspring with an imprecise and knife-free kitchen task may hold some appeal, a rolling pin or sturdy spoon will suffice for most domestic-scale sauerkraut stomping (and I feel any aromas added by *kinder fuß* will hardly be missed).

One root cause of the aforementioned cabbage aversion is surely the smell that it emits when cooked – caused by dimethyl sulphide, a chemical which in very low doses adds a truffley complexity to red wine, in slightly higher amounts begins to smell of the sea (because plankton also produce it), and beyond that starts to smell pretty farty. The chemical is present in much higher amounts on the outer leaves of cabbage, and the smell gets worse the longer it's cooked for, so if using raw cabbage rather than sauerkraut in a recipe, remove the first layer of leaves and don't keep it on the hob much longer than half an hour. Analysis of sauerkraut has shown dimethyl sulphide is almost entirely eliminated in fully fermented sauerkraut (though this can take 3–4 weeks, so if you're very sulphide-sensitive, aim for a mature kraut).

Another possible cause for our hostility to the cruciferous cultivar may in fact be genetic. Much as some lucky souls cannot, due to some evolutionary quirk, smell the malodorous consequences asparagus wreaks upon their urine, about half the population (including myself, happily) do not perceive cabbage as tasting bitter. The fault lies with a single gene (TAS2R38) which masks sulphur-containing compounds called glucosinolates in cabbage and other brassicas like Brussels sprouts and kale (unsurprisingly, as a glucosinnocent I love both). Happily for all, this scent is nullified by fermentation, which destroys these bitter-tasting chemicals (after 3–5 days of fizzing they're almost entirely eliminated).

Unfortunately, the chemical in cabbage (and also beans) that's responsible for unspeakable post-prandial effluvium – raffinose (a coincidental conflation of 'ruffian' and 'nose') – is hardy to the sauerkraut fermentation process. Cruel, room-clearing raffinose cannot be digested by human stomachs – it requires the enzyme alpha-galactosidase, which we do not produce (though it can be purchased in the form of some preposterously titled supplements such as Beano, BeanAssist and Bloateez). Once it reaches our large intestines, raffinose runs into gut bacteria that do possess the appropriate enzyme to break it down into gases (which some people reabsorb better than others), and flatulence ensues. There is hope for the cohabiting sauerkraut enthusiasts, however. It turns out that raffinose is not generated by cabbages simply to spite us, but to help plants resist cellular damage from frost, and they only produce it in winter – it's triggered by the shortening of daylight hours rather than cold temperatures. Summer sauerkraut may thus fill your fridge without clearing the room.

As Captain Cook found, sauerkraut is tremendously good at staving off scurvy, though it would be many years before researchers discovered that this was down to the abundance of vitamin C. The scientific name for vitamin C

Goats produce the equivalent of more than 180 oranges' worth of vitamin C every day. Humans produce none.

– ascorbic acid – is even derived from its anti-scurvy or 'antiscorbutic' properties. We humans are rare beasts, sharing the company of guinea pigs, fruit bats, and a smattering of simians as the only mammals thus far discovered that are unable to make our own vitamin C. This biological quirk is truly remarkable – thousands of other mammals happily produce their own vitamin C in large amounts (so, for the vast majority it isn't a supplemental 'vitamin' at all). It's currently theorized that the evolution of our ape ancestors didn't selectively favour this ability as they were consuming so much vitamin C in their diet. Goats are therefore (in at least this regard) far better equipped for long sea voyages than us. In light of this shortcoming, we have adapted to become incredibly efficient at absorbing and recycling the vitamin C that we can get hold of, to the extent that we can derive our quota from just one orange a day, while our seafaring goat will produce the equivalent of over 180 oranges' worth in the same time.

Vitamin C is not the only substance of nutritional value that sauerkraut provides. While cabbage has barely a third the calcium content of milk, twice as much is bioavailable to us in cabbage. Some vegetables with very high amounts of calcium, like spinach, also contain compounds (largely oxalate and phytate), referred to as 'antinutrients', that bind with the calcium, preventing us from absorbing it. Cabbage is already quite low in oxalate and phytate anyway, but fermentation is able to break down the small amounts that exist, leaving almost all the calcium available to us. However, I suspect a heaping portion of sauerkraut over our morning muesli will be a hard sell for even the most healthful among us.

In recent years there's been a huge amount of focus on the salutary properties of all fermented foods, but some have suspected this for a long time. In 1950 Miklos Worth wrote a wonderfully hyperbolic book on the stuff, subtitled 'How Sauerkraut Regulates Digestion, Prolongs Youth, The Natural Way', in which he declared that 'to our knowledge, no other food offers as much for health as sauerkraut – except cabbage, from which it comes'. He goes on to ascribe benefits to it in almost every area, from heart to lungs to complexion, observing that 'among the people who use sauerkraut as a staple food, rosy cheeks seem to be a national characteristic'. A significant portion of the curative properties Miklos ascribes to sauerkraut relate to its ability to prevent constipation, though, prefiguring current research into fermented foods, intestinal health, and the gut microbiome.

While there have since been dozens of studies investigating the potential benefits of sauerkraut on the gut, and for irritable bowel syndrome sufferers in particular, there is no scientific consensus thus far. What we know is that the ecology of everyone's microflora is uniquely complex (to the point that microbiome fingerprinting is an emerging field in forensics), and specifically that the balance of microbes in our guts is individual too. Disruption to this intestinal environment, for instance by diet or disease, has been associated with diarrhoea, gastroenteritis, constipation, inflammatory bowel disease and IBS. Probiotics – defined by the WHO as 'live microorganisms which when administered in adequate amounts confer a health benefit on the host' – can help to equalize our gut microbiome in a way that helps combat these ills. The best evidence so far shows that probiotics can shorten the course of infectious diarrhoea and ease constipation, with signs that it could prevent relapse of Crohn's disease too. Unfortunately more research is still needed to determine exactly which microbes are most helpful before we can assert which foods should help with particular conditions (and so it is probably best to eat a range of them regularly). At the very least, we can say without doubt that as a delicious, vitamin-rich food, sauerkraut should surely occupy a regular place in your fridge, but turning once more to Miklos, we echo the caveat that 'the author of this book does not advocate the sole use of sauerkraut in the daily diet, to the exclusion of all other vegetables'.

While it is, for the most part, a pleasingly simple endeavour, when making your own sauerkraut there are a few pointers and pitfalls to observe to ensure your best chance of success. There are alien species of bacteria, yeasts and moulds which would dearly love to colonize your kraut, given half the chance – but by following the instructions laid out here, they shan't get a look-in! However, if you detect off flavours/smells, extreme softness or weird colours,

The humble cabbage has too long remained in the shadow of its brassican cousins, broccoli and kale. Sauerkraut is the pedestal on which it can shine.

your poor ferment is probably hosting unwelcome guests. These generally thrive in contact with air, so you should make sure you keep all your vegetables submerged, either using weights or a well-wedged outer cabbage leaf. If you find something funny growing on the top, you might be able to scrape off the top layer and see if the good guys win out, but given that cabbage comes cheap it's probably best to pitch it and start again.

I've only once suffered from slimy or 'ropy' kraut – where it appears that someone has snuck egg whites into your jar – so I think it may be quite rare. The likely culprits are enzymes producing a sugar called 'dextran', but you usually need a bit more sucrose (e.g. from carrots) for this issue to raise its head. As long as you make sure you use clean implements and containers when making and handling your sauerkraut, use the correct amount of salt, and are fastidious about keeping your vegetables within the bounds of normal room temperature (18–22°C) during fermentation and well submerged within their brine, all should go well. There's a rumour that using iodized salt (with minute amounts of iodine added to prevent iodine deficiency) will render your ferment entirely inert. This is not the case. Similarly, anyone who advises you need to use some exotic variety of salt, such as that imported from the Himalayas, is either misguided or a charlatan.

One issue that you will almost certainly encounter with sauerkraut, especially when it's thriving, is 'heaving'. When sauerkraut produces carbon dioxide, as it should, instead of bubbling up through the brine, it tends to get trapped in the compacted veg. Eventually the entire mass is lifted up by the gas as one, forcing the vegetables to the surface and out of the brine, and even pushing the brine out of the jar. If you lose a significant amount, just make up more 2.2% brine as per the recipe below and top up. To avoid this, you should leave a good 5cm clear at the top of your container for expansion, and either weigh down your veg, or regularly push the sauerkraut back into the liquid with a clean spoon – either way, you'll need to open the jar regularly to release gas. For a more hands-off solution, an airlock lid in tandem with weights will allow your sauerkraut to breathe without you pretty well – though I find that I rather enjoy the health check of 'burping' all my jars a couple of times a day. Don't fuss them too much though – a bit of CO_2 build-up at the top will keep your jar free of nasties.

Sauerkraut

*This is a really simple ferment, but even so there's a couple of things
to take particular care over. First, try your best to shred the cabbage
evenly, so it's all equally crunchy – easier if you're using a mandoline, but
perfectly possible with a sharp knife. Second, it can be a battle keeping all
the cabbage submerged, since white cabbage doesn't put out half as much
liquid as the Chinese leaf in kimchi. If pushing firmly doesn't provide
enough, simply make up a little 2.2% salt brine (mix 500ml of water
with 11g of salt) and use as much as needed to top up. If you're partial
to caraway seeds, adding a few to the jar will lend a bittersweet nuttiness
with a hint of aniseed, whereas juniper berries impart a green, piny taste.*

TIME / 1–4 weeks
YIELD / 1.25kg sauerkraut
KIT / Large narrow jar OR
   fermenting pot (enough
   to hold 1.5 litre water)
Large bowl
Mandoline (optional)
Weight (optional, see page 9)

INGREDIENTS
1 large white cabbage
   (~1.5kg once cored
   & outer leaves removed)
2.2% salt (e.g. 33g for
   a 1.5kg cabbage)

1 tablespoon caraway seeds OR
   10 juniper berries (optional)

1/ Core out the tough centre of the cabbage, and remove the outermost
   leaves, reserving the largest one.

2/ Shred the rest of your cabbage into ~1–2mm slices. This is a very
   satisfying use of your sharpest knife, or fast work with a food processor
   slicing blade or mandoline if you have one.

3/ Put the cabbage into a large bowl, weigh, then add the 2.2% of the total
   weight in salt (and caraway or juniper, if using), and mix it thoroughly
   (don't be afraid to bruise it a bit). It will instantly begin to wilt before your
   eyes, but leave it for at least a couple of hours. You should see it putting
   out plenty of brine – if it doesn't, you need to mix it more, and even give it
   a bit of a pounding to break open some cell walls and get the salt in there.

4/ Put the cabbage and brine into your fermenting crock or jar, and press it down slowly but firmly until the liquid covers the veg entirely. Press! No, press even more. You're aiming to create something with the density of a cabbage neutron star here. The narrower your container, the less surface there will be and the more likely the brine is to cover everything. When you're done, there should still be 5cm of headroom above your brine line in the jar to allow for expansion.

5/ Put your reserved outer leaf on top of your sauerkraut-to-be, and if necessary add a weight on top to keep it all down. The aim is to keep all the cabbage entirely submerged, otherwise you'll risk mould developing.

6/ Leave your sauerkraut at room temperature, out of direct sunlight and away from radiators.

7/ After 24 hours you might start to see a bit of fizz – after 48 hours you almost certainly will. Make sure to open the container daily (or more often if it's warm) to stop pressure building up too much and creating a kraut-geyser.

8/ You can start tasting your kraut from 4 days in, but you'll probably find it won't be ready before a week, possibly longer if you prefer it really sour. You can leave it for a month or more – just make sure to keep pushing the cabbage down under the brine. Once it tastes to your liking, stick it in the fridge to slow fermentation – it will keep souring, but at a glacial pace.

TROUBLESHOOTING / If your Sauerkraut is...

Forming a white film on top of the brine (during fermentation)	This is likely something that's commonly called 'kahm yeast' (see page 170), which can be a particular problem with longer ferments. It's not harmful, but can affect flavour slightly. Skim it off the top, keep the cabbage below the brine (top up with a bit more brine if necessary) and try fermenting in a cooler spot.
Going mouldy (raised fuzziness in any colour - black, blue, green or even pink)	If you can't confidently identify anything visibly growing on your sauerkraut as kahm yeast (as above) you should discard the batch as it may be harmful. Next time, make sure you're using enough salt, not too large a jar (it should be about 70-80% full to limit the amount of air) and that all the cabbage is covered in brine (a narrower jar will help with this).
Explosively fizzy	This is normal! Gently open the jar over the sink to release pressure, push the veg under the brine and then seal it. If it tastes ready, put it in the fridge (this will calm it down). Also, keep your fermenting jar on a side plate in case of overflow.
Gathering white sediment at the bottom	These are just dead bacteria, and nothing to worry about. They lived a good life, doing what they loved.

Classic Reuben Sandwich

*Chunks of salt beef (what Americans confusingly call 'corned beef')
are ideal here, but if you don't live near a Jewish deli or bagel shop then
pastrami may be easier to obtain. The Russian dressing, source of much
confusion, is often muddled with Thousand Island, which involves
mayonnaise and is quite a bit sweeter, whereas the authentic stuff should
have a kick of spice from the horseradish (get the root rather than the
sauce if you can) – though if we're being true traditionalists it should also
involve caviar, but making a sandwich shouldn't require a loan. Most
importantly though, you do not want to use 100% rye bread – it is far too
cakey and will stick to the pan and go soggy – but rather a mixed wheat/
rye bread (often in delis it will be sourdough, and that works very well).*

TIME / 20 minutes
YIELD / Sandwiches for 2
KIT / Non-stick pan

FOR THE SANDWICHES
4 tablespoons sauerkraut,
    drained
4 slices pastrami/salt beef
100g gruyère, grated
4 pieces light rye bread
    or sourdough

FOR THE DRESSING
2 tablespoons yogurt
½ tablespoons ketchup
1 teaspoon grated horseradish
    root
½ clove of garlic, crushed
½ teaspoon hot sauce
1 tablespoon pickled
    cucumber, finely diced

1/ Mix all the dressing ingredients in a bowl and set aside.

2/ Preheat a non-stick pan on medium heat.

3/ Butter one side of each slice of bread. Spread Russian dressing on
the unbuttered sides. Next, top half the slices on the sauce side with
sauerkraut, pastrami and cheese, then close them up with the remaining
slices, butter side up.

4/ Place the sandwiches in the pan, turn heat down low and cook for
4–5 minutes, pressing with a spatula regularly to keep everything together,
then flip and repeat.

Mushroom & Sauerkraut Pierogi

I've yet to meet a dumpling I don't like, and Poland's pierogi are no exception. Sauerkraut makes an excellent filling and foil against a range of autumnal flavours. My favourite way to serve these is to make three different filling varieties and have them as an autumnal pierogi 'salad' with a bit of sour cream or kefir mixed with dill. It may sound as much like I'm a glutton for punishment as a garden variety glutton, but once you've made the dough, the fillings come together in a trice. If you find yourself in some kind of dumpling desert island scenario, and must choose just one type though, I'd go with the mushrooms – truffle oil works well with these, as the primary chemical which imparts its scent (dimethyl sulphide) is also present in cabbage.

Time / 40 minutes
Yield / 15–20 pierogi
(dinner for 2 or starter for 4)

For the Dough
145g plain flour
½ teaspoon salt
½ tablespoon butter, melted
60g sour cream

For the Filling
½ an onion, finely diced
100g mushrooms, finely diced
75g sauerkraut, drained and finely chopped
30g pine nuts, chopped
Truffle oil, to finish (optional)

1/ Mix plain flour with salt, butter and sour cream, add 2 tablespoons of water and knead gently for a couple of minutes until it comes together into a dough – if it feels too sticky, just add a tiny bit more flour. Leave this to rest in a ball for 20 minutes.

2/ Meanwhile, to make the filling, heat 2 tablespoons of vegetable oil in a pan over medium heat, then add the onions and fry for 3 minutes, stirring until softened. Next add the mushrooms and cook for a further 5 minutes, then add sauerkraut and cook for a minute more, and finally add two-thirds of the pine nuts off the heat. Season with salt and pepper and set aside.

3/ Roll the dough to 1mm thickness and cut using a circular cutter around 5cm in diameter, or a glass.

4/ Fill with about 1 teaspoon of mushroom mixture (err towards under rather than overfilling) and seal, pinching the edges together starting from the centre and moving your fingers outwards as you crimp the edges. Make sure to close the edges tightly, or they'll burst in the pan.

5/ Bring a large pot of water to the boil, and drop in the pierogis. They should be done after 3 minutes. Remove with a slotted spoon to a plate smeared with butter. Avoid the temptation to drain them in a colander – your pierogi will stick together. Scatter with pine nuts (and truffle oil, if you wish) and serve.

Some more fillings:

Blue Cheese & Walnut
Mix 130g drained, finely chopped sauerkraut with 50g crumbled blue cheese, 15g sour cream and 70g finely chopped walnuts and proceed to fill the pierogi as above.

Beetroot & Horseradish
In a blender blitz together 130g drained, finely chopped sauerkraut with 130g cooked beetroot, 1 tablespoon horseradish sauce and ¼ teaspoon paprika into a rough paste and proceed to fill the pierogi as above.

Choucroute Garnie

Choucroute garnie *(dressed sauerkraut)*, *German* schlachtplatte *(slaughter plate) and Swiss* berner platte *(Bernese plate) all follow the same principle: combining sausages and sauerkraut infinitely improves both. The French fancied up the dish after the annexation of Alsace, and would eventually create* choucroute royale *– a version of the peasant pig farmer dish which substitutes champagne for the traditional riesling. Personally, I think the wine is less important than the sausages here, so put your efforts into sourcing those. Polish supermarkets provide ripe pickings, especially for the smoked varieties which always seem to be eaten first. This is not the kind of dish that suffers too badly for substitutions though. If you find one of the cuts of pork tricky to obtain, or have a surplus of sausages, just mix and match as suits. The Estonian sauerkraut and pork dish* mulgikapsad *adds pearl barley too – a nice way to soak up excess broth.*

TIME / 3.5 hours

YIELD / Dinner for 6–8

INGREDIENTS

400g boneless pork shoulder, chopped in half

2 onions, finely sliced

4 carrots, roughly chopped into 2cm pieces

2 cloves of garlic, crushed

400ml dry white wine, such as pinot blanc/gris or Alsace riesling (not German sweet variety)

250ml chicken stock

6 juniper berries

8 whole black peppercorns

3 whole cloves

3 bay leaves

600g smoked ham hock, skinned (skin reserved), chopped in half

750g mixed sausages (French, e.g. Montbéliard or Morteau; Polish, e.g. *swojska*, *żywiecka* or *wiejska*; or German, e.g. frankfurters, bratwurst or *weisswurst* – make sure some are smoked)

400g pork tenderloin

1.5kg sauerkraut, drained (rinse it under the tap if it's very sour)

1.2kg russet potatoes, peeled & quartered

Dijon and wholegrain mustard, to serve

The day before:

1/ Cover the pieces of pork shoulder all over with ½ tablespoon of salt. Refrigerate overnight in a shallow dish – some liquid will be released.

On the day:

2/ Preheat the oven to 130°C (or 110°C if fan-assisted). Heat 1 tablespoon of vegetable oil in a very large casserole dish or oven-proof pot with a lid over medium-low heat. Add onions and carrots and cook, stirring often, for 10 minutes or so – you're looking to catch them before the onions brown.

3/ Add garlic, cook for around 30 seconds until fragrant, then add the wine, stock, spices and bay leaves, and then the pork shoulder and ham hock. It might not all quite be covered by the liquid, but nestle it in as best you can. Increase the heat to bring the pot to a simmer, then put the lid on, transfer to the oven and cook for 2 hours, turning the meat over every half hour or so.

4/ Meanwhile, heat 1 tablespoon of vegetable oil in a large frying pan or griddle over medium-high heat, and sear the tenderloin for about 4 minutes until browned on all sides, then set aside. Repeat the same process with any unsmoked sausages – they won't need as long, likely 3 minutes or so.

5/ After the shoulder has been cooking for 2 hours, add the sausages, cover with sauerkraut and replace the lid slightly ajar. Turn up the oven to 180°C (or 160°C if fan-assisted) and cook for a further 30 minutes.

6/ Next, nestle the tenderloin under the sauerkraut and give it 40–45 minutes more in the oven so the tenderloin is just cooked (63°C, if you have a probe thermometer). Meanwhile, simmer the potatoes in a pot of water for 15–20 minutes until tender, and drain.

7/ Remove the casserole from the oven and ladle the sauerkraut on a large serving platter, reserving the cooking liquid, and dot it through with the potatoes. Cut the pork shoulder, ham and tenderloin into large pieces, then arrange with the sausages over the sauerkraut. Ladle a little of the cooking liquid over and serve, accompanied by mustards.

Chapter two
Kimchi

KIMCHI WAS MY GATEWAY into living fermented foods. I made it for a pop-up restaurant one time, got hooked and before long was eating it straight from the jar. For Christmas I was given a large (or it seemed large back then) clay kimchi pot, called an *onggi*. In my excitement I made too much, so I started selling it door-to-door, tweaking my recipe until it was ready to take to shops, and now it's pretty much my full-time job. Therefore, while I love all the fermented foods and drinks elsewhere in this book, I must admit to slight favouritism here. But it is not a myopic infatuation, for 'kimchi' does not describe a single product, but an entire style of Korean vegetable fermentation. From the basic fundamentals of the kimchi method, there are myriad directions you can set your compass to. So, while you'll most often find kimchi in the form of a spicy, garlic and ginger-laden Chinese leaf cabbage fermented pickle, don't be deceived – this is only one variety of the 180 kimchis that are found across Korea. To bundle them all up into one definition beyond 'fermented food with seasonings' is tricky. The word 'pickle' makes for a good comparison, as this too describes a process which can be equally applied to everything from onions to herring, but is generally used as a briny synecdoche to mean a pickled gherkin. In the same way as pickling, then, it's helpful to think of 'kimchi' as a process – one for making vegetables (and sometimes meat or fish) last longer and taste better. As Deuki Hong and Matt Rodbard put it in their book *Koreatown*: 'Kimchi is a verb, not a noun.'

The origins of kimchi are lost to the sands of time, but the first known written record of kimchi is in a twelfth-century pastoral poem, entitled 'Six Songs on the Family Garden', which says, 'Preserved in soybean paste, radish tastes good in the summer, preserved in brine it makes a good preparation for the winter.' So not only is it by then clearly a well-established food, with seasonal variations, but the verse also highlights how the harsh peaks and troughs of Korea's climate made kimchi an ideal way of preserving harvests. Mountainous Pyeongchang, in the east, swings from highs of 33°C in July down to –29°C in January, and Seoul can be nearly as extreme on a bad year. Thus, having a way of keeping the autumn's bounty through freezing winters and sweltering summers was essential, and kimchi was the answer.

Despite appearances, Chinese leaf is more closely related to the turnip than it is to Savoy or white cabbage.

The 'cabbage' that's used in kimchi is *Brassica rapa* subsp. *pekinensis* – what in the UK we usually call 'Chinese leaf'. I've spent a long time pondering this rather beautiful vegetable (having chopped roughly ten thousand of them myself). Its ovate, curving leaves make it look more like a crisp romaine lettuce heart than its stout European cousins. Within the venerable ancestry of brassicas, it's much younger than the traditional roundhead cabbage, dating back to fifteenth-century Beijing. Occasionally you'll find it called 'napa cabbage', and even though this name is more commonly used in America, it has nothing to do with the Californian wine-growing region (which has Native American etymological roots), having instead been adopted from the colloquial Japanese word for 'vegetable leaves'. In Korean, it's called *baechu*, which is also the name given to the typical kimchi that's made with it. It has a slightly sweeter taste than garden-variety Savoy, and a little more pepperiness too.

While it's now seen as integral to many types of kimchi, chilli didn't arrive in Korea until after the 'Columbian Exchange' of the late fifteenth century, when the Spanish explorer returned to Europe from the Americas with tomatoes, potatoes and chillies (leaving smallpox and colonialism in return). The chilli likely arrived in Korea when it was invaded by Japan about fifty years after Portuguese missionaries brought it to Nagasaki as part of the *Nanban* ('Southern Barbarian') trade. Korean cuisine would transform the chilli into two magnificent ingredients – a fermented chilli paste called *gochujang*, which lends its sweet/savoury spiciness to wonderful dishes like spicy stir-fried rice cakes (*tteokbokki*) and the quintessential Korean *bibimbap* rice bowl; and a red pepper powder named *gochugaru*. This is magical stuff, truly different from any other chilli powder. It's deep cherry red in colour, and usually ground coarsely into flakes large enough to lend their hue to your kimchi without fully dissolving into it. Unlike the more common chilli flakes you might find on the supermarket spice shelf, it is seedless, so its lovely shade is totally uniform. Counting against it, though, I've discovered that it also possesses some of the less charming qualities of glitter, being able to hide away in the least likely places and becoming remarkably adhesive when wet. Days after making a batch of kimchi I'll find a fleck of it in the hinge of my glasses, or staring down at me from the ceiling.

Despite the intense colour, *gochugaru* is surprisingly mild, tipping only 2,500 on the Scoville scale – about half as spicy as Tabasco. While kimchi (or *baechu* kimchi at least) certainly has a kick, heat isn't its prime culinary directive – it's not a hot sauce or chilli oil. Correspondingly, *gochugaru* isn't just a capsaicin delivery vehicle – it also has lovely sweet, smoky notes, and it's these flavours that are really important in kimchi. I'm afraid to say though, that *gochugaru* is the only essential kimchi ingredient that you might have trouble finding – the other elusive element in kimchi, *jeotgal* (preserved fermented fish), has a couple of substitutes, but alternative chilli flakes and powders won't stand in for *gochugaru* very well. Chinese supermarkets sometimes stock it, but Korean ones are obviously a safer bet, and there are many stockists online.

Before the arrival of chilli, of course, kimchi would have been a much milder affair. Though not as globally well known, these types survive today: one of my favourites is the pale 'winter kimchi' (or *dongchimi*, see page 56) made with radish. The earliest Korean cookbook (*Sanga Yorok*, written by the royal family doctor, Jeon Soon) suggests that turnip kimchi was all the rage in the 1450s, and that 'hot vegetables' like ginger, green onion, garlic and spring onion were really taking off (as a precursor to the heat that chilli peppers would later impart). By the end of the sixteenth century, Koreans may have been flirting with cabbage kimchi, but radish is very much the mainstay – a recipe involving the leafy pretender to the throne isn't definitively recorded until much later, in 1766. Around this time, there's an explosion of kimchi creativity – experimentation with ingredients blossoms as both chilli and preserved fish become prevalent. Suddenly recipes become much more complex, with accenting flavours ranging from fresh blowfish and salted large-eyed herring to aubergine, pomegranate and pear, and herbs like Korean angelica, leaf mustard and oyster thief seaweed. By the middle of the nineteenth century, cabbage has become synonymous with kimchi, and makers begin to ferment whole heads of it to add a touch of presentational flare (or maybe due to cabbage chopping fatigue).

Much like hyper-localized pastas in Italy, over time kimchis have become heavily regionalized. For example, in the south-west province of Chungcheongdo, kimchis are typically made without fish products, instead leaning on fermentation alone to lend umami notes, and this has given rise to more delicately flavoured ingredients like chestnuts and mushrooms being used. In coastal Gyeongsangdo, kimchi tends to be more heavily salted to preserve it for longer in the hot weather. On the temperate, volcanic Jeju Island, winter seafood kimchis like abalone are popular as there's no need to ferment vegetables to store them through winter.

Kimchi isn't even limited to vegetables and fish. A favourite of mine, *kkaennip* kimchi, is made by fermenting the herb perilla – it has a strong menthol and thyme flavour which contrasts admirably against the earthy spiciness of the sauce. It's very easy to grow, so worth keeping a pot in your garden for salads, infused soy sauce (page 87) and *bossam* (Korean pork shoulder lettuce wraps).

Adding to the breadth of styles of kimchi, even the common *baechu* cabbage kimchi has different uses depending on its maturity. Kimchi reveals different flavours with age – initially the strongest constituents (the garlic and chilli) stand out, but as it ages these meld into a more rounded flavour, and as fermentation slows down the fizziness also drops off while the acidity increases, before eventually becoming quite dominant. Before it begins fermenting, it is called *geotjeori*, which is more akin to a salad or a kind of kimchi-style coleslaw, made to be eaten immediately. At its next stage, when it's fermented and fizzy, but still relatively young (at around 1–4 weeks), it's at the ripe stage, which is typically when it would be eaten. Then, as it matures further, it gets much more sour, and this opens up a whole new range of recipes. 'Old' kimchi or *mugeunji* has often been fermenting for 6 months or more, and is best for dishes like *hongeo samhap* (a preparation of steamed pork and fermented skate with old kimchi), where it contends with the pungency of the fish (which excretes uric acid through its skin, turning into ammonia as it's cured). If you're caught without any fermented skate, the slightly less intimidating (and

Though there are hundreds of types of kimchi, the most common and widely beloved is made with Chinese leaf.

phenomenally tasty) *kimchi jjigae* stew with pork shoulder and tofu is an excellent reason to forget a jar of kimchi at the back of the fridge. Its cousin *budae jjigae* (army base stew), is a riff on the recipe created in the aftermath of the Korean War using surplus US rations, incorporating ham, spam, frankfurters and even baked beans alongside the kimchi. In 1966, as South Korea was expanding its role in the Vietnam War, US President Lyndon B. Johnson flew over for a state visit and remarked that he loved the stew, giving rise to its nickname *Johnson-tang* ('Johnson soup').

The Vietnam War played an unexpected role in the evolution of kimchi technology – were it not for Korean involvement, kimchi may never have been put into a can. To entice South Korea to commit further to the war effort, Lyndon B. Johnson agreed to help fund the supply of kimchi, after president Park Chung-hee explained that, besides outdated equipment, Korean troops were being held back by their ferment-free rations. Johnson concurred that familiar food was essential for morale, and US food scientists worked with South Korea to improve their canning plants, allowing them to produce long-life kimchi that could safely reach the furthest outposts and withstand conditions in the jungle. Though canned kimchi would eventually be replaced by pouches, it's still a part of Korean military rations today.

By the early 1990s, Korean tech companies had essentially perfected kimchi storage. The 'kimchi refrigerator' was created with the specific aim of keeping kimchi in prime condition for longer, by providing lower temperatures and more stable conditions than your average fridge, which, due to the way that cold air is circulated, often has 'cool' and 'hot' spots. Instead, in a kimchi fridge, the cooling elements surround the food, meaning that the temperature is much more consistent, keeping the lactic acid bacteria in stable stasis and thus preventing the kimchi from getting too sour. Fancy models have separate temperature settings for each drawer, to allow multiple batches of kimchis to ferment (or not) at different rates. I must admit, I am really rather envious of this feature. One manufacturer even boldly claims that milk can last for months in one, though using it for anything other than kimchi somewhat defeats the point of having a fridge where you can quarantine its insistent odours away from the rest of your food.

What did Koreans do before kimchi fridges? Well, they used regular fridges, obviously, but long before that there was a more basic, but equally effective, storage method. At Beopjusa, the head temple of Korean Buddhism, a massive pot was found buried up to the lip in the ground; it was placed there in the year 720 and is said to have held kimchi for up to three thousand monks. Like the subterranean pots that many families around Korea would bury their kimchi in, it would have acted as a simple but effective refrigerator. Because soil acts as a very effective insulator, the temperature even one metre below ground is much more stable, to the point where it isn't really affected by differences between day and night. This, coupled with the salt in kimchi which prevents it from freezing, means that a buried pot is actually a fantastic way to store kimchi (as long as you don't live on the thirtieth floor of a Seoul apartment block).

Every year, Koreans get together to make kimchi in a collective practice known as *kimjang*. It could be compared to a harvest festival, but marked by communal kimchi-making rather than scythes and corn dollies. When kimchi was a dietary and nutritional staple food, making enough to ensure it would last the winter could have been a stressful time, so engaging in it with the entire town or village would have made it a celebratory affair, while counterbalancing any discrepancy in supply. As Koreans moved to cities, however, the annual event began to present some unique problems. The enormous surge in demand for ingredients meant that by the 1930s temporary *kimjang* markets would appear each November, with stalls stacked high with cabbage and radish. These were in turn accompanied by water shortages, as a whole city would attempt to wash their veg at the same time, and newspaper reports about enormous piles of discarded cabbage trimmings left over from kimchi processing. It's remarkable that even in our era of

Kimjang *is a kind of seasonally orchestrated collective labour, where communities cooperatively make and share kimchi to ensure that all have enough to last through winter.*

culinary pan-seasonality, at a time when Korea has moved from being an agrarian society to an intensely urbanized one, the tradition of *kimjang* is as popular as ever, with thousands of rubber-gloved kimchi devotees gathering around long tables in Seoul Plaza each autumn to ferment together.

Inscribed in 2013 on the List of the Intangible Cultural Heritage of Humanity, *kimjang* is a kind of collective labour, acting as a reminder of the shared power of neighbours working as one. In recent years Korea has further embraced kimchi as part of their culinary heritage, rather than sidelining it in favour of newer, more 'exciting' dishes (in contrast to trends around other nationally iconic foods around the world). An essay in an academic journal entitled 'Cultural Sovereignty of Kimchi Overcame the Power of Cheese' (brilliant already) explains that in the 1960s, when owning a camera was a status symbol, people would pose for photos and say 'cheese' (the foreign food being another indicator of affluence). However, a modern Korean family is more likely to chorus 'kimchi' as the shutter descends, the voiceless postalveolar affricate 'ch' sound being similarly followed by a close front unrounded vowel to generate a smile, but now accompanied by a note of domestic culinary pride.

Kimchi is a major export too – not just as a product, but as an idea. In terms of soft power, China has pandas, the US has rock and roll and South Korea has kimchi. Over the past decade or so, having witnessed Thailand's extraordinarily effective gastrodiplomacy program (which began in 2002 with the government handing out loans and restaurant blueprints and saw the number of Thai eateries worldwide double in a decade), South Korea has been on an international mission to spread Korean culture and cuisine (called *Hallyu*, or Korean Wave). As part of this, the World Kimchi Institute was established. The four-storey complex acts as a kind of kimchi MIT, focusing on everything from kimchi hygiene and packaging development, to its global promotion and research. Its academic staff have been responsible for papers on topics ranging from kimchi genomics to how antioxidants within kimchi could extend the shelf life of sausages. The Institute also has an economic function, working to support domestic kimchi producers in order to increase exports and reduce Korean reliance on cheaper imported Chinese kimchi (for many years Korea has run a kimchi 'trade deficit', buying up to ten times as much foreign kimchi as they were selling abroad). Much like the UK has a Retail Price Index, measuring inflation by the cost of a typical shopping basket, Korea has a kimchi index, tracking the price of kimchi constituents like garlic, *gochugaru* and salted shrimp for a family of four. The rising costs of these ingredients is what pushes more and more Koreans to buy Chinese kimchi, which can be nearly seven times cheaper (in 2016, the average kimchi export price was $3.36/kg, versus $0.50/kg when imported from China).

As ever-more kimchi is made outside of Korea, ever-increasing amounts are consumed globally. Making kimchi at home means it's possible to eat it unpasteurized, which not only tastes better, but means it remains full of living probiotic bacteria, and avoids racking up food miles too. On the subject of kimchi abroad, in 2008 the Korean Atomic Energy Research Institute had a truly ambitious plan for kimchi – they developed a special recipe for South Korea's first astronaut, Yi So-yeon, knowing that in the cold foreignness of space, it would be critical in maintaining her comfort and morale. As one researcher put it: 'If a Korean goes to space, kimchi must go there, too.' The 'space kimchi' was engineered to be bacteria-free – a technique which apparently preserved 90% of the flavour, while resulting in a less fragrant kimchi – a kindness to Yi's fellow travellers, as the ISS is not very large. The head of South Korea's Astronaut Program reckoned it would be a popular addition to the ISS meal rotation for space scientists 'tired of their bland menu' – but records do not indicate whether kimchi has remained a fixture following Yi's return to earth.

Kimchi has an amazing diversity of ingredients and microbes, which combine to create a flavour that's at once totally unique and utterly recognizable.

OF ALL THE FUNDAMENTAL FERMENT recipes in this book, kimchi has the most ingredients (still no more than six or seven, but sufficient to be 'complex' by the standards of its effervescent cousins). Looking at them, it possesses what I'd call 'active' and 'passive' ingredients – the ones that are 'active' make a major difference to the biochemical processes, while the 'passive' ones solely contribute to the flavour. Kimchi is a 'wild ferment', more like sauerkraut and kvass than yogurt and soy sauce, so it relies entirely on the native microbes that are naturally present in its ingredients – there's no starter required. You'd be forgiven for suspecting Chinese leaf to be the primary bacterial carrier, given that it's so iconic to *baechu* kimchi. However, it's actually garlic that acts as the party train for lactic acid bacteria, with ginger helping out with a limited rail replacement role, and cabbage only providing a rural weekend bus service.

Korean researchers have enumerated the microflora of a clove of garlic, and found that it contained fifty-one species of lactic acid bacteria, forty more non-lactic acid bacteria, as well as fifteen yeasts (the garlic was sourced prepeeled in their study, meaning more species proliferated, but at least twenty-six types of bacteria were identified within a newly peeled clove). Of these, various strains of *Leuconostoc mesenteroides* occur the most frequently – the very same bacteria that is found in many fermented foods including hot sauce and sauerkraut. So, we have our culprit. It's curious that garlic is such fecund ground for certain microbes, given that it's also well-recognized for its antimicrobial properties against others (like *E. coli*). As soon as you cut into garlic, a compound called allicin is formed. This happens as two chemicals, which exist in separate cells, combine together – a bit like the way a glow stick lights up after you bend it. It's a defence mechanism, which protects the plant from attack by insects (to which it's also toxic) and bacteria. The desirable lactic acid bacteria that helps ferment kimchi is resistant to allicin's effects, however, meaning that garlic actually encourages these strains to thrive by killing off their competition. Allicin is also responsible for a large part of garlic's smell, and when it reaches your stomach it breaks down into an array of sulphurous compounds which give rise to garlic breath (as well as sweat and urine, if you eat enough). Incidentally, you can mitigate this by drinking full-fat milk after (or for best results, with) garlic. In kimchi, you'll notice that the garlic tastes quite strong before it is fermented, but once ready it becomes much more harmonised with the rest of the ingredients – indeed, this is one of the simplest ways to easily tell that your kimchi is done.

Curiously, while garlic provides a kickstart, the red pepper flakes actually slow down the early stages of fermentation (although not the latter stages), allowing kimchi to become more microbially diverse and in particular, more habitable to the bacterial genus *Weissella* – a group so intrinsically linked with kimchi that two unique species which were discovered in 2002 were named *Weissella kimchi* and *Weissella koreensis*.

The microbial activity that kimchi processing promotes, which prevent the vegetables from simply rotting, are impressively multi-faceted – especially given that they were developed without any knowledge of what microbes were. First, the kimchi is salted. This is usually done by 'direct salting', which is to say, simply rubbing salt into the vegetables if they have a high water content, like cabbage; however, if the kimchi is being made with veg that won't put out a lot of water when salted, they can be 'wet brined' in salty water instead. Either method achieves the same results. This briny stage kills off plenty of bacteria, but, critically, not the strains needed for fermentation, which then have free rein to get to work without too much competition. The amount of salt used is important in determining the final quality of the kimchi, as it is both a powerful way of selecting the right microbes, and controlling the speed at which they work – if too little is used the kimchi will ferment too quickly and become very sour. Around 2–3% salinity is the ideal ratio in the final product, but because some of it will be rinsed off, recipes will start with more salt than this.

After salting, the second most powerful 'lever' that we have to control how kimchi ferments is temperature. Compared with some fermented foods, kimchi is fairly relaxed about warmth – unlike soy sauce or yogurt it doesn't require onerously high temperatures or particularly narrow bounds, but this isn't to say that warmth has no effect. Like any of us on a winter morning, the good bacteria in kimchi can be slow to get going in colder climes. On the other hand, while kimchi will very happily ferment at up to 30°C, at these higher temperatures it will do so incredibly quickly, in around a day, but taste a bit one-dimensionally sour. By shooting somewhere in between, you'll end up with a broader range of microbes and a finished product that doesn't become overly tart too quickly to be eaten at leisure. I've found that temperatures around 10–15°C yield the best kimchi.

The final tool with which we can control how our kimchi ferments is the simplest – patience. If your kimchi isn't ready yet, you can of course just check back in with it tomorrow. If you've got a shed or cellar in your house where it can cruise along at 10–15°C, it should be ready in about nine days. Much cooler than this, it will take forever to ferment. You can make great kimchi at room temperature too, where it should be ready in as little as two or three days – it will likely be fizzier, as the microbes which produce a lot of carbon dioxide thrive in these warmer conditions. As it ferments, you'll notice the taste of kimchi changes distinctively from raw to tangy and rounded, and after a few batches you'll become familiar with the scent of volatile aroma compounds that declare it is done. The scent that tells me kimchi is ready is somewhere between pear drops and ripe bananas, with a slight sour note.

Once your kimchi is as fermented as you like, refrigeration will slow the process right down, though it will still continue to crawl along (which is why you may still need to open the jar in your fridge every so often to let gas escape, especially if it was initially fermented at a higher temperature). Different people prefer it at different stages of maturity, and there are some great recipes (like kimchi *jjigae*, see page 60) that really benefit from your ripest kimchi vintages. As it ages, it turns from bright red, crunchy and tangy, to a deep maroon as it softens and becomes really sour. I'm yet to have any good kimchi turn bad, though – it just seems to be very stable stuff.

At a microscopic level, the timeline of kimchi fermentation goes something like this. In the early stages, *L. mesenteroides* is first out of the gates, along with some other *Leuconostoc* species, and these are responsible for creating initial acidity. As the pH drops, they hand the baton to other bacteria (primarily *Weissella koreensis*) which help push the fermentation process along, further lowering the pH to below 4.4, at which point it becomes largely out-competed by a third major player called *Lactobacillus sakei*. While this is what most commonly happens, the degree of variation between different kimchi samples is huge – bacteria that are present in one batch may never show up in half a dozen others. In relation to this, there's a common phrase to describe the idea of food being 'hand-made' in Korean cuisine – *son-mat*, which means 'hand taste'. Expanding on the Western concept, it has as much to do with literally imparting a flavour with your fingers as the idea of food being made with care and attention. As kimchi-making involves a lot of manhandling, the concept of *son-mat* is particularly apt. It's much easier to get *gochugaru* in between each cabbage leaf by hand than it is using a spoon or spatula, and that's how it's traditionally made. Our skin is part of our microbiome, and plays host to our own unique mix of microbes – there was a great experiment conducted by the Radiolab podcast where they established that a simple handshake could alter the microbiota (the community of microbes) on someone else's skin for months. In much the same way, it's easy to see that the bacteria on your hands could affect how your kimchi turns out, giving it a more literal 'hand taste'.

The constituent elements that make kimchi (*baechu* kimchi specifically) taste the way it does are sour, spicy and savoury (or 'umami'). The acidity balances and brings out other flavours, and fermented foods have 'sour' in spades. That's why kimchi goes so fabulously with anything rich that needs a bit of cut-through, especially foods like stews, barbecued meats and anything fried. Its spiciness works particularly well rubbing up against comfort foods with 'muting' fats like avocado or melted cheese, which is why kimchi macaroni cheese is such an excellent idea.

The savoury flavour is the aspect of kimchi which often seems to surprise people (well, apart from the fizzing vegetables and the unique smell). It's the fish. It gives the essential element of savouriness (or umami) to your ferment jar. Traditionally you'd use some pretty pungent salted fermented seafood called *jeotgal* to impart this, of which there are more than eighty varieties, including salted sea pineapple (*meongge-jeot*), salted horned turban (*sora-jeot*) and salted pollock eye (*taean-jeot*). Most of these are relatively hard to obtain outside of Korea – but happily for the rest of us there are alternatives. If you want to keep your kimchi traditional, look for salted shrimp (*saeujeot*) – it usually comes in a little plastic jar in brine and will last a long while in the fridge. Failing that, you can use fish sauce – preferably Korean, or otherwise Thai or Vietnamese (the best ones declare the amount of nitrogen proudly, e.g. '60°N', with a higher number being better).

Even if you can't get hold of *jeotgal*, or prefer your kimchi to be vegan, I would say don't ignore the *jeotgal* element – the savoury flavour it contributes is crucial. You'll find some commercially available kimchis do, but in my eyes they're really just selling spicy sauerkraut. Instead, there's a couple of very solid fish-free substitutes to give your kimchi a savoury kick – I often use either *doenjang* or *aka* miso. Both are fermented soybean pastes – the former Korean and the latter Japanese – and both are enormously savoury. *Aka* miso or red miso paste is the longest-fermented of the misos, much darker, more assertive and less sweet than the common white (*shiro*) miso used to make soup. *Doenjang* is similar, though a bit saltier and less robustly funky.

The sea pineapple is one of the many types of seafood used to flavour kimchi.

I'm aware that by suggesting substitutions in making a centuries-old Korean food I run the risk of gastronomic colonialism, and I'd caution you not to replace the fish unless your diet demands it. I'd be doing kimchi a greater disservice, though, if I gave the impression that it is a singular and immutable thing. The beauty of kimchi is that it is a whole realm of ferments unto itself, and to that realm, *baechu* kimchi is merely the gateway. Looking beyond *baechu,* then, to the breadth of other varieties, none of the ingredients, bar salt, are truly essential (*dongchimi*, for instance, is neither spicy nor fishy), but the broad concepts behind how brine, temperature and time interact to transform vegetables into fermented delights remain constant. Through familiarizing yourself with these, you will have the knowledge and instincts to 'kimchi' almost anything.

Chinese Leaf Kimchi (*Baechu Kimchi*)

Chinese leaf heads vary enormously – they can weigh up to 2kg, or as little as 500g (but puzzlingly they're priced by piece not weight). They can be dense and compact or light and leafy, and anything from ivory-coloured to pine-green. For kimchi, I'd usually opt for the dense, heavyweight, paler variety – but you'll find these much more easily between the months of October and March. I've yet to meet a specimen that can't be fermented successfully, though, so go with what you can get.

TIME / 3–7 days (depending on ambient temperature)
YIELD / 2kg kimchi
KIT / Food processor
Large bowl
Rubber gloves (optional, but strongly advised)
Large (1.5 litre) jar with a weight to fit (see page 9)

INGREDIENTS (DAY ONE)
1 bunch of spring onions (~150g)
250g carrots, peeled
2 heads of Chinese leaf (~2kg)
120g coarse sea salt

INGREDIENTS (DAY TWO)
5cm ginger, peeled and roughly chopped
10 cloves of garlic, peeled
95g *doenjang* OR *aka* miso OR 40g preserved shrimp (*saeujeot*)
10g caster sugar
60g *gochugaru* chilli flakes

1/ Chop the spring onions into 5cm lengths and separate whites from greens. Put the greens in a large bowl, and the whites aside in the fridge for making sauce the next day.

2/ Chop the carrots into 5cm batons about the thickness of a pencil and add to the onion greens.

3/ Remove any damaged outer leaves plus the bases from the cabbage and discard (retaining a large outer leaf as a weight, if desired). Chop the cabbage into 5cm-wide strips and combine with the carrots and spring onion greens.

4/ Combine the salt with the chopped veg, mix thoroughly and leave covered overnight. The veg will shrink and wilt substantially as water is drawn out of it.

5/ The next day, thoroughly rinse the salted veg twice.

6/ Combine the ginger, garlic, reserved spring onion whites, miso, sugar and *gochugaru* in a food processor, and pulse until you have a paste a little looser than peanut butter. You may need to add a little water.

7/ Combine the chilli paste with the rinsed veg (rubber gloves are advised), getting it between every leaf.

8/ Once thoroughly mixed, put the kimchi in your jar, and cover with weights – as the cabbage releases brine this will keep everything submerged. Make sure there's a little headspace at the top of your container (5–10cm). Seal, and leave in a cool place if you can – around 10–15°C is ideal – and out of direct sunlight.

9/ Check your kimchi daily for signs of fermentation (bubbling and a change in smell – you might notice a 'pear drop' aroma) and continue to open the jar twice a day to let gas escape once it has begun fermenting. Watch out, if it's particularly fizzy it might try to escape the jar – wrapping a piece of kitchen roll over the lid as you open it will save your clothes and worktop from kimchi spatter.

10/ Three to seven days after fermentation has begun, your kimchi should be ready – it'll be quicker if you've put it somewhere warmer. Try it, and if it tastes good, refrigerate. If it still tastes a bit raw, leave it for another day. Once in the fridge, it will keep for well over a month, but loosen the lid every few days to prevent gas build-up.

Weird and slimy, a bit like egg whites	If the kimchi still smells the same, then this is most likely dextran – a sugar derivative that some *Leuconostoc* bacteria produce when they're a bit warm. This strain isn't necessarily undesirable, though if you're seeing slime it means that it's taking over a bit too much. You'll likely find that it will disappear in a day or so, as the kimchi ferments, but to avoid slimy kimchi in future, check the temperature isn't too high, and that you're adding enough salt.
Flat/raw tasting	It's not ready yet. Ferment it for longer, or in a warmer spot.
Mouldy	Likely the veg became exposed to air. Start again, stick to the salt measurements, and make sure you keep it submerged under the brine (which may mean regularly opening the jar and pushing it down if it makes enough gas). I've never experienced kimchi going mouldy when following the above recipe, however.
Explosively fizzy	This is normal! Gently open the jar over the sink to release pressure, push the veg under the brine, then seal it and (if it tastes ready) put it into the fridge (this will calm it down). Also, keep your fermenting jar in a dish in case of overflow, and if this is a problem use a bigger jar for your next batch.

Kimchi-pickled Eggs

Kimchi brine is a delicious by-product from making a lot of kimchi yourself. Pickled eggs made with it are as beautiful as they are delicious. After a short dunk they get a neat 'pink rim' and a little spiciness, but if you let them keep going for 2–3 days the flavour fully permeates the white exquisitely. You'll want to jam them into their pickling jar as tightly as possible to minimize the amount of kimchi brine you need (since it can be a rare commodity if you're not making industrial quantities of kimchi). Use the smallest jar you can squeeze them into, and if you still don't have enough brine, top up with a little more rice vinegar.

TIME / 48–72 hours
YIELD / 4 pickled eggs
KIT / A small jam jar

INGREDIENTS
4 hard-boiled eggs
100ml kimchi brine
30–50ml rice vinegar

1/ Pack the eggs into the jar, pour over the kimchi brine and 30ml vinegar, and push them down so that they are covered, adding a little extra vinegar if necessary. If you're still short, you can pack a little kimchi in with them.

2/ Refrigerate for at least 48 hours and up to a week.

Radish Winter Kimchi (*Dongchimi Kimchi*)

One of my favourites, radish winter kimchi is a real departure from the classic, spicy stuff. Its paste is really easy to make and it's relatively quick to ferment too. The radish is not the small, pink sphere popular in Europe, but the much larger, winter-cultivated Asian variety. Traditionally, Korean radishes (called joseonmu*) are the type to use – they are shorter and a bit spicier than the more commonly spotted white daikon (or mooli), but the latter variety work well for our purposes too. The extra-spicy green Chinese Qingluobo variety are also great. Once fermented, the radish really retains its crunch and is superb chopped into salads or coleslaws. The brine is also a great ingredient in itself: excellent in salad or noodle dressings, and a few drops with some gin make for a fiendish dirty martini.*

TIME / 36–48 hours	**INGREDIENTS**	6 cloves of garlic
YIELD / 1kg kimchi	1kg Korean radish	(approx. 30g), peeled
KIT / Food processor	OR daikon/mooli	20g ginger, peeled
Large bowl	45g salt	3 long green chillies
Muslin OR a strainer	3 spring onions	(approx. 25g)
Large jar	1½ Nashi/Asian pears	
	(approx. 330g), peeled,	
	cored and roughly chopped	

1/ Peel the radish, split down the middle and chop into 1cm thick half-moons. Add 40g of salt, mix and leave in a bowl at room temperature for 4 hours.

2/ Reserve the radish water which has collected in the bowl, then rinse the radish twice.

3/ Separate the spring onion greens from the whites, and blend the whites with the pear, garlic and ginger in a food processor. Chop the spring onion greens into 5cm lengths and set aside.

4/ Squeeze the pear paste through a muslin or strainer and mix with the reserved radish water.

5/ Chop the chillies into 1cm pieces and mix with the spring onion greens and radishes, then pack them into the smallest jar that they will fit in. The narrower the better, as it will allow you to keep them below the 'brine line' as much as possible, rather than floating.

6/ Mix 5g salt with 250ml water to make a 2% brine.

7/ Cover the veg with your radish & pear water, then top up with the brine until it covers the veg by 0.5–1cm or so.

8/ Seal the jar and leave at room temperature for 36–48 hours, checking in on it about every 12 hours, loosening the lid to check for gas production. Once you see it beginning to become fizzy, try it, and if it's starting to taste sour, refrigerate. If it still tastes a bit too raw, leave it for one more day.

9/ Once in the fridge, it will keep for a month, but loosen the lid every few days to prevent gas build-up.

Shiitake & Chestnut Kimchi (*Bossam Kimchi*)

*These little kimchi wraps are traditional celebration food from Kaesong,
the capital of Korea for four hundred years until the end of the fourteenth
century, now part of North Korea. Like any wrapped food, whether ravioli
or dumplings, you'll get the hang of folding as you go, so don't worry if
a couple at the bottom of the jar split, they'll still be delicious. You should
be able to find the wrinkled, dried red jujube dates in most Asian grocers.*

TIME / 3–9 days
   (temperature dependent)
YIELD / 1.2kg kimchi
   (6–8 wraps)
KIT / Food processor
Large bowl
Large (1.5 litre) jar
   (not too wide)

INGREDIENTS
100g salt
1 large head of Chinese leaf
   cabbage (1.5kg)
1 bunch of spring onions
   (~150g)
7 dried shiitake mushrooms
   (~35g)
1 tablespoon rice flour OR
   1 teaspoon potato starch
1 tablespoon sugar
9 chestnuts

10 dried red jujube dates
½ Nashi/Asian pear (~110g),
   cored
7 cloves of garlic, peeled
3cm ginger, peeled and
   roughly chopped
30g *gochugaru* chilli flakes
4 tablespoons fish sauce OR
   40g preserved shrimp
   (*saeujeot*)
2 tablespoons toasted
   sesame seeds

1/   Mix the salt into 1.5 litres of warm water in a large bowl until dissolved.

2/   Remove any damaged outer leaves plus the bases from the cabbage
and discard (unless using as weight, see page 9). Separate the cabbage
out into leaves which will be used as wrappers, stopping when they
are smaller than about 10cm near the core. Add the leaves and core
to the brine. Separate the spring onion whites from the greens, and put
the greens into the brine, refrigerating the whites for making sauce later.

3/   Soak the mushrooms in enough boiling water to cover them (weigh them
down if they float). Leave them and the veg for about 8 hours or overnight.

4/   Combine the flour and sugar with 250ml of water in a small pan. Bring
to the boil and simmer for 3–4 minutes while stirring, then leave to cool.

5/ When the cabbage leaves are soft enough to bend in half, rinse them and the spring onion greens twice, then wring them out gently and proceed with making the filling.

6/ Slice the chestnuts into 3mm thick pieces. Deseed the jujubes and slice them similarly. Once the mushrooms are rehydrated, cut out and discard the stems and slice them in the same way.

7/ Blend the flour roux, onion whites, pear, garlic, ginger, *gochugaru*, fish sauce/*saeujeot* and cabbage core until you have a thick paste.

8/ Pull apart the brined spring onion greens into 2 pieces each, then tie pairs of them together to make long pieces of 'twine'.

9/ Line a small bowl with 2 lengths of onion greens laid in a cross, followed by 2–3 cabbage leaves laid at right angles with their spines along the onion 'twine' so they flop over the sides of the bowl. Make parcels by spreading the leaves with 2–3 tablespoons of the paste, followed by a layer of the chestnuts, jujubes, sesame seeds and mushrooms, then 2–3 tablespoons more of the paste, and then fold the sides and ends up towards the middle to close them and tie up with the onion greens. Place the wrapped parcel in a large jar, and repeat, stacking them on top of each other until either the leaves or sauce are used up.

10/ Push the wraps down gently in the jar until brine comes up to cover them, using a chopstick to poke down and dislodge any large air bubbles, and top with any leftover sauce, leaving at least 5cm headroom at the top. Seal, and leave out of direct sunlight at room temperature (18–22°C) for 2–3 days, or cellar temperature (10–15°C) for 5–7.

11/ Check your kimchi jar daily for signs of fermentation (bubbling and a change in smell – you might notice a 'pear drop' aroma) and continue to open the jar once or twice a day to let gas escape once it has begun fermenting. You may need to push the wraps back down into the brine as the fizziness pushes them up (a chopstick or whisk may prove useful).

12/ Three to five days after fermentation has begun, your kimchi should be ready – it'll be quicker if you've put it somewhere warmer. Try it, and if it tastes sour, refrigerate. If it still tastes a bit raw, leave it for another day. Once in the fridge, it will keep at its best for well over a month, but loosen the lid every few days to prevent gas build-up.

Kimchi Stew (*Kimchi Jjigae*)

Kimchi jjigae *is, for me, consolation for the end of summer. The sun's gone, the clocks have turned back, but it is also now time for the autumnal prince of suppers.* Jjigae *is Korean for stew, and like all great stews, this one keys into one of my particular culinary turn-ons: using up leftovers. This is where the kimchi you lost at the back of the fridge finds a home. The stuff that's gone super-sour, where the cabbage has started to become translucent. And, like any good stew, it's almost infinitely adaptable. Prefer it veggie? Lose the pork, swap the stock, add some sweet potato. Got beef brisket? That'll work just fine.*

TIME / 3–4 hours
YIELD / Enough for 4 people
KIT / A large heavy-bottomed pot

FOR THE PORK

600g rolled boneless pork belly, skin-on
125ml water
25ml Shaoxing wine
25ml soy sauce
½ tablespoon *doenjang* OR *aka* miso
½ tablespoon *gochujang*
1½ tablespoons honey
2 spring onions, roughly chopped
2 cloves of garlic, crushed
1.5cm ginger (~5g), roughly chopped

FOR THE JJIGAE

2 white onions, thinly sliced
1kg kimchi
650ml good chicken stock
4 tablespoons mirin
300g silken tofu, cut into 2cm cubes
2 spring onions, thinly sliced

1/ Preheat the oven to 140°C. Place the rolled pork belly in an ovenproof pot and set aside.

2/ Mix the remaining pork ingredients in a small saucepan and stir over a low heat until the *gochujang* and *doenjang*/miso dissolve, then pour over the pork belly and put it into the oven.

3/ Cook for around 2–3 hours, or until fully tender, turning it a few times to baste it.

4/ Meanwhile, to make the *jjigae*, heat 2 tablespoons of vegetable oil in a large heavy-bottomed pot over a medium heat and add the white onions and a pinch of salt. Sweat for 5 minutes, stirring frequently, and as they start to soften, lower the heat and cook for another 20 minutes, until they begin to caramelize.

5/ Turn up the heat to medium, add the kimchi and stir until it starts to sizzle and is fully combined (about 5–10 minutes). Set aside until the pork is ready.

6/ Once it is fully tender, remove the pork from the pan, allow to cool slightly, then chop into bite-sized pieces.

7/ Add a few spoonfuls of stock to the pork cooking pan and deglaze, then add this along with the rest of the stock and the mirin to your kimchi pan and bring to the boil.

8/ Add the chopped pork to the pot, then lower the heat to a simmer. Cook for 25 minutes, then add the silken tofu, stir very carefully so as not to scramble it, and cook for one more minute.

9/ Sprinkle over the spring onions and serve over white rice.

Goat's Cheese & Kimchi Quesadilla

Any grilled cheese sandwich goes gloriously with kimchi, from the simplest white bread and cheddar to the gruyère-gilded croque monsieur. The inspiration behind this fusion sandwich, though, is the Salvadoran pupusa *(stuffed flatbread), which is often served with* curtido *(a kind of central American fermented sauerkraut). Making your own flour tortillas only adds 20 minutes' more effort, and improves the quesadilla immeasurably – not to mention you'll have leftover tortillas, which can only be a good thing. The citrusy, minty freshness of perilla leaves really lifts the quesadillas, but supermarket-friendly coriander works well too.*

TIME / 1 hour
(30 minutes active
+ 30 minutes proving)
YIELD / 4 quesadillas

FOR THE TORTILLAS
60g all-purpose flour
40g bread flour
1 teaspoon baking powder
½ teaspoon salt
40g room temperature
 salted butter
50ml warm water

FOR THE QUESADILLAS
120g *baechu* kimchi
1 tablespoon *gochujang*
 (optional)
125g soft goat's cheese
2 tablespoons finely chopped
 coriander, perilla or
 shiso leaves
4 small tortillas (see recipe)

1/ Mix the flours with the baking powder and salt, then mix in the butter by hand, rubbing until you have a mixture resembling coarse sand. Slowly add the warm water (you may not need all of it) while mixing until it comes together into a soft dough.

2/ Knead for 5 minutes, then leave covered in a bowl for 15 minutes.

3/ Divide into 4 golfball-sized spheres. Leave for another 15 minutes, covered.

4/ Heat a non-stick pan over a medium-high heat. Gently roll out each ball on a floured surface with a floured rolling pin (or tortilla press) until they're about 15–20cm in diameter. As each is rolled out, carefully place in the pan and cook for about 40–60 seconds until speckled golden brown, then flip and cook for 30 seconds more. Repeat with the rest of the tortillas.

5/ Wrap in a clean tea towel to keep warm until needed.

6/ For the quesadillas, drain the kimchi as thoroughly as possible, returning the brine to the jar, and chop roughly.

7/ Crumble the goat's cheese and combine with the kimchi and herbs.

8/ Spread a quarter of the *gochujang* (if using) and quarter of the kimchi mix over one half of a tortilla, then fold, and repeat with the other tortillas.

9/ Heat a non-stick pan over a medium-high heat and add 2 tablespoons of vegetable oil. Add 2 folded tortillas side-by-side to make a circle, cook for about a minute, or until golden, then flip and repeat. Repeat with the other 2 tortillas. Serve while piping hot.

Kimchi Pancakes (*Kimchijeon*)

Who likes pancakes? Oh, that's right, everyone. This is a pretty common Korean snack and the second most common use for kimchi in my house (after toasted cheese sandwiches). The rice flour, along with frying them in a generous amount of oil, will help to really crisp them up.

Time / 15 minutes
Yield / 2 pancakes

For the Pancakes
60g plain flour
60g rice flour
  (or potato starch)
1 spring onion, cut in 2cm
  diagonal slices
75g *baechu* kimchi, drained
  and finely chopped
60g *baechu* kimchi brine
2 teaspoons *gochujang*
1 egg, beaten

For the Dipping Sauce
2 tablespoons rice wine vinegar
2 tablespoons light soy sauce
1 teaspoon sesame oil
1 teaspoon toasted sesame
  seeds
1 teaspoon caster sugar

1/ Combine the flours in a bowl, then add the spring onion, kimchi, kimchi brine, *gochujang*, egg and 2 tablespoons of cold water. Mix the batter until it's just combined and refrigerate while you make the dipping sauce.

2/ Preheat the oven to 80°C to keep the pancakes warm. Combine the dipping sauce ingredients in a small bowl.

3/ Heat 2 tablespoons of vegetable oil in a non-stick pan over a medium heat. When the oil is shimmering, spoon in half the batter and spread it evenly across the pan. Reduce the heat to medium-low and cook until the edges are just turning golden brown (~3 minutes), then flip (using a plate, spatula or pure confidence) and cook for a further 3 minutes. Keep the first pancake warm in the oven and repeat to cook the second, allowing the oil to heat again (topping it up if necessary).

4/ You can serve the pancakes whole, or (as is traditional) pre-cut into small triangles for handling with chopsticks. Either way, serve with dipping sauce.

Chilled Radish Noodle Soup (*Dongchimi Guksu*)

This is a recipe that somehow becomes much, much more than the sum of its very simple parts – indeed I'd say it's worth making your own dongchimi *for. With a refreshing, vinegary tang, it makes a great starter, or a light lunch on a summer's day. Despite* dongchimi *meaning 'winter kimchi', as the pickle was usually made in November, this tastes delicious all year.*

TIME / 45 minutes
YIELD / 2 bowls
   (lunch or starter)

INGREDIENTS
250ml *dongchimi* brine
   (see page 56), chilled
2 tablespoons rice vinegar
1 teaspoon sesame oil
2½ teaspoons sugar

75g thin wheat noodles
   (e.g. somyeon/somen)
60g *dongchimi*, cubed
¼ of a cucumber, julienned
1 teaspoon sesame seeds
10cm x 10cm *gim*/nori
   seaweed sheet, finely sliced

1/ Mix the *dongchimi* brine with 200ml of cold water, the rice vinegar, sesame oil and sugar.

2/ Put the brine mixture in the freezer for 20–30 minutes, until very well chilled.

3/ Meanwhile, cook the noodles according to the packet instructions, then drain and refresh in iced water until chilled.

4/ Split the noodles between two bowls and spoon over the cold soup, then top with *dongchimi*, cucumber, sesame seeds and seaweed.

Feta & Kimchi Muffins

The process of making and cooking with kimchi will give you a bit of leftover brine, and baking makes excellent use of it. Replacing water with the brine gives your dough an almost sourdough tang, but with just a hint of heat (though as there isn't sufficient yeast in kimchi, you'll still have to add some). If you haven't yet made your own kimchi, you will need to drain the liquid off a couple of jars of the commercial stuff to make this. The salty nuggets of feta and chopped kimchi punctuating these fluffy orange muffins are the ideal counterpart to avocado and a poached egg.

TIME / 20 minutes active + 1¾ hours rise/bake
YIELD / 6 muffins
KIT / Metal cooking rings (optional)

INGREDIENTS
300g strong white flour
1 teaspoon salt
1 packet (6g) instant dried yeast
2 eggs, beaten
15g butter, cut into small cubes
60g *baechu* kimchi brine
120g feta
60g *baechu* kimchi, drained and finely chopped
Semolina OR polenta, for dusting

1/ Combine the flour with salt and yeast in a bowl, then add the eggs, butter and kimchi brine and bring together into a soft dough.

2/ Turn out the dough on to a clean, lightly floured surface and knead for about 10 minutes, until soft and glossy. It should bounce back quickly after a gentle poke.

3/ Crumble the feta into small pieces, around the size of a raisin, and combine with the chopped kimchi. Knead this briefly through the dough until just combined. Add more flour if needed.

4/ Place the kneaded dough in a lightly oiled bowl, cover and leave to rise for 30 minutes.

5/ Split into 6 roughly equal pieces and roll them lightly into balls. Squash these into 2.5cm thick circles, dust with polenta/semolina, and place on an oven tray lined with baking paper. If you own metal cooking rings, placing your muffins in these will force them to rise upwards rather than outwards.

6/ Leave to rise for another 60 minutes, then preheat the oven to 200°C.

7/ Bake for 15 minutes (in rings if using), or until golden.

Chapter three

Soy Sauce

SOY SAUCE IS PROBABLY THE WORLD'S favourite condiment, with about £32 billion worth sold globally in 2018 (that's more than ketchup and mayonnaise combined). It's traditionally fermented from soybeans, wheat, salt brine and *koji* fungus, though nowadays it's often made by other, faster methods. It's also incredibly ancient, with origins first documented in China around two thousand years ago.

According to the epic Chinese creation myths in *Hei An Zhuan* (or the 'Epic of Darkness'), the god-king *Shennong* ('divine farmer') discovered the humble soybean and decreed it to be one of the five sacred plants, along with wheat, hemp and two varieties of millet. Five is a fundamental number found throughout Chinese culture and mythology – there are five standard colours, five seasons, five ancient corporal punishments (ranging rather steeply from tattooing to execution), five Confucian virtues and, of course, five-spice powder. Further to this holy accreditation of soy, evidence from some of the oldest archaeological sites in China shows that the soybean has been cultivated there since the Bronze Age. Little did those ancient farmers know that the furry little podded beans would one day be among the most heavily sown plants in the world, used to feed animals, make oil, crayons and candles, masquerade as meats and milks, and at their most glorious, of course, be stewed, brewed and fermented into soy sauce.

The soybean also falls into that curiously alluring category of foods that are poisonous when raw, along with cassava (bursting with cyanide), cashew nuts (shells akin to poison ivy) and kidney beans (just a few can cause vomiting). As a defence mechanism, soy plants contain a chemical which prevents proteins from being digested – this can be circumvented by those with multiple stomachs (e.g. cattle), or the ability to cook (as the toxin is destroyed by heat – if you've ever wondered why packets of edamame carry a warning against eating them raw). Once they're cooked, soybeans can be processed in all sorts of ways. Most commonly they're either blended and strained to make milk (and subsequently tofu), or fermented to make soy sauce, tempeh or a variety of pastes like miso, *gochujang* or *doubanjiang*.

The earliest iteration of fermented soy was as douchi – *wizened, salty, sun-dried nuggets which provide the umami backbone to mapo tofu and black bean sauce.*

The very first soy ferment, though, was the simplest – salted and fermented *douchi*, or 'black beans' as they're generally known in the West (though not to be confused with the black turtle beans popular in Latin American and the Caribbean, which are nicknamed similarly). These wrinkled black umami neutron stars are mostly associated with the black bean sauce ubiquitous to Chinese takeaways, though they are also key to making twice-cooked pork and *mapo tofu* – which is alone reason enough to own a bag. They have been a delicacy for over two thousand years, as we know from the incredible tomb of a marquise found in Hunan province. Lady Dai's body, despite being interred in 168 BC, was so remarkably (and creepily) well-preserved that her skin was still supple, her joints still moved – she even had her eyelashes, as well as 138 undigested honeydew melon seeds in her stomach. You'd imagine she'd died a couple of weeks ago. Evidence of her diet derives from foods buried alongside, including meat skewers, lotus soup and the little fermented soybeans.

It's unfortunately not quite so clear when soy sauce was first concocted, as the evolution from fermented meat or fish paste to soy sauce is linguistically hazy – they were all originally referred to broadly as '*jiang*' (meaning simply 'sauce'). The modern Chinese name that was eventually given to soy sauce is quite different, in that it uses a Chinese character (油) which in other culinary senses means 'oil', but its first singular name seems to have been 'clarified sauce' (清酱). This name, dating back to at least 40 AD, indicates that these *jiang* pastes were being transformed into liquids. *Jiang* pots from the Han Dynasty (202 BC–220 AD) have been found with taps at the bottom, supporting the idea that the liquid part must have been drawn off as a separate product (unlike whey from yogurt or brine from kimchi, it is the solid paste that floats on top, as you'll find out when making soy sauce). This alone, however, doesn't indicate that this 'clarified sauce' was made from soy instead of meat or fish. Helpfully, in *Science and Civilisation in China*, Huang Hsing-Tsung cites a medical text from around 215 BC which refers to the 'dregs of soy paste' as being useful as a haemorrhoid cream, thus inferring that there was also a liquid part – perhaps our first soy sauce. Within a few hundred years fermented fish fell out of favour in China, and ever since Asia has remained divided sharply into condiment zones, with Cambodia, Thailand and Vietnam flying the flag for fish, and China, Japan and Korea sticking to soy (fermented meat sauce didn't remain particularly popular anywhere until it was revived by the endlessly inventive René Redzepi and David Zilber at Noma, making it with squirrel, swan and grasshoppers).

In Japan, soy sauce took on a whole new character (but not literally – the same logographic characters are used in Mandarin and Japanese, though the pronunciation is different). The condiment took a long time to establish itself – in the oldest extant collection of Japanese poetry from the seventh century, *hishio* (a chunkier version of *jiang*) is still more fashionable than sauce. A choice verse from it reads: 'I want to eat sea bream and wild onions dressed with *hishio* and vinegar. How dare you show me soup of hollyhock!'

The evolution of fermented soy was hastened in 675 when Buddhist convert Emperor Tenmu banned the consumption of horse, cattle, dogs, monkeys and birds (but not deer, as they were hunted by nobility). This period of enforced pescatarianism lasted for nearly 1,200 years, and when the edict was finally lifted in 1872, several monks died trying to storm the Imperial Palace in protest. In this meat-free era, soy popularity exploded to fill the protein gap, and this resulted in a series of iterative improvements in the world of fermented soy condiments. First *hishio/jiang* was refined into miso, then out of miso came gluten-free *tamari* sauce (literally – *tamaru* means 'to accumulate', as the liquid would have done at the bottom of the miso), and finally soy sauce (or *shoyu*) evolved from *tamari* with the addition of roasted wheat.

The final chapter of the *shoyu* origin story has ascended into something of a legend. A Buddhist monk, Kakushin, having spent many years travelling in China, was said to have settled in the small town of Yuasa, 100 kilometres south of Osaka. There in around 1254, the tale goes, Kakushin started making a miso adapted from his time abroad, using soy, *koji* starter and salt, as well as *ume* plums, aubergine, melon, shiso leaves and ginger. Critically, the worldly monk also added much, much more water than usual, before fermenting it all for three months. His unorthodox, high-hydration method resulted in a looser soy mash called *moromi*, which was pressed to extract the liquid, with the leftover mash being used for animal feed. The tables had turned – from *tamari* being a by-product of the fermented paste, it was now the paste that was the waste. The final sixteenth-century innovation that led to modern Japanese *shoyu* was the addition of roasted, cracked wheat in a similar proportion to soybeans, rounding out the richness with a sweeter, lighter flavour. Marking it out from traditional Chinese soy sauce, the dark, roasted wheat also changed its colour quite dramatically – this new style was dubbed *koikuchi* (meaning 'dark mouth' or 'rich flavour'), and it remains the most popular type of *shoyu* even today.

Their version of soy sauce now perfected, this was surely the time for Japan to share it with the world. Trade with Europeans had been underway for just seventy years, and had brought such prodigious quantities of silk that Japan was spending half its entire silver production with Portuguese fabric traders. However, as more enormous carracks docked in Japan, they began to bring with them Jesuit fathers. The Catholic mission was a resounding success, and by the 1590s it was estimated that there were 200,000 Japanese Christians. Though the religious incursion was initially tolerated by local leaders, after a suppressed Christian uprising in 1637 the military government enacted a policy of *sakoku* ('closed country'), expelling all foreigners and banning Christianity. Dutch traders had a unique position in Japan, though, both economically and geographically. The sole European trade relationship permitted by the seclusionist shogunate was with the Netherlands, and this only via a tiny man-made offshore island slightly bigger than a football pitch. Through Dejima (meaning 'exit island'), the Dutch East India Company enjoyed sole access to Japan for over two centuries – so it was they that were responsible for introducing coffee, chocolate and beer to the Land of the Rising Sun, and for exporting soy sauce around the rest of the world.

The first European mention of 'soy' is found in a handwritten letter from a Dutch merchant in 1647 trying to approximate the Japanese '*shoyu*' – he calls it *soije*, and it's from this that the words 'soy', 'soybean' and 'soya' all derive (incidentally, in Japanese the word for 'soy' as a legume is quite separate – *daizu*). By 1679 the English philosopher John Locke wrote in his journal that he had come across it, though I wouldn't want to presume that tasting soy sauce influenced his theory that all knowledge must derive from sensory experience. By 1790, the condiment was popular enough (and a sufficient

Many traditional Japanese colours have wonderfully evocative names, such as 'steamed chestnut', 'stylish persimmon', 'pot peering' and 'flirtatious indigo tea'.

marker of status) that Sheffield glass-makers were selling 'soy cruets' for table service (the Metropolitan Museum of Art has one in its collection).

The finest house-blend restaurant soy sauces, often combined with ingredients like bonito flakes or mirin, are referred to as *murasaki*, meaning 'purple' – a noble colour, once reserved by law for the upper echelons of society. Japan has a plethora of evocatively named traditional colours, from 'steamed chestnut' (a straw yellow) and 'stylish persimmon' (a blush orange – distinct from the other five persimmon-named colours) to 'pot peering' (the blue of the inside of a bottle of water) and 'flirtatious indigo tea' (dark green). *Murasaki*, however, is just simple purple – a word which you'll often see printed on premium soy sauce bottles today, as a mark of quality.

Soy sauce has always inspired unique and interesting containers and receptacles. The Japanese industrial designer and former Buddhist monk Kenji Ekuan took three years and over one hundred prototypes to settle on the iconic Kikkoman bottle, with the red cap and shape evocative of a sake bottle. The innovative, dripless spout is 'based on a teapot's, but inverted', and combines with a double-dispenser to allow the user to slow the freeflowing condiment down to a single drop by capping one end with a finger. It has sold over three hundred million bottles in more than seventy countries, and was

Yoshihisa Sawada created a book categorizing seventy-six fish-shaped plastic soy sauce bottles by genus and species.

displayed in New York's Museum of Modern Art in 2015 as part of their show *This Is for Everyone: Design Experiments for the Common Good*.

There's a good chance that the last soy sauce container you purchased isn't a bottle though, but a fish. The little fish-shaped disposable soy dispenser that you get with takeaway sushi, though it may seem inconsequential, is in fact part of a whole ersatz plastic piscine biome – a moonlighting Japanese entomologist has compiled a book documenting seventy-six different kinds of soy fish, categorizing them into six families and twenty-one genera. The reason for their shape is simple enough – they accompany takeaway sushi, and are thus reminiscent of the fish beside which they're served – and yet, there's a neat historical echo to the form as well, given that some of the earliest soy sauce precursors were themselves fermented with fish. The little 'bottles' have now become a kind of design icon in themselves: during the Covid-19 pandemic in 2020, a Japanese hand sanitizer company, finding themselves short on containers, repurposed the soy fishes, giving them blue caps reminiscent of face masks.

At the other end of the scale of soy sauce containers sit the enormous wooden barrels in which it was traditionally brewed. They're truly incredible objects. At 2.3 metres tall, they tower over their owners on Shōdoshima (literally, 'small bean island') in Japan's Inland Sea – one of the few places they're still made. Shōdoshima was once an industrial hub for soy sauce breweries, with natural resources of sea salt and spring water, and easy access to soy and wheat via the shipping lanes criss-crossing the inland sea it is set within. By these same ships the islanders also had access to huge discarded barrels that had seen out their usefulness making sake in nearby Nada. Already three decades old, these barrels were rich in flavour, and ideal for making soy (much like the bourbon barrels repurposed for Scotch). Named *kioke*, they are carefully made with cedar planks held together by wooden pins and split bamboo. Between many batches and across many years, the wood becomes steeped with the *koji* mould that ferments soy sauce, and so the barrels themselves become intrinsic to the sauce's microbial profile.

For centuries the *kioke* coopers were in constant demand, with hundreds of sake and soy sauce breweries using thousands of barrels. However, the immense modern popularity of soy sauce has been to the detriment of the *kioke*, and the bacteria that once called them home. As the manufacturing process has been industrialized, the microbial workforce has been laid off and replaced by a much faster chemical method where, instead of fermentation, the soybeans are broken down by pressure-cooking in hydrochloric acid. An alkali is then added to neutralize the acid and make the sauce edible. This 'acid-hydrolyzed' soy sauce is missing many of the aromatic characteristics – esters, alcohols, carbonyl compounds – which would develop through the fermentation process, though, so additives such as caramel, corn syrup and lactic acid are added to mimic the appearance and flavour of a traditionally fermented soy sauce. The new method takes days rather than months, and in the period after the Second World War it became hugely popular with Japanese manufacturers. Replaced by stainless steel vats, the wooden ageing barrels were surplus to requirement. Nowadays less than 1% of Japanese soy sauce is made by wooden barrel fermentation.

But there's hope yet – in recent years there's been a revival in the craft of making soy sauce the old way, led by brewers like Yasuo Yamamoto of Shōdoshima. When Yamamoto inherited the business from his father, he needed new barrels. He found the last company who still made *kioke*, but discovered that they had all but closed up shop, merely repairing old barrels without having taken a single order for a new one in seven decades. Yamamoto knew this business wouldn't be around forever, so he requested their tutelage, and soon started making his own barrels. Using more than forty pieces of century-old Yoshino cedar, he straps the 4,000-litre barrels together using braided bamboo hoops, setting everything precisely to avoid any leaks. There's been a lot of curiosity about Yamamoto's work, with fifty thousand people visiting his brewery per year, and a consequent growing demand for *kioke* across Japan. This has led him to start the Kioke Revival Project, hosting coopering workshops to bring in new blood and craft more barrels.

The modern history of soy sauce in Japan is one of loss and revitalization. When waves more than five times the height of his sauce barrels crashed over the town's sea defences during the 2011 tsunami, Michihiro Kono, ninth-generation president of the Yagisawa Shoten brewery, was left without a factory. He kept his staff on while he figured out what to do next, and managed to raise $1.3 million in crowdfunding to restart his business. But nothing could buy back the lost heirloom microbial cultures that had been handed down through the two hundred-year-old company's history. A researcher happened to hear about Kono's story from a TV report, and contacted him, since Kono had previously donated some of his *moromi* to a nearby university for cancer research. The institute, built on the seafront, had also been severely damaged by the tsunami, but in a locker on the second floor, 4kg of Kono's *moromi* was found. Three years after the earthquake he resurrected the soy sauce, dubbed *Kiseki*, or 'miracle'.

CONSIDERING HOW SOY SAUCE is made, it's really quite amazing it exists at all. Like coffee, it's a part of everyday life for billions of us, yet its creation requires so many unintuitive steps it seems as though it must surely have sprung into culinary existence fully formed.

First, before fermentation begins, the dried soy beans are soaked and boiled, while the wheat grains are roasted and milled. Soy sauce doesn't usually rely on the caprice of wild fermentation these days, but instead employs a specific strain of spores (*Aspergillus oryzae* and/or *Aspergillus sojae* – called *koji* in Japanese) which are sprinkled over the cooked beans and wheat. Even though they are fungi, these spores don't produce mushrooms – they're of the 'filamentous' type (also known as mould). The beginnings of the development of the soy sauce method would have required these spores to be in the soybean storeroom by chance. After discovering that these beans were particularly piquant, someone must have realized that adding a few of them to a fresh batch replicated the trick, and thus soy sauce brewers began to culture what would eventually be known as *koji*. Many, many generations later, the process has been streamlined sufficiently that *koji* can be freeze-dried, powdered and sold on the internet.

So, what does the *koji* do? It contains a whole range of enzymes (enzymes being chemicals that accelerate reactions) which allow it to break down difficult-to-digest foods like soybeans. As the *koji* grows on the soybean/

wheat mixture, its enzymes consume the protein and starch, turning them into amino acids (which are delicious) and sugars (which can then be fermented by yeasts and lactic acid bacteria). But *koji* is also a very fussy fungus. It likes to be warm (but will die if it gets too hot), damp (but will drown if it gets too wet), and well-aerated (without getting too cold or too dry). Strangely, however, it's better for the final product if the *koji*'s just a little bit stressed out. With such demanding conditions it's not hard to make it slightly uncomfortable (microbial cruelty, I know, but needs must). By keeping the temperature a little below what it would really like (37°C), we can force it to spend more energy producing enzymes to transform our soy, and less trying to make reproductive spores. Though the spores, which manifest as a dusty green powder, will not ruin the soy sauce, they are slightly detrimental to flavour, so it's best to try and keep the temperature under control. To really fine-tune soy sauce production, the temperature can be nudged downwards into an even more exacting range (25–30°C) to encourage the *koji* to produce more protease (protein-consuming enzymes, which will in turn produce tasty amino acids) – with the drawback that at these lower temperatures the *koji* takes longer to colonize the soybeans and so it becomes a greater challenge to stop other, unwanted microbial invaders.

When koji *is slightly stressed by cold it produces more savoury amino acids in our soy sauce, so go on and give it a hard time.*

While this initial process takes just a few days, the second stage (during which the *koji*-colonized beans are submerged in a salt brine) is much, much slower. The amount of salt added is up to ten times higher than in other salty ferments, like kimchi, sauerkraut or hot sauce, and this slows things down to an almost glacial pace – this secondary phase lasts a minimum of three months and up to three years. It's not the *koji* doing the fermentation now, though, since the salt kills it off; instead, a whole new family of microbes moves in. Soy sauce is one of a number of ferments (including kefir, kombucha and vinegar) that rely on a symbiotic relationship between different organisms which aid each other to reach the end product. As we force the soy sauce to undergo a dramatic change in environment (by lowering the temperature while increasing the salinity and moisture) it suddenly becomes hospitable to very different beasts. The salt encourages a lactic acid bacteria named *Tetragenococcus halophilia* (*halophilia* meaning 'salt-loving') – a microbe extremophile able to survive where other microbes fear to tread. Once this bacteria has succeeded in making the salty soybean mash (or *moromi*, as it's called) even less hospitable by reducing its pH, an intrepid yeast (*Zygosaccharomyces rouxii*) accompanies it into the briney, acidic unknown.

This range of microbes fermenting away across many months gives rise to an unusually large array of chemical reactions, and it is these which are responsible for soy sauce's remarkably complex flavour (around three hundred different flavour molecules have been identified in soy sauce). During the first stage, the protease enzymes from the *koji* break down the huge quantities of protein in the soybeans into amino acids called glutamates. Glutamates are molecules responsible for the savoury flavour common to Marmite, fish sauce, blue cheese and mushrooms – what is known as *umami*. You might also know the name from MSG or monosodium glutamate, which is simply a very concentrated version of this flavour (the idea that it's somehow harmful has consistently been disproved, and is possibly rooted in xenophobia due to its use in Asian fast food).

At the same time, amylase enzymes (similar to the ones in your saliva) break down starch in the wheat and soy into sugars. The balance between protease and amylase enzymes in the *koji* thus determines how sweet or savoury the finished product is. The process for making miso (similar to soy sauce, but using less brine and, typically, rice in place of the wheat), requires higher protease for the more savoury red or dark *aka* miso, and a greater ratio of amylase for the sweeter white *shiro* miso. Some soy and fish sauces will list a 'TN' or 'total nitrogen' percentage – this is a mark of quality, showing how much savoury glutamate is present (1.5% is necessary for 'special grade' soy sauce classification in Japan).

The ageing process is intrinsic to the final flavour of soy sauce. It is at this point that the yeast transforms some of the sugars from the wheat (released by the amylase) into alcohol. Now, getting drunk from soy sauce would be a real challenge, as it ranges from 1–2.5% ABV (and it's a bit too salty to do shots of), but the alcohol helps lift the heavy soy aromas with a bit of heady volatility, and adds fruit aromas, as well as providing sweetness to balance the salinity. Non-fermented modern soy sauces sometimes have concentrated ethyl alcohol added as a preservative, whereas traditional *shoyu* produces enough alcohol from wheat fermentation on its own.

The yeast is also responsible for another key flavour in soy sauce, a burnt caramel-scented compound called HEMF (with a name too obscenely long to print in full). This only appears in later fermentation – you should really notice it about two months into the brewing process (so if your soy doesn't smell much like soy at first, take heart). It's been found to be most concentrated in soy sauces made with 16% salt – having said that, my recipe shoots slightly higher at 18.75%, because this lowers the risk of contamination.

When buying soy sauce, there's a couple of things to look out for. First, try to avoid the words 'defatted' or 'hydrolysed' in the ingredients. These signify shortcuts to minimize brewing time, not a somehow superior product. Using the acid-hydrolysed method it is impossible to recreate all the aromas which are woven together through the myriad reactions of fermentation. Instead, you'll often see added flavourings and colourings which take blunt aim at them. Secondly, the vast majority of the sauces you'll find on the market will have been pasteurized to improve shelf life and colour – 50% of the colour in commercial fermented soy sauce typically comes from heating during pasteurization. Though this makes less of an impact with such a slow ferment as soy sauce (as it's never going to be particularly lively), the pasteurization process does add more 'meaty' notes while removing the 'raw' flavours as well as destroying the yeast and enzymes which would otherwise cause the taste to continue slowly changing on your shelf. If you are seeking unpasteurized versions, you should look for *nama-shoyu* or *ki-joyu* varieties from Japanese brands – Kikkoman do one with a clever squeezy cap to prevent air getting back in – but these are quite hard to find, which is an excellent reason to make your own.

Though Japanese soy sauce is probably the most famous around the world, there are regional varieties all across East Asia. Chinese soy sauce, for example, is divided into 'light' and 'dark' varieties. Dark soy sauce is more

The finest soy sauces are truly sophisticated creations, containing up to three hundred different aroma components ranging from fenugreek to popcorn.

viscous, with a heavier, caramel flavour; you might expect it to be saltier, but it's actually the opposite. Light soy sauce has more salt, and this suppresses production of HEMF, which would otherwise darken the soy sauce. In Chinese cooking, dark soy sauce tends to be used in smaller amounts for colouring and as an accent, due to its stronger flavour, and is often combined with milder, thinner light soy sauce. In Japan, light soy sauce is relatively uncommon, with 'dark soy' making up 80% of sales – 'light soy' (*usukuchi*) is really a Kansai regional specialty. You're more likely to see wheat-free *tamari* – a good option for coeliacs. On the other end of the spectrum, white soy sauce, or *shiro shoyu*, is made almost entirely from wheat, with only a small amount of soy, so has a mild, sweet taste – it works especially well in egg dishes or cocktails, as much for reasons of colour as flavour. The most popular Korean style of soy sauce, *guk ganjang*, most commonly used in soups, is also favoured for its shade – being slightly lighter it doesn't muddy the broth as much as other varieties. Like *tamari* it's made without wheat, and being saltier than other types it should be used in smaller quantities.

Though it is common for fermented soy brewers to age their sauce for a year or less, the top producers often set some aside to mature. Two to five year vintages are common, but the oldest I've come across, at thirty-eight years old, predates me. Older soy sauces tend to express more bittersweet chocolate and caramel flavours, and are more viscous. There's also double-fermented soy sauce, where soy sauce is added to the *moromi* mash instead of brine, to achieve the most concentrated flavour.

Beyond straight and unadulterated soy, there's a plethora of Japanese blended styles for use as dipping sauces, incorporating other flavours from *yuzu* (an aromatic citrus fruit), to *katsuobushi* (dried, fermented and smoked skipjack tuna), firefly squid, seaweed and smoke. You can also make some really delicious infusions with soy sauce at home – it combines beautifully with a number of herbal flavours, like lemongrass, Thai or holy basil, coriander and shiso/perilla leaves.

Soy sauce lends itself well to many other dishes from around the world – a little light soy to brighten a broth, or *koikuchi* to deepen a mushroom risotto. It's also an excellent way of adding savoury umami flavour if you're looking for a vegan substitute, such as over polenta in place of parmesan. Surprisingly, a little light soy sauce even makes a lovely accompaniment to vanilla ice cream – the contrast is a little like the ever-so-popular salted caramel.

The best soy sauces have a lot in common with whiskies, being expensive, artisanal and endlessly varied. Actually, comparing high-end soy sauce and whisky is quite apt – both are made in small batches which are aged for years, and their producers often speak proudly of their local water quality. Maybe if Japan can make great whisky, Scotland should have a shot at *shoyu* . . . With this in mind, I hope you won't think it too odd if I entreat you, when buying and trying soy sauce, to sip it by itself. It's strong, salty stuff – but by tasting it on its own, or even better alongside other examples, you'll get a much better idea of the diversity that exists within the simple fermented soybean.

It's even been suggested that soy sauce is too complex to be bound by the standard parameters of flavour. In a 2020 paper entitled *Chemical and Sensory Characteristics of Soy Sauce*, Carmen Díez-Simón *et al* asserted that the five taste categories (salty, sweet, sour, bitter and savoury/umami) were insufficient for describing its full depth – astringency and *kokumi* (or 'heartiness') must also be considered. Astringency – the mouth-puckering sensation commonly associated with rhubarb, red wine or strong tea – is a measure of texture and mouthfeel, and in the case of soy sauce it is commonly caused by phenolic acids created during wheat toasting and *koji* fermentation. *Kokumi* is a more modern concept, proposed by Japanese researchers in the 1990s, embodying the amplitude of richness and fullness of flavour. It is closely associated with many fermented foods such as cheese, soy sauce and fermented fish, though as these are also all very high in umami it can be hard to distinguish this 'heartiness' specifically from savouriness. However, if you take into account that *kokumi* compounds are most concentrated in dark and least in white soy sauce, it's easier to discern it by the lingering quality that the former has. Thinking about these two extra categories when tasting soy sauce really helps you assess it in a more three-dimensional way, which is only fair for a ferment that goes through so much to reach your plate.

Soy sauce didn't arrive in Europe till 1647, but now you'd be hard-pressed to find a kitchen cupboard without it.

Soy Sauce

The process of making soy sauce may be quite involved and take the better part of a year – but to have bottles of your own shoyu slowly fermenting away is immensely satisfying. (Babies take about as long to gestate, and don't go half as well with rice.) You'll also get a lovely kind of miso paste as a by-product. Don't be intimidated by the length of my instructions – they are only so detailed because I've described it all very thoroughly, since I know information on making soy sauce is hard to find.

Briefly, we'll soak and cook the soybeans before covering them in koji, then incubate them in a cool box for two days, and finally brine them for six months. The first step is selecting the right dried soybeans. Bypass the small, green variety and instead seek out the larger white and mature specimens, which are about the size of a garden pea. They might have a dark 'spot' (the 'hilum') on them from where they were attached to their pod, which is fine, but the paler this is, the better (this generally indicates a higher quality in most white varieties). The koji spore starter is best purchased online – try fermentationculture.eu – if they are marked 'undiluted' or 'concentrated', they should be diluted with some all-purpose flour.

You'll need a consistently warm spot (27–36°C) to incubate your koji spores for the first few days. A bank holiday weekend is an ideal time to babysit your soy sauce – warm weather helps keep the necessary temperature, though traditionally it was considered that winter shoyu had the best flavour and sold for the highest price (probably because it was the hardest to make). A cool box containing a hot water bottle works well for providing an appropriate climate, but you'll need to check it a few times a day. I've also had great success using a sous vide water circulator as a heater. Whatever method you go for, a thermometer is really essential here, and if it happens to have an alarm, all the better – for this is a serious business. I've heard seedling heat mats, dehydrators and bread-makers can be repurposed too (if they can be set to just the 'proving' step).

Lastly, as with all ferments (but doubly necessary for one that takes so long), make sure that all utensils and pans are very clean so as to prevent any other bacteria taking hold.

Time / 6–12 months
Yield / 1.5 litres light *shoyu* soy sauce
Kit / Food processor
Large pot
Shallow oven tray (~26 x 35cm), lined with baking paper

A cool box or similar
Digital thermometer
A 5 litre bottle (or multiple smaller bottles)
Muslin or cheesecloth for straining

Ingredients
500g dried soybeans (large white ones are best)
30g all-purpose flour (optional)
500g wheat grain (you'll find this in health food stores)
1g *koji* spore starter for *shoyu*
300g salt

Cooking:

1/ Rinse the dried beans, picking out any that are discoloured, then soak in plenty of water, making sure there's enough room for them to double in size. Leave overnight.

2/ The next day, drain the beans and put them into a large pot. Cover with cold water and bring to the boil, then reduce the heat and simmer for 5–6 hours, topping up with water as necessary, until they're soft and break easily. You may find their skins slip off and float to the top – discard them. Once the beans are cooked, drain and set aside to cool.

Inoculation & Incubation:

1/ If your *koji* starter is marked 'undiluted', you'll need to mix the tiny amount required with flour to make it easier to spread. Toast the flour in a pan for a few minutes, stirring constantly until light brown, then let it cool.

2/ Once cool, combine with the *koji* starter. We won't need all of the mix, but the rest will keep for 6 months in an airtight bag in the freezer.

3/ Meanwhile, toast the wheat grain in a large pan over a low heat, stirring for around 10 minutes until it starts to turn golden brown – a few grains might 'pop'. Leave it to cool for 5 minutes.

4/ Blend the wheat grain coarsely in your food processor – the aim is to break open each grain, not to pulverize them. It may take a little while, depending on how much you toasted them.

5/ Mix together the ground wheat and cooked, drained soybeans in the paper-lined oven tray. It shouldn't be more than 2.5cm or so deep. Allow the mixture to cool, checking with a thermometer until it reaches around 35–40°C.

6/ Using a sieve to help with even distribution, stir 2 teaspoons of prepared *koji* starter through the wheat/soy mixture thoroughly, and, once you're done, make troughs every 10cm through the mix to stop the *koji* getting too hot – it'll create quite a bit of warmth as it starts colonizing your soy mix over the coming days.

7/ Cover the mixture with cling film, piercing it a few times to allow airflow, and put it into your cool box with a hot water bottle, large Tupperware or pan filled with 35°C water under the tray.

8/ Stick a thermometer into it, making sure the temperature of the *koji* is between 26–35°C, mixing a bit of cold water into the hot water bottle if necessary.

9/ Check on it every few hours or so to make sure the temperature remains at 26–35°C (preferably at the lower end of this), replenishing the hot water as necessary.

10/ Once white mould begins to grow, pay particular attention to the temperature, and once you notice it is rising rather than falling, jettison the hot water.

11/ Going forward, each time you check on it, stir the mixture up a bit, breaking up any clumps – this will cool it down slightly, as the *koji* heats itself up when it's clumped together. Lifting the edges of the baking paper can help break it up too. You may even need to add some ice and leave the cool box open, depending on how vigorous it is.

12/ After 36–48 hours or so, your *koji* mix should be covered entirely with white or yellow mould – even small areas of pale green are OK, though they signify that it is ready to use right away (this is the *koji* beginning to produce spores). You are really trying to catch it just before it begins to produce spores, but I will forgive you for not keeping a nocturnal vigil. Discard any parts that have turned dark green or black. You can now remove it from your makeshift incubator. The hard bit is over, well done.

Brining:

1/ Mix 1.6 litres of water with 300g of salt and stir until fully dissolved (you can use slightly less salt, but it increases the risk of nasties – 250g is the absolute lowest I'd go).

2/ Break up your *koji* mix (now called *moromi*) into a large jar and pour in enough brine solution to cover it, then cover the mixture with a tight-fitting lid. Label with your inception date.

3/ Leave your soy-sauce-in-training somewhere warm (ideally around 22–25°C), and stir or shake it daily for the first 10 days. After that, stir or shake it once a week for the next 6 months.

4/ After 6 months it will be ready, but you can leave it to age for up to another 6 months or more (or divide it in two, and keep one bottle ageing). Strain your soy sauce using the muslin, squeezing out all the liquid, and bottle it up. The leftover paste can be used like miso. Your soy sauce may appear lighter than commercial versions, but that won't affect the flavour. It should keep for at least 1 or 2 years in a sealed container, and almost indefinitely if you pasteurize it – to do this, heat the soy sauce to 70°C and keep it at this temperature for 30 minutes before bottling.

TROUBLESHOOTING / If your Soy Sauce is...

Not clumping or turning white/yellow (in the koji *stage)*	This means your *koji* hasn't survived, or the temperature/humidity isn't right. If you have more *koji*, you could try adding it, but the soy needs to be covered in white/yellow mould before you can proceed.
Smelling like ammonia (in the koji *stage)*	This is likely caused by too much of a bacteria called *Bacillus subtilis*, which prefers hotter, wetter environments than you should have. It's used in making another Japanese ferment – *natto* – but this isn't what we want here. I'm afraid you'll have to chuck it and start again, being extra-careful about temperature and airflow.
Entirely green (in the koji *stage)*	This means it has started 'sporulating' (creating spores) and is past ready – get it into the brine right away and it should be all right, but this may affect the flavour.
Growing mould on the moromi *(in the jar)*	The jar should be agitated more often, especially in the first weeks (to keep everything wet with salt). If the mould is the same colour and smell as during the *koji* stage, you can probably scrape it off and proceed, but otherwise discard the batch.
Pale red or brown in colour (in the jar)	This is normal, and shouldn't affect the flavour, but if you'd like to darken it, leave the bottles in a sunny spot for a few months. The soy and wheat particles also make it appear lighter, so if you want to remove more of them, filter it through a coffee filter (you may have to change it a number of times).

Flavouring Your Soy Sauce

The robust taste of soy sauce can easily be infused with other ingredients without being overpowered. Kombu seaweed's oceanic aroma pairs perfectly with the saltiness of soy sauce, shiso's complexity is untangled by the brine, and garlic shoyu *is so good I've been caught sipping it.*

Garlic: Put 5 peeled cloves of garlic into a small jar and cover with 100ml soy sauce. Refrigerate for at least 24 hours. The garlic works well in stir-fries, and the sauce is great for dipping. It will keep in the fridge for a month.

Shiso: Put 10–15 shiso (or perilla, which is very similar) leaves into a small jar, cover with 100ml of soy sauce and refrigerate for at least 48 hours. The leaves can be used to wrap around rice for a delicious snack, and the sauce will be infused with a delicate mint, liquorice and thyme aroma, which makes for a lovely fresh dipping sauce for tempura. After removing the leaves, it will keep for at least a month in the fridge. Shiso can be tricky to find in the UK but is easy to grow – I have a pot which has established itself as a perennial without any particular effort.

Toasted Kombu: Cut a 5cm square of kombu seaweed and place in an unoiled pan over a medium heat. Dry roast for 3–4 minutes, until aromatic. Remove to a small jar and cover with 100ml of soy sauce. Refrigerate for 24 hours, then remove and discard the kombu. The sea-scented sauce complements broccoli and asparagus very nicely, and will keep for a month in the fridge.

Soy Sauce Butter: This umami delivery system is one of those embarrassingly simple tricks which, once tried, presents itself as an almost universal condiment. Use it for finishing noodle soups, punching up steamed veg, brushing over steak, dressing polenta, or even, as Yotam Ottolenghi does, on savoury porridge (he should not be questioned – this is delicious). Heat 2 tablespoons of unsalted butter with ½ tablespoon of soy sauce until it's just melted, then whisk to form an emulsion. Apply liberally to anything you'd like to make delicious.

Soy Caramel Dark Milk Chocolate Tart

I am a total sucker for a chocolate tart, and I will always order it anywhere I find it on the menu. It took me some years before I came to the dreadful realization I could cook it at home. Soy caramel is like salted caramel squared. Or cubed. No, it's the butter that should be cubed. As for the chocolate, I find that dark milk (over 50% cocoa) works perfectly. You can adjust the amount of soy sauce slightly to taste. Anyway, I impart this to you with my apologies to your tailor if you find it as addictive as I do.

TIME / 2½ hours
   (+ 4–5 hours refrigeration)
YIELD / 1 tart (12 slices)
KIT / Food processor
23cm tart tin with removable
   base
Baking beans (OR dried beans)

FOR THE CRUST
250g all-purpose flour
1 teaspoon caster sugar
½ teaspoon salt
1 medium egg
125g unsalted butter,
   in 2cm cubes
60ml ice-cold water

FOR THE FILLING
280g unsalted butter
240g light brown sugar
240g double cream
60ml soy sauce
280g dark milk chocolate,
   in 2cm chunks

1/ Sift the flour, sugar and salt into a bowl, then heap it and make a well in the centre.

2/ Add the egg to the well and mix, bringing in a little flour from the sides until there's no more liquid.

3/ Add the butter cubes and flatten each of them with your fingers.

4/ Now mix in the water little by little, kneading lightly, until it comes together into a smooth dough – you may not need all the water. Turn the dough out, roll into a ball, then flatten to form a thick disc. Wrap with cling film and refrigerate for at least an hour.

5/ On a lightly floured surface, roll out the pastry into a 30cm circle, turning regularly, then lay gently in a 23cm tart tin. Fold the edge under itself to form a roll of crust atop the lip of the tin and prick the base with a fork, then line with baking parchment, overlapping the edges to prevent burning, and fill with baking beans. Cover the pan with cling film and refrigerate for another 45 minutes. Preheat the oven to 180°C.

6/ Remove the cling film, bake for 20 minutes on a tray, then carefully remove the weights and paper and pop it back in for 15–20 minutes more until it's golden brown. Remove and leave to cool.

7/ Now make the filling. Put the butter and sugar into a large saucepan over a medium heat. Stir for 4–5 minutes, until the sugar has dissolved, add the cream and soy sauce and stir for 2 minutes more, then remove from the heat and whisk in the chocolate until melted. Try it and add a few drops more soy sauce to taste. Pour the mixture into the baked tart case, allow to cool slightly, then refrigerate for 4–5 hours to set.

Soy-cured Egg Rice

This traditional Japanese snack, known as tamago gohan *(egg-rice) is essentially egg-fried rice without the frying: a bowl of soy sauce-seasoned hot rice, stirred through with a raw egg yolk. I prefer a soy-cured egg yolk, but they can be a bit too jammy to mix into the rice properly, so I add another, unadorned yolk at service. The eggs' marinating time is flexible, but this is a great breakfast dish, and the length of a good night's sleep is the sweet spot. It is also superbly well-paired with some of the pickles on pages 133–5, which likewise can be prepared the day before. A note about eggs – in 2017 British eggs were declared safe to eat raw (or lightly cooked, as here) provided they have the Lion stamp.*

TIME / 15 minutes
(+ 8 hours marinating)
YIELD / Brunch for 2
KIT / A bowl and a small
saucepan

INGREDIENTS
40ml soy sauce,
plus 1 teaspoon
½ tablespoon mirin
4 egg yolks

150g long- or medium-grain rice
Furikake, shichimi togarashi
or sesame seeds (optional)

1/ Mix 25ml of soy sauce and the mirin in a small bowl, then slide in two of the egg yolks, topping up with soy to make sure they're covered. Cover the bowl with cling film and refrigerate for 8–10 hours. Give them a swirl halfway (but only if you happen to be awake).

2/ To cook the rice, first wash it three times in a small saucepan to remove excess starch, then add 300ml of water and bring it to the boil over a high heat. Once boiling, reduce the heat to a bare simmer, cover with a lid and cook for 8 minutes.

3/ Remove the rice from the heat and leave for 10 minutes, still covered, to finish cooking.

4/ Divide the hot cooked rice into two bowls. Add an unmarinated egg yolk along with ½ teaspoon of soy sauce to each bowl, and stir through vigorously so that the yolk gently cooks as it coats the rice. Top with a marinated egg yolk and a sprinkling of *furikake*, *shichimi* or sesame seeds.

Soy Sauce Pickled Cucumbers (*Shoyuzuke*)

A neat alternative to the more familiar gherkin. Instead of being pickled in vinegar, these cucumbers are preserved largely by the saltiness of soy sauce. The same technique can be applied to a whole range of vegetables, from daikon radish to cime di rapa.

TIME / 30 minutes
   (+ 6 hours pickling)
YIELD / 120g pickles
KIT / A small (~300ml) jar

INGREDIENTS
½ a cucumber (150g)
½ teaspoon salt
90ml soy sauce
30ml sushi vinegar
25g caster sugar

1/ Cut the cucumber into 3mm slices, and mix thoroughly with the salt. Leave to sit for 20 minutes.

2/ Fill your jar and its lid with boiling water to sterilize them.

3/ Bring the soy, sushi vinegar and sugar to the boil, then reduce to a simmer and stir until the sugar has dissolved.

4/ Rinse and drain the cucumber slices, then pack them into the empty jar. Pour the soy mixture over, pushing them down with a clean spoon to make sure they're covered, then lid. Leave to cool, then refrigerate for at least 6 hours before using. They will keep for around 2 weeks in the fridge.

Wafu Mushroom & Soy Butter Spaghetti

Fusion food – so often shorthand for 'we couldn't get the proper ingredients, and/or didn't think you'd like them, so . . . how about this?' Personally, I think this Japanese take on pasta con funghi *is a shining example of fusion done right. It takes the central tenet shared by Italian and Japanese cuisine of letting ingredients shine, and applies it to soy sauce and mushrooms – so use the best that you can. It's far from essential, but if you happen to have some kombu kelp to hand, add a bit to the pasta water while it's cooking. By the way,* wafu *simply means 'Japanese style', just as the 'wa' in* wagyu *signifies 'Japanese beef'.*

TIME / 20 minutes
YIELD / Dinner for 2
KIT / A large saucepan and heavy frying pan

INGREDIENTS

220g spaghetti, dried
4 tablespoons unsalted butter
350g button or chestnut mushrooms, cut into 5mm slices
1 red onion, finely diced
3 cloves of garlic, finely sliced
2 tablespoons mirin
2 tablespoons soy sauce
1 teaspoon rice vinegar
2–3 spring onions, green part only, sliced
2 tablespoons sesame seeds, toasted
Parmesan (optional)
15cm x 15cm nori seaweed (¼ of a sushi sheet), finely sliced (optional)

1/ Heat a heavy pan over a medium-high heat. Once it's hot, add 1 tablespoon of butter, and once it's foaming add half the mushrooms and fry for about 3 minutes, stirring once. You want them brown and softening but not totally flimsy. Transfer the cooked mushrooms to a bowl and set aside, then repeat with the rest.

2/ Heat the pan over a medium heat and add 2 tablespoons of butter, followed by the onion. Cook for 4–5 minutes, then add the garlic and cook for 1 minute more. Add the mirin and let it sizzle for 10 seconds, then add the soy sauce, cooked mushrooms and vinegar, reduce the heat to a minimum and cook for 5 minutes more.

3/ Meanwhile, bring a large pan of water to boil over a high heat. Add 2 teaspoons of salt and 1 tablespoon of olive oil to the water followed by the spaghetti. Cook until almost al dente (~7–8 minutes) and just before you drain it, remove ~100ml of the cooking water and set aside.

4/ Add the pasta to the frying pan (run it briefly under running water if it's sticking together) and toss everything together over a low heat until it's very well combined, adding as much of the pasta cooking water as necessary to bring it all together. Remove from the heat, add the spring onion greens and sesame seeds and stir thoroughly, then serve (optionally garnished with parmesan and seaweed slices).

Chapter four
Hot Sauce

A CROSS-CULTURAL CURE-ALL for sandwiches, leftovers and eggs of all kinds, hot sauce can augment almost anything using the holy trinity of sour, salt and spice. At current count, my fridge door heaves with seven different varieties of hot sauce, bolstered by three more waiting their turn from the larder; it routinely comes out at breakfast, lunch and dinner, and gilds most late-night snacks. My adoration is by no means unusual. The depth of the hot sauce market reflects this, and in efforts to stand out on this crowded field, naming conventions have descended into the violent ('Heartbreaking Dawn's Cauterizer'), the cautionary ('One Fuckin' Drop At A Time') and the puerile ('Professor Phardtpounder's Colon Cleaner!'), with bottles shaped like coffins, grenades and blood vials. Fanciful branding may belie the dedication and craft which goes into layering flavours within these condiments, taking them in all manner of directions beyond pure, aggressive spiciness. Mexican chipotle sauce is made from smoke-dried jalapeños; Bajan pepper sauce takes mustard heat as a base, supercharged with Scotch bonnets and accented with turmeric; while in Michigan, BLiS brand hot sauce is made from three chilli varieties before being aged for a year in barrels that have already been used for ageing bourbon, maple syrup *and* stout.

Before hot sauce though, there was the chilli pepper. It can be traced back to Mexico, where it's been consumed by humans for around eight thousand years. It was one of the first self-pollinating crops, meaning a single chilli could replicate itself without relying on other plants, or bees to cart its pollen around. This meant that they could get established and survive even in ecosystems where insects hadn't become attuned to the deliciousness of their nectar. The chilli pepper needed only birds. Birds could airdrop their seeds into clifftop crevices, undiscovered islands and isolated oases, where the new arrivals could replicate and thrive. Mammals, by contrast, were far less attractive seed dispersers – with teeth instead of wings they could only deposit the seeds nearby, and would likely chew them into impotence anyway. Chilli peppers therefore developed capsaicin. This fiery defence mechanism made them repellent to mammals (as well as pest insects and some moulds – yes, fungi can 'taste' spiciness), yet still attractive to birds, who are without

the necessary taste receptors to notice heat. Like so many of nature's adaptations, this worked very well until humans came along. Us, with our stuffed jalapeños and ghost pepper challenges, our phaals and Sichuan hot pots. We bloody loved chillies. We loved them so much that we gave their defence mechanism a new vector (converting it to an attractor) and started breeding them ourselves.

Hot sauce makers have crafted bottles in shapes ranging from vials of blood to coffins.

The diminutive, blueberry-sized *chiltepin* (roughly, 'flea chilli') is believed to be the ancestor of all chillies. Ironically, however, it's fiercely resistant to human-led domestication, so it remains difficult to buy even today. Its name is Aztec in origin; archaeobotanists have found chilli remnants on ancient Aztec millstones, so we know that they used ground chillies. From there, it's not hard to imagine that they might have combined these chillies with water and salt and left them to sit in the sun to ferment.

The *chiltepin* might have been similar to the first chillies brought from the West by Columbus in 1493, but he dubbed it a 'pepper' not because of its peppercorn-like dimensions, but to increase its marketability. Far away in the Mediterranean, the Italian maritime city-states like Venice, Pisa and Genoa had become wildly rich through their monopolies on the spice trade over the past five hundred years. Columbus, as a Genoan, would have grown up surrounded by fortunes built upon cinnamon, clove and grains of paradise (a popular contemporary substitute for black pepper). In the Middle Ages, spices (particularly black pepper) had become the most valuable commodities in Europe, and so, by the fifteenth century, explorers were feverishly searching for new routes to the 'Spice Islands' of Indonesia and the 'Malabar Coast' of India. Columbus had been tipped off that a westerly passage might exist to Asia, and thus embarked on the voyage that would bring about the European 'discovery' of the Americas. Keen to reassure himself of the commercial success of the expedition, upon visiting the Caribbean island of Hispaniola Columbus noted in his journal, 'The land was found to produce much *ají*, which is the pepper of the inhabitants, and more valuable than the common sort [of black pepper].' When he returned from what he insisted was west Asia with these spicy plants, 'peppers' is therefore what he called them.

This new 'pepper' didn't catch on instantly in Europe, except as an ornamental curiosity cultivated in the gardens of aristocrats and monasteries.

However, over time it gained traction in the kitchens of southern Europe as 'the pauper's pepper', giving farmers a way of invigorating bland dishes. Demonstrating the importance of culture as much as ingredients in cooking, it was only when European settlers 'rediscovered' the *chiltepin* through Native American and Mexican cuisine in the American Southwest that it was really incorporated into their food.

An early missionary to Sonora in Mexico found himself on the receiving end of conversion in 1687, when offered a taste of the *chiltepin* by his Othama neighbours. The German priest (called, in an incredible stroke of nominative determinism, 'Ignaz Pfeffercorn') wrote to his fellow Jesuits:

> *It is a bit more bitingly sharp than the [black pepper], yet it is manna to the American palate, and is used with every dish with which it harmonises . . . After the first mouthful the tears started to come. I could not say a word and believed I had hell-fire in my mouth. However, one becomes accustomed to it after frequent bold victories so that with time, the dish becomes tolerable and finally agreeable.*

God bless Ignaz and his 'bold victories'. Meanwhile, back in Europe, chillies were beginning to weave their way into recipes and food cultures. In Hungary, the paprika peppers first cultivated by monks would eventually go on to become so popular that by the 1820s they had supplanted other spices and transformed the national dish of *goulash* into *paprikash*.

The tiny, wild, berry-like chiltepin is forefather to the many hundreds of other chilli varieties.

While it may have taken time for Europeans to absorb the smouldering spice into their diets, it quickly set the rest of the world on fire. In Tunisia, roasted red peppers were combined with garlic, cumin, caraway and coriander seeds to create glorious harissa (a word deriving from the Arabic *harasa*, meaning 'mash'). Portuguese traders took it across the span of their empire, from Mozambique in the south (where it caught on as the 'peri-peri') to India in the east. Once the chilli had made the crossing to Goa, it sped through China, India, Korea and Thailand, seeding itself in local dishes from curries to kimchi to hot pot – foods that all predated the chilli but now seem so inherently linked to it that it feels faintly ridiculous to imagine them without it.

Plenty of these early adopters of the chilli pepper discovered ways of turning it into a condiment. Koreans folded chillies into a sweet/savoury fermented bean paste that had for centuries been spiced with black or Sichuan pepper, and in doing so the wondrous *gochujang* was fashioned (all fridges should have a tub – I've used it in a few recipes in the kimchi chapter). In China, Sichuanese cooks had a similar idea, creating spicy *doubanjiang* with fermented broad beans and chillies (another delicious fridge staple). Indonesians grind chillies with shallot, garlic, shrimp paste and a plethora of other ingredients to make a range of condiments called *sambals* (there are hundreds of varieties across the archipelago).

If we're being pedantic, none of these quite count as 'hot sauce' as we'd recognize it today – one that's predominantly made of chilli, salt and maybe a little vinegar and other flavourings. Hot sauces, in a way, embody the American Dream. There are hundreds of homebrew hot sauce start-ups, many of them hoping that one day they might be half as popular as the titans of industry, but knowing in a year or two half of them will be replaced. The behemoths of hot sauce that they may aspire to follow are both American, both immigrants who started their businesses in the wake of wars, and both accused of taking 'inspiration' from other recipes.

Colonel Maunsel White emigrated from Ireland to the American South in 1796, when he was thirteen. For most of his life, he was a slave-owner and cotton trader in Louisiana, but in his old age he began growing chillies. He was a well-known *bon vivant* in New Orleans, at a time when the city was the wealthiest in the country, with the fourth largest port in the world, built on the suffering traded through North America's largest slave market. All the city's many inhabitants, from the original French colonizers and their Creole descendants, to Spanish and German immigrants, to enslaved West Africans – each brought with them their own ingredients and recipes. A common thread in this uniquely variegated cuisine was a singular love of the chilli pepper. White, who regularly hosted dinner parties for the well-to-do of New Orleans, started making a hot sauce which he served to his guests. It became so popular that he occasionally provided barrels to local stores and left them to bottle it, but (perhaps because he was already fabulously wealthy) this was more a culinary act of municipal largesse than serious commercial endeavour – he never made the effort to market it further afield. A New Orleans paper, the *Daily True Delta*, noted in 1850:

> *Col. White has introduced the celebrated tobasco [sic] red pepper . . .*
> *Owing to its oleaginous character, [he] found it impossible to preserve it*

by drying; but by pouring strong vinegar on it after boiling, he has made a sauce or pepper decoction of it . . . The use of a decoction like this, particularly in preparing the food for laboring persons, would be found exceedingly beneficial in a relaxing climate like this.

It should be said that, certainly in White's case, 'laboring persons' meant the two hundred enslaved men, women and children who worked his plantations. Hot sauce unmistakably has roots in the worst parts of American history.

Another well-to-do resident of the city, the banker Edmund McIlhenny, would soon develop his own sauce using the same type of peppers. McIlhenny had already made a fortune in New Orleans lending valuable Louisiana currency, when the Civil War forced him and his wife Mary to flee to Texas. After their return they moved to Mary's family sugar plantation on Avery Island, which was no longer profitable following the emancipation of its workers by Union soldiers. The island, however, was blessed with a rare natural resource, being sited atop a massive 'salt dome' (the largest on the Louisiana coast). With a steady supply of the valuable commodity that was salt, Edmund toiled away in the old pigeon coop, improving on White's hot sauce manufacturing technique. Instead of simply boiling the tabasco peppers with vinegar, he used the salt to dry-brine them and left them to ferment in bourbon barrels for six weeks, before adding vinegar just at the end.

In 1869, McIlhenny packed his first bottles – which were very similar to those sold today – and delivered them to stores. Wholesalers promptly bought up his entire supply for a dollar a bottle (about $18 in today's money). Soon, assisted somewhat ironically by word-of-mouth spread by Union troops returning home, he had distribution over most of the country. Keen to protect his new hot sauce, he filed a patent for 'E. McIlhenny Tabasco Pepper

The first batches of Tabasco sauce were packaged in small cologne bottles, which were corked and sealed in green wax.

Sauce', detailing his production method carefully. Puzzlingly, he included in the patent method 'bisulphate of lime' to 'retard further fermentation', though the McIlhenny company historian has claimed that this was never an actual ingredient, and thinks it may only have been included in the patent as a 'ruse' to throw off would-be imitators. The sauce was a huge hit, and within three years he set up an outpost in London to handle European orders.

Tabasco sauce went on to have many successes, but one of McIlhenny's most wonderfully whimsical legacies was to inspire the 'Burlesque Opera of Tabasco', an 1894 show in Boston which featured a giant papier-mâché Tabasco bottle and a surprising spectrum of hot-sauce-centred seduction, cross-dressing and assassination attempts. After arranging that Tabasco miniatures be given out in the interval (the first time these tiny bottles had been manufactured), McIllhenny's son gave the show his blessing. You can hear a rendition of the opera's overture by the Czech Hradec Králové Philharmonic Orchestra on YouTube, which naturally I must recommend.

Meanwhile, on a beach far, far away on the eastern shore of the Gulf of Thailand, another hot sauce phenomenon was brewing, and in an interesting parallel with the story of Louisiana's spiciest son, it was not the early bird that would go on to catch the global market share. The chilli pepper had proved a wild success within Thai cuisine since its arrival with the Portuguese in the sixteenth century. In the 1930s Thanom Chakkapakhad from Si Racha (sometimes spelled 'Sri Racha') devised a three-month fermented hot sauce made with spur chillies (milder than the more commonly seen 'bird's eye' variety) to pair with local seafood, and after encouragement from her friends, started selling it to shops and restaurants. Her sauce (known as Sriraja Panich) is still sold in Thailand today, but you're probably more familiar with a later evolution of it that started life in neighbouring Vietnam. David Tran's family chilli farm was struggling after the Vietnam War, so they started experimenting with chilli sauce, which they sold in repurposed Gerber baby food jars left by American aid workers. Eventually forced to evacuate by the war in 1978, Tran set up a new factory in California, and after trying a few other chilli sauce styles, he hit upon making sriracha with local red jalapeños, combined with garlic, sugar, salt and vinegar. The bottles, labelled with roosters (his Chinese zodiac birth sign), and crowned with green nozzles, have been a worldwide phenomenon, spawning everything from keychain 'pocket bottles' to socks to lip balm. At David Tran's factory in Irwindale, even the fire extinguishers are emblazoned with the famous rooster.

THE CHILLI PEPPER is an intensely geekified ingredient – it even has a measurement scale. The Scoville scale describes the concentration of capsaicinoids, which are the chemicals that make chillies 'hot'. The original way this 'scale' worked was somewhat idiosyncratic. To assess a chilli's heat in Scoville Heat Units (SHUs), a small amount would be dried, mixed into a solution and then tasted by a panel of expert tasters, then diluted, tasted, diluted again and tasted repeatedly until the heat was no longer detectable. The number of dilutions was used to determine the SHU – and thus how much of a certain chilli pepper you'd need to use in a dish in order to achieve the desired level of heat. These days the process involves a bit more chemistry and a bit less subjectivity, but the scale remains the same. The '7 Pot' Trinidadian pepper, at 1.1 million SHU, is said to provide enough wallop for seven pots of stew – which indicates that a Scotch bonnet pepper, at 225,000 SHU, would be enough for about 1.432 pots.

The chipotle is only one of at least a dozen types of dried chilli in Mexico – even the smoked jalapeño itself comes in two styles (the more pliant and fruity morita, *and the intense, heavily smoked* meco).

It's very useful to have a method for objectively quantifying our personal preference for chillies of a particular capsaicin concentration. While you might pour on Dunn's River hot sauce (~1,000 SHU) like ketchup, your chilli-averse friend may find a couple of drops cause searing pain. However, one side-effect of being able to gauge spiciness has been a chilli arms race, with the venerable Realm of Bhut Jolokia (the 'ghost pepper') shoring itself against the guerrilla forces of the Carolina Reapers, as the Trinidad Moruga Scorpions jostle for position. This is a very recent culinary phenomenon – until the 1990s the hottest measured chilli was the humble habanero, and even after the Red Savina pepper (a slightly hotter habanero) was cultivated, it remained the new champion for twelve years until 2006. Then it really started. Guinness World Records assessed the Bhut Jolokia, which India's Defence Research Laboratory had already been researching for weaponization, and found it to be at least twice as hot as the Savina. Since then, a flurry of competitive capsaicin cultivation has led to the record being broken five more times, with chillies that can only be reasonably considered useful for economizing mace production and YouTube challenge videos.

Given the pain that chillies can cause us, it may seem paradoxical that it can alleviate it too, and it's this dual purpose which has led capsaicin recently to be banned from competitive equestrian events. Capsaicin has been deemed a 'doping agent' because it can be used to hypersensitize horses to touching a pole while jumping, but also, despite seeming to *cause* pain, it can actually act as an analgesic. The reason that we sense heat when eating (or touching) chillies is that receptors in our skin (called TRPV1s) which sense high temperatures (above 43°C) are also stimulated by capsaicin, as well as compounds found in mustard, wasabi, ginger and black pepper. (We have different receptors for cold temperatures, which are similarly baffled by menthol.) The mechanism by which this apparent pain *prevents* pain is not fully understood, but it's thought that by overstimulating these receptors we deplete the chemical which sends signals to our brain, which may also be why we can build tolerance by eating lots of spicy food.

One might imagine that the heat of chillies and hot sauces is something that can be measured purely in amplitude – the greater the Scoville rating, the fiercer the burn – but there's more nuance than that. While capsaicin is the best known 'heat chemical', comprising nearly 70% of the 'capsaicinoids' in a typical chilli, more than twenty other similar compounds have been identified. The amounts of these vary hugely in some chillies – *Capsicum pubescens* varieties (which are the literal black sheep of the chilli family, being the only peppers with dark seeds) can have only small amounts of capsaicin, but large amounts of dihydrocapsaicin. These different chemicals give different kinds of 'burn' – nordihydrocapsaicin is mostly detected in the front of the mouth and fades quickly, while homodihydrocapsaicin lends a late-blooming heat, but can stick around for hours.

The hierarchy of heat by which we categorize chillies disregards their other culinary properties. Chillies cover an amazing range of flavours, from the robust, toasted aroma of the dried 'facing heaven' pepper in Sichuan cuisine to the tropical fruit bowl that is the habanero. In fact, back in 2002 the excellent Chile Pepper Institute at New Mexico State University developed a new variety, the NuMex Suave, with all the citrus/apricot flavour of the scorching habanero, but the heat of a sweet red pepper. It's a constant staple in my garden. These gustatory nuances can be highlighted in hot sauces. When you start pairing one (or two) of the head-spinning number of cultivars up with the huge array of other ingredients that ferment well, the breadth of flavours you can achieve is almost endless. Scotch bonnets pair beautifully with tropical flavours like mango, kiwi and lime, while peach is a great friend to habanero and watermelon is curiously good with the serrano pepper (this is the miniature jalapeño-shaped type one you'll usually see in supermarkets as unnamed 'red' or 'green' chillies).

The traditional way of making hot sauce is to create a 'mash' – that is, to blend up the peppers with a bit of salt (2–5% the weight of the peppers) and then leave them to ferment, submerged under the small amount of liquid they'll shortly put out. This method tends to get the most flavour out of the chillies, but, because it's harder to keep all the mash submerged, it's more prone to errant yeasts and moulds. Though you can scrape these off, there's a more reliable method, whereby you chop the chillies into large pieces and then cover them in a salt brine (as if making pickled cucumbers). When your sauce is fully fermented you'll simply strain out the chillies, blend them up, and then add back just enough of the brine to reach your desired consistency. This means, of course, that you'll lose some of the flavour to any leftover brine, but it is pretty tasty stuff so I always tend to find a home for it (great in guacamole for simultaneous spice, sour and salt).

When dreaming up new hot sauces, I most often reach for fruit to add new flavours. Mango, peach, kiwi, cherry, plum and orange – all resonate with the natural flavours of so many varieties of pepper, but particularly the *C. chinense* types in the habanero family. You can add the fruit along with the chillies at the beginning, in which case it will ferment along with them, but you'll lose its sweetness, or you can add it at the bottling stage and retain more of its original character. If you opt for 'late' fruit addition, though, you run the risk of restarting fermentation – those extra sugars are fresh food for your lactic acid bacteria – which could result in a hot sauce explosion in your fridge. So, if adding fruit at the end, it's best either to just blitz up a portion

The floral and fruity aromas typical of habanero marry splendidly with ripe peach.

of the hot sauce with the fruit as required and keep for no more than a couple of days, or, if you want to keep it for longer, add 10–20% of the sauce weight in vinegar to tame fermentation and make sure the pH stays low enough to preserve the finished product. You could even pasteurize your hot sauce by simmering it for ten minutes – this will arrest fermentation by killing off all microbes. Ginger and garlic should usually be added at the beginning, and will add a secondary heat dimension, but don't be alarmed if your garlic turns green or even bright blue (this happens when garlic is exposed to acid – a favourite dumpling restaurant in Beijing lines their walls with huge glass vessels full of cobalt-coloured cloves, which guests are free to plunder).

As for spices, for the most part it matters less when you mix them in, and more how much you add. Cumin and coriander are great base notes, and can be added relatively freely. Star anise and allspice are also delicious – but err on the side of caution, as they can develop quite dominant flavours. Mustard seeds are classic in Bajan-style hot sauce, and if you add them early they'll have time to properly soften up, so they blend nicely.

Once you've got everything together, added the salt and left it to ferment, what's actually happening? Similarly to other vegetable ferments like kimchi and sauerkraut, the first signs of life will come from *Leuconostoc mesenteroides*, which is going to start work on making your hot sauce a bit more acidic, but will primarily be providing fizziness. If you see bubbles in the first two or three days you're off to a flying start – they will often be accompanied by the brine becoming cloudy (this is the cells of the microbes floating about). This is only the beginning, though. Chillies are slow fermenters, and this will be a long ride. I should explain that it's not the chillies slacking off here, but the bacteria that's breaking them down into a nice, acidic hot sauce. Studies have shown capsaicin is actually bactericidal, and can kill off listeria and streptococcus quite effectively – and thus not only does it deter hefty mammals from eating chillies, but also discourages tiny little lactic acid bacteria from having a go at them too. Anyway, even if it takes a while, the second stage of fermentation (with *Lactobacillus plantarum*) will reduce the pH by producing lactic acid, which will eventually sour the hot sauce enough that it can be considered 'safe' from pathogens.

The hot sauce isn't necessarily finished once your chillies are fermented. If you've left the chillies in large chunks, you're going to need to turn them into something more pourable, probably with the aid of a blender. Having said which – Hawaiian pepper water and Puerto Rican Pique sauce are simply left in this separated state, using the brine or vinegar that the chillies have been steeping in as the condiment (one of the earliest known hot sauces from 1850s New York was a bird pepper-infused vinegar in this style). Most makers blitz the chillies though, and gradually add the brine back until it reaches the desired consistency. If you want something like the Louisiana hot sauce with the little dropper bottle however, you'll need to strain the chilli solids back out – and even then you'll notice that it's probably far too thin to easily 'dose'. Deploying a thickener is very helpful here – xanthan gum is most common, and works well as it is flavourless, doesn't need to be heated and works in minute quantities (start with a shy one-eighth teaspoon per 150ml and make sure you add it *while* blending, or it'll seize up). Sure, it's got a weird name, but it's totally safe (as reviewed by the strict European Food Safety Authority), and it's actually a product of fermentation itself – bacteria produce it after munching on sugar. It's easiest to buy online, though you may find it in the supermarket with other thickeners like arrowroot, which is also an apt substitute, but you'll have to use a tiny bit more and heat it just slightly first. (To avoid heating your hot sauce, if you don't want to pasteurize it, make a slurry of arrowroot with a little water, warm that until it thickens, then add a teaspoon or so per 150ml hot sauce once it's cooled a little.)

You may notice that many hot sauces have vinegar as a main ingredient. With non-fermented hot sauces this is, of course, essential in order to make them sour – but it's often added to fermented hot sauces too. Why? Because manufacturers don't want to wait a month or more for their hot sauce to be ready, and they want to be sure that every bottle is consistently sour. Often this is done at the same time as pasteurizing the hot sauce. Of course, at home we don't need to do this, but the vinegar can be a big part of the flavour, especially in Louisiana-style sauces, so feel free to add a couple of tablespoons at the end to taste (or if you want to use your hot sauce before it's quite finished fermenting). Apple cider, rice and white wine vinegar all work well, and by making hot sauce at home you can use higher quality vinegar than would ever be considered for commercial manufacture – the pinnacle being, of course, your own homemade vinegar (see page 116). Note also that fermentation slightly reduces the heat of chillies, as the bacteria consume some of the capsaicin, so you'll find that fermented hot sauces are marginally less spicy than their vinegary cousins (don't worry, hotheads, the effect isn't significant), but will have greater potential complexity and depth.

Everyday Hot Sauce

I implore you to please wear the gloves. When working with large numbers of chillies, it's almost impossible to avoid getting capsaicin particles in unwanted places. If you are without gloves, rub your hands with oil before soaping them (the oil-soluble capsaicin will dissolve more easily than in water, and then you can wash the whole mess off).

TIME / 3–12 weeks
YIELD / 150ml hot sauce

KIT / Food processor
~300ml jar
Blender
Rubber gloves
Shot glass or other small
   weight

INGREDIENTS
150g chillies
   (any variety or a mix)
9g salt (to make a 3.6% brine,
   which the 150g chillies will
   dilute to 2.25%)

1/ Remove the stems and, with gloves on, chop the chillies into wide slices, then pack as tightly as possible into a jar.

2/ Mix the salt with 250ml of lukewarm water and stir until fully dissolved, then pour over the chillies until they are just fully covered (you probably won't need all the brine). Push down any that try to float – if you have a small weight it will be helpful here.

3/ Seal the jar and leave it on a counter out of the sun, checking once a day for fizziness – once it begins, open the jar once a day to let any gas escape. After it's started fizzing the brine will cloud over, then a few days later the fizzing will stop, but it's still fermenting. The longer you leave it, the better it will be, but as a guideline shoot for a minimum of 3 weeks and 12 or more if you want to really age it. Taste it (gingerly!) to check if it's ready – you're looking for a sour, vinegary flavour.

4/ Pour off and reserve the brine, and blend the chillies. Slowly add back as much brine as you like to achieve the desired consistency – you can strain too if you'd like a smooth sauce. Transfer to a jar or bottle and refrigerate – it will keep for several months.

A Few of My Favourite Blends

Many of the recipes in this book are really starting points, and this is particularly true of hot sauce. The vast range of chillies, fruits and spices that you can use while following the same basic steps mean that you absolutely ought to experiment with different ingredients – it would be churlish not to have at least two or three versions on the go. I've adjusted the salt in each of the below to account for the extra ingredients.

Bird's Eye & Peach: As above, substituting the chillies with 150g of bird's eye chillies (roughly chopped) and 1 peach, peeled and chopped into large pieces. Add the peach to the jar, wedging in the pieces to prevent floating, followed by the chillies and brine, upping salt to 12g (plus weights if using).

Red Habanero, Bell Pepper & Onion: As above, substituting the chillies with 60g (~4–6) of red habaneros, ½ a red pepper, deseeded, and ½ a white onion, all chopped into large pieces. Add the onion, pepper, chillies and brine (with 11g salt) to the jar (plus weights if using).

Mango, Orange Scotch Bonnet & Ginger: As above, substituting the chillies with 60g (~4–6) of orange Scotch bonnets, the flesh of ½ a mango, a 1cm piece of peeled ginger and ½ a white onion, all roughly chopped. Add the ginger to the jar, followed by the mango, onion, chillies and brine, with 11g salt (plus weights if using).

Scotch Bonnet, Mustard & Turmeric (Bajan): As above, substituting the chillies with 60g (~4–6) of orange Scotch bonnets, 50g of fresh peeled turmeric and ½ a white onion, all roughly chopped. Add 1 teaspoon of yellow mustard seeds to the jar, followed by the turmeric, onion, chillies and brine, with 11g salt (plus weights if using). The turmeric amplifies the habanero flavour, making it somehow seem even fruitier.

Pineapple & Garlic: As above, using a larger 500ml jar and substituting the chillies with 300g of ripe, chopped pineapple (approx. ½ a pineapple), 20g of garlic (~4 cloves) and 75g (~5–7) of red habaneros, deseeded, followed by the brine (increasing the salt to 15g).

TROUBLESHOOTING / If your Hot Sauce is...

Not fermenting	Chillies can be very slow to get going, especially in the high-salt environment we place them in. If they take more than a couple of weeks, you may have to start again – though if there's no sign of mould, you may as well leave your problem batch running. Make sure the amount of salt is correct, and try fermenting somewhere slightly warmer.
Forming a white film on top (during fermentation)	This is likely something that's commonly called kahm yeast (see page 170), which can be a particular problem with longer ferments, especially if there's a lot of sugar (e.g. when adding carrots). It's likely not harmful, but can affect flavour slightly. Remove and continue fermenting. In hot weather, you may need to increase the brine to 5% (12.5g salt to 250ml water) to counteract this.
Forming a white film on top (once bottled)	This is rarer, but still likely kahm yeast. Add a little vinegar (a tablespoon per 150ml should do).
Too spicy	There's not a lot you can do about this, except try making it again with milder chillies. Mixing it with mayonnaise will subdue the heat (but you could also just give it away – I'm always happy to receive a bottle of hot sauce).

Green Chilli Fermented Salsa

This is a very mild 'hot' sauce – the kind of stuff you can consume in ketchupesque quantities, and even use as the basis for entire dishes. If you've ever come across Mexican recipes that call for tomatillos, you'll know that these papery-husked sour fruits are a rare and exotic find in the UK, even in their canned form – I never saw them fresh until I grew them in my garden. If you don't want to grow them, this recipe makes a passable substitute. You can use any mild green chilli – there's a couple of good Turkish varieties, or the 'Scoville roulette' types such as Padrón or shishito – and if you can only find slightly hotter chillies (jalapeños, say), then try combining with a green pepper. You can also apply the mash technique here with any of the above hot sauce recipes too, optionally straining it at the end and adding xanthan gum (see page 105) if you want a thin, pourable sauce (but I think chunky salsa style is perfect for a mild sauce like this that you'll use in larger quantities).

TIME / 1–6 months
YIELD / 300g salsa
KIT / Small/medium jar
Blender

INGREDIENTS
300g Padrón, shisito or other
    very mild chilli OR 270g
    green pepper + 30g jalapeño

2 cloves of garlic
9g salt

1/ Remove the stems from the chillies/peppers and deseed, then blitz them with the garlic and salt into a chunky paste. Pack into a clean jar, making sure the inside surfaces of the jar are scraped down.

2/ Seal the jar and leave on a counter out of the sun, checking once a day for fizziness (once it begins, open the jar once or twice a day to let any gas escape). Press down the mash with a clean fork to push out bubbles every couple of days while it's fizzing, and be vigilant for any mould on the surface in the first few days. Mashes age particularly well – try and leave it going for at least a month (and anywhere up to 3–6 months). Once it is soured to your liking, it will then keep for many months in the fridge.

Satay Prawn Noodles with Cucumber Achat

Peanut or sesame mixed with chilli is one of those wonderful flavour combinations which manages to easily exceed the sum of its (already excellent) parts. From the simplest honey and chilli roast peanuts, through to dan dan *noodles with chilli oil and Chinese sesame paste, it just works. Satay sauce is an excellent example of this delicious marriage – peanuts with coconut milk is good, adding hot sauce makes it better, and red curry paste (not only traditional, but essential) makes it so delicious I often find it hard to bother making the rest of the dish and not just eat it out of the bowl. The cucumber* achat *quick pickle (below) which usually accompanies Thai satay does a superb job of cutting through the sticky sauce.*

Time / 20 minutes
Yield / Dinner for 2
Kit / A wok

For the Sauce
80ml coconut milk
3 tablespoons smooth peanut
    butter
2 teaspoons red curry paste
1 tablespoon garlic-based
    hot sauce (e.g. pineapple
    & garlic or sriracha)
2 teaspoons tamarind paste
2 teaspoons fish sauce

For the Noodles
180g dried chow mein noodles
160g raw prawns, peeled
1 small carrot, peeled and
    julienned
1 clove of garlic, finely
    chopped
2 spring onions, finely sliced
2 teaspoons sesame seeds
½ lime

1/ Thoroughly combine the coconut milk with the peanut butter, then add the other sauce ingredients and mix well.

2/ Boil a medium pan of water, add the noodles and cook for 4–5 minutes, stirring occasionally, until flexible but al dente. Drain, thoroughly rinse under cold water, and set aside.

3/ Heat a large wok over a high heat until just smoking, add 2 tablespoons of vegetable oil, swirl quickly and drop the heat to medium. Add the prawns and cook until just pink (1–2 minutes), then add the carrot and garlic and cook for a minute more.

4/ Add the spring onions, noodles and sauce to the wok, and combine all thoroughly. Cook for a little longer until all warmed through, adding 1–2 tablespoons of water to loosen the sauce as necessary.

5/ Serve in warmed bowls, topped with sesame seeds and a squeeze of lime. Sprinkle the cucumber pickles over as you eat it.

Cucumber Achat

While the name is similar to 'achar' in Hindi-Urdu, Tamil, Nepali and other languages, Thai achat, unlike most familiar South Asian pickles (such as the ubiquitous lime or mango varieties) is quick-pickled.

INGREDIENTS
⅓ of a cucumber
80ml white vinegar
1½ tablespoons sugar

1 teaspoon salt
1 bird's eye chilli, finely chopped
2 tablespoons shallots, finely chopped

1 tablespoon coriander leaves, finely chopped

1/ Quarter the cucumber lengthwise, then chop into small pieces. Next, heat the vinegar with the sugar and salt until they just dissolve, then remove from the heat.

2/ Add the cucumber, chilli, shallots and coriander to the vinegar, mix thoroughly and leave for 15 minutes to cool in a small jar or bowl.

Thai Crab Cakes with Avocado Hot Sauce

Crab is a delicate flavour, easily lost under the weight of too many breadcrumbs or crushed beneath a wave of spices. By sticking to the gentler end of Thai aromatics and offloading the chilli into a creamy condiment, the tender crustacean's shy demeanour is spotlit. Avocado is a step beyond traditional Thai flavours, I know, but it just bridges the hot sauce and crab cakes so well that I must request your indulgence. This goes nicely with coconut rice, for which you can cook rice as usual (page 90), replacing the water with two-thirds coconut milk and one-third water, plus a sprinkle of fish sauce to taste.

TIME / 45 minutes

YIELD / Dinner for 2 with rice

KIT / A large non-stick frying pan

INGREDIENTS

200g crab meat

110g panko breadcrumbs

4 minced *makrut* lime leaves (thick central 'stem' removed)

3 finely sliced small spring onions

1 clove of garlic, crushed

2 teaspoons chopped coriander leaves

1 teaspoon minced ginger

Zest and juice of 1 lime

1 teaspoon fish sauce

1 teaspoon mayonnaise

2 teaspoons fish sauce

1 egg, beaten

1 teaspoon salt

1/ Mix the crab with 50g of breadcrumbs and the rest of the ingredients, except the egg and salt.

2/ Form into 4 patties and put into the fridge for half an hour.

3/ Mix the egg with the salt, then dip the cakes in the egg followed by the remaining breadcrumbs.

4/ Heat 2 teaspoons of vegetable oil in a large non-stick frying pan (use two pans if necessary) on medium-high until shimmering, then fry the cakes for about 3 minutes a side, or until dark golden.

5/ Serve with avocado hot sauce and, optionally, coconut rice (as per above).

Avocado Hot Sauce

This recipe is very loosely based around 'guasacaca', a Venezuelan avocado salsa with a smoother texture than guacamole. I'll leave the hot sauce choice up to you, but the Bird's Eye & Peach goes very nicely.

INGREDIENTS
1 avocado
1 clove of garlic, crushed

3 tablespoons finely chopped
  coriander
1 lime, juiced

~1 tablespoon hot sauce
  (depending on heat)

Mash the avocado, mix in the other ingredients and add salt to taste.

Spectral Mary

Clarified tomato juice doesn't just look cool – its lack of body makes for a less filling drink, and good quality cherry tomatoes impart an intense flavour.

KIT / A blender
A coffee filter (or muslin)
TIME / 3 hours
YIELD / A single cocktail

INGREDIENTS
200g cherry tomatoes
  (about 10)
⅛ teaspoon celery salt
Ice

50ml vodka
10ml lemon juice
8–10 drops Everyday
  Hot Sauce

1/ Blitz the tomatoes and salt for about a minute in the blender.

2/ Set up the coffee filter in a glass, securing it with a rubber band. Pour the tomato pulp over the filter and refrigerate for at least 3 hours.

3/ Pour 85ml of the filtered tomato juice into an ice-filled highball glass followed by the vodka, lemon juice and hot sauce. Stir and serve.

Chapter five

Vinegar

VINEGAR IS MAGICAL STUFF – surely the only substance equally beloved of chefs, alternative medicine practitioners and whoever writes those articles about how to eliminate stubborn stains from around the home (always accompanied by bicarbonate of soda). I have no idea whether a 'cleansing vinegar rub' is truly able to cure shingles, but I do know that vinegar is one of the first things I reach for when a stew, soup or stir-fry needs 'something' (and that 'something' isn't salt).

Unlike soy sauce, kefir or sauerkraut, it's not hard to see how vinegar was discovered. Its Old French etymology offers a clue – *vin* (wine) which is *aigre* (sour), though it goes back much further than medieval France. In Old English it was *æced* (the name of a ferment-focused house music label, you mark my words), but tumbling further down the etymological rabbit hole to Latin it was known as *vinum acer* (sour wine), which also links to the *acetobacter* genus of fermenting bacteria responsible for making it.

Around 400 BC Hippocrates noted that mixing vinegar with honey would treat a cough. The first vinegar we know of wasn't made of grape wine though, but dates. Five thousand years ago Babylonians wrote of leaving palm fruits to shrivel in the sun to concentrate their sugar, before mashing them into a syrup, which would be left to ferment to alcohol and then vinegar. Even today, date vinegar is a good home-style substitute for balsamic.

Vinegar's current status as a (largely) cheap commodity stretches back to ancient Rome, where soldiers and slaves drank *posca* (vinegar diluted with water). The saying went '*posca fortem, vinum ebrium facit*' ('posca makes you strong, wine makes you drunk') – at the very least, while on the march *posca* would have been slightly better than weeks-old water. Our earliest records of it from Egypt (around 3,000 BC) show it to be valuable stuff, with pottery shard receipts showing jars of vinegar were used as payment.

The Flemish painter Jacob Jordaens's depiction of *The Banquet of Cleopatra* (held at the Hermitage, St Petersburg) shows the queen winning a bet with Mark Anthony that she could splash 10 million sesterces on a single meal.

The painting shows her sitting smugly, with a puppy curled on her lap and a parrot held above her head, as she drops a pendulous pearl earring into a goblet of vinegar; so the story goes, it dissolved in the acid and Cleopatra was able to drink it. Modern scholars, unfamiliar with vinegar's sink-scrubbing powers, were suspicious of this tale, so Prudence Jones (Associate Professor at Montclair State University, New Jersey) tested it herself, only to find that a small pearl will indeed dissolve in around 24 hours, neutralizing the acidic vinegar at the same time, making it more palatable for drinking 'neat'.

As Roman viticulture began to regionalize wine, so too vinegar began to settle into regions and cities acclaimed for their terroir, style and quality. One of the oldest of these is Orléans in the centre of France. On the banks of the Loire, the city is the closest river port to Paris (the Seine, which bisects the capital, was not favourable for transport as it has more twists than an escargot) and became the clearing house for wines. A proportion of these had soured en route, and a brand-new industry emerged to take advantage of the unsaleable plonk. In 1394 the artisans of Orléans formed a guild of *vinaigriers*, *sauciers*, *moutardiers* and *buffetiers* (meaning waiters – the name inspired that of the Beefeaters), to protect the quality of their trades. The vinegar makers in Orléans also took an oath not to reveal their manufacturing process, and with their secret they managed to create a burgeoning industry from bygone burgundies. They had achieved a near monopoly by 1800, producing 80% of all the vinegar in France.

Their great innovation was the '*Methode d'Orléans*'. The Orléanais left a little old vinegar (or 'mother') in the barrel when new wine was added, to reliably kickstart the fermentation process. The lengthwise-laid barrels were then only halfway filled with the fresh wine, and holes drilled in the top side, to maximize air flow. Though the *vinaigriers* may not have known this, the acetic acid bacteria need a good amount of oxygen to get to work. Louis Pasteur would later analyse this method, proving that a bacteria was responsible, and naming it *Acetobacter aceti*.

The Orléans vinegar makers continued to thrive up until the French Revolution, when the rights and protections of the guild were removed and production was thrown open to the free market. New producers flooded in, techniques were modernized, and the riverside vinegar stronghold became best known for lending its name to a recently founded city over on the other side of the Atlantic, in French Louisiana.

Nearly eight centuries earlier, in northern Italy in 1046, Henry III, king of Germany, Italy and Burgundy (all one guy – quite busy), had just dealt with three men claiming to be Pope, and was on his way to be crowned as Holy Roman Emperor (by his chosen Pope, quite coincidentally). He stopped off at Piacenza in Emilia Romagna to visit the most powerful north Italian prince of the day, who gave him a silver barrel filled with vinegar, drawn on a cart by two white oxen. Scribes in the royal entourage wrote of the gift, and this is how what we'd now call balsamic vinegar first made its way into the history books. For centuries balsamic vinegar remained a regional familial delicacy, little known outside Emilia Romagna, as is too often the way in Italy. It was something that was kept slowly fermenting in the larder and passed down from *nonno* to *papà* – 'slow food' from a time before 'fast food'. Until 1977, that is, when the founder of the US kitchenware brand Williams Sonoma decided to import some 12-year aged *aceto balsamico* from Modena to sell in his stores. American chefs fell in love with the sweet-sour ambrosia, and their love promptly crushed it half to death. It's not an easy thing to mass-produce a vinegar that is only just ready after the length of three presidential terms, but the demand was so enormous that producers were tempted into shortcuts. Nowadays, nearly 100 million litres of balsamic are produced every year.

The way that proper balsamic vinegar is made starts with grape must (juice) cooked down for 12 hours or more until it's reduced into a darkened syrup called *saba*. Next, the *saba* is overwintered in wooden barrels while it ferments into alcohol (a kind of very sweet wine called *vino cotto*, rarely made for drinking). After this, it progresses slowly through a series of barrels, each decreasing in size like unstacked matryoshka dolls – a little is decanted from each one every year and passed to the next by a technique called 'fractional blending' (very similar to the *solera* method used in sherry). Of course, that isn't what's happening with the cheap, supermarket own-brand Balsamic Vinegar of Modena.

As balsamic vinegar ages, it's moved through a shrinking series of barrels, much like matryoshka dolls.

So, how can you tell what type of balsamic you're buying? The simplest way, I'm afraid, is price. You're never going to find a 25-year aged vinegar for £10 or £20 (and if you do, please message me). The key term for the posh stuff is 'Traditional Balsamic Vinegar', which is PDO-protected, and carefully specified in every single aspect, ranging from the grape variety *and* growing region, to the bottle shape and size (always 100ml), to the ageing (12 years minimum, but can be up to a century), to the colour, viscosity and flavour (the latter judged by a panel of experts). All of that being sufficiently onerous as to make it impossible to make a cheap Traditional balsamic, the powers that be instead created a run-off Protected Geographical Indication (PGI) designation called 'Balsamic Vinegar of Modena', which has *some* regulations, but is much less restrictive. Producers are required to use grapes that are processed in Modena (though they may be grown anywhere), and the vinegars must be aged for a minimum of just 2 months, may be sweetened and coloured with caramel, and are often blends of *saba* and regular wine vinegar. Because of this, you can find 'of Modena' vinegars ranging from supermarket white-labels all the way to 10-year aged Leonardi retailing for £25.

Then there are *condimento* balsamics, which are free-wheeling vinegars constrained by no special production requirements at all. These can still be fantastic if, for instance, if they're a second grade vinegar made by producers of 'Traditional Balsamic' without the required bottle size or sufficient ageing, or are created outside of Modena. Who knew that vinegar could be such a marketing minefield? If you want guaranteed great balsamic, buy one labelled 'Traditional' – but I can appreciate that not everyone wants to shell out a minimum of £35/100ml (or even if you do, that you might want another bottle to splash more liberally). So, in order to aid you in searching out the best versions of the cheaper 'of Modena' and '*condimento*' vinegars, I'm going to try and simplify things with a list of indicators.

Some Things that Indicate Particular Quality:

Simple ingredients – A good 'of Modena' example will include just 'cooked grape must' and 'wine vinegar' (in that order, indicating it's mostly grape must).

Flavour – A good balsamic should have a balanced sweet-sour taste, with a developing complexity and hints of wood. Unfortunately you'll have to buy it first to check this.

Producer background – If a manufacturer sells a condimento as well as 'Traditional Balsamic', then the cheaper condimento is likely to represent great value as it may only miss the mark by virtue of being aged for, say, 6 years instead of 12.

More Questionable Indicators of Quality:

Viscosity – 'Traditional' balsamics are always denser, however manufacturers of cheaper vinegars have found plenty of cheap, fast ways to thicken vinegar.

Label colour – 'Traditional' balsamic labels are coloured to indicate age. Red means 12 years, silver means 18 years, and gold means 25 years. Some sneaky 'of Modena' producers emulate these colours to hint at a maturity they don't possess.

Age – If it's labelled invecchiato (aged) then even 'of Modena' balsamics must have been kept for 3 years – but some producers will leave it sloshing about in an oil tanker rather than a small oak cask.

IGP/PGI *(Indicazione Geografica Protetta)* – Certificates are great, but a producer could create a fantastic balsamic which isn't processed in Modena or uses the wrong grapes, and is thus excluded, while another may coast the lowest requirements to get IGP on the label.

All this, and we haven't even considered fruit balsamics! You can just as well press, ferment and age other fruits to make apple, fig or even pomegranate balsamic; the sour behemoth that is Italian balsamic largely overshadows these, but they're definitely worth a look, especially as it means supporting local food producers. There are some excellent West Country apple balsamics – fantastic for making *beurre blanc* – look out for those made solely with apples, rather than by adding balsamic vinegar, which isn't quite the same.

Sherry vinegar is a simpler thing. Though the fortified wine vinegar of Cádiz is also region-protected, it has never quite reached the levels of balsamic mania. It has humbler origins, long regarded as a waste product from spoiled wines to be sold out the back door. During the nineteenth century, however, interest in sherry vinegar slowly built – especially from France, where (perhaps) they'd grown tired of the same old stuff from Orléans. As it's grown in popularity, its producers have become more careful with their methods. Rather than leaving it to chance, wine-makers started using the same *solera* method for vinegar that they had long employed to age sherry. Much like with balsamic, this involves transferring it between barrels little by little, so each new vintage is 'balanced' with its sisters, as it ages for between six months (for *vinagre de Jerez*) to two years (for a *Reserva*) and a whole decade (for *Gran Reserva*). Instead of the vinegar passing through barrels that decrease in size (like balsamic) though, *solera* ageing occurs by transferring vinegar down a pyramid of barrels, which certainly looks jauntier. The designated growing region is similarly shaped – the Jerez triangle, as it's called, encompasses nine regions in which nothing that enters may escape unpickled. Within the nine regions there are (primarily) three varieties of grapes – the dry and crisp Palomino Fino, the ultra-sweet and raisiny Pedro Ximénez, and the floral, honeyed moscatel. If no grape is mentioned, your sherry vinegar is most likely from Palomino stock, which should be relatively neutral. Ximénez vinegars are easy to spot once poured, due to their dark umber shade (which verges close to soy sauce), and are similarly impactful on the palate, with high acidity (all sherry vinegars must be 6–8% acidity, compared to cider or malt vinegars which are closer to 4%) matched by deep jamminess – an aged Ximénez is a great place to start exploring the depths of sherry vinegars. Moscatel vinegars are probably the rarest, falling somewhere between the other two in both shade and sweetness, but bringing some of the floral characteristics shared with the sherry.

Meanwhile, China has been slowly nurturing a different kind of sour brew. While balsamic vinegar may seem popular by European standards, the Chinese vinegar market is absolutely enormous. Each year China ferments over a billion gallons of vinegar – forty times as much as Modena. The brand Jiangsu Hengshun Vinegar alone doubles the total output of the most common 'of Modena' type of balsamic. The history of vinegar in Chinese cuisine stretches back more than three thousand years. Confucius wrote about it, and incidentally, his image along with Buddha and Laozi (founder

Chinese black vinegars from Baoning, Zhenjiang and Shanxi are all delicious and well worth hunting down.

of Taoism) dipping their fingers into a barrel of vinegar is a traditional subject in classical Chinese religious painting. Their facial expressions show their attitudes to life: Confucius scowls, reflecting on the moral decay of society vinegar represents; Buddha frowns, thinking of the suffering brought by disappointed desire attached to such worldly things; Laozi smiles, because he accepts the sourness of vinegar as being just as it should be.

In ancient China, vinegar was an aristocratic pleasure; a text from around 250 BC relating to bureaucracy and governance makes it clear that any self-respecting state should appoint an official vinegar maker. Twenty-four common types of vinegar are described in a sixth-century tome on agriculture, and diversity is something Chinese vinegars have held on to – while vinegar companies in Europe and America have largely been conglomerated, merged and monopolized, in China there remains a much broader range of local brands and styles. The most common, though, is the vinegar of Zhenjiang – sometimes known simply as 'black vinegar'. You'll most commonly see this in a yellow-labelled bottle, often dubbed with the old name of Chinkiang. This vinegar has been around for about 1,400 years, with the most popular current brand (Jiangsu Hengshun) dating back to 1840, when it was started in the aftermath of the First Opium War. The city of Zhenjiang is down the Yangtze river from Shanghai, which the British fleet had just captured in June 1842, after Chinese officials had seized opium that the British East India Company had been selling to Chinese merchants. The battle at Zhenjiang was bloody and decisive, resulting in the unequal Treaty of Nanking, which forced the Chinese government to pay crippling reparations, and to grant the British a small island named Hong Kong. After the war, one local wine producer decided to switch production to vinegar – that company is today worth £2 billion, and in 2012 Zhenjiang vinegar was granted the same European geographical protection (PGI) as balsamic.

Zhenjiang vinegar is made from steamed glutinous rice – though it may seem a pedantic semantic difference, Chinese vinegars aren't made with rice wine, though the rice still becomes alcoholic before it turns to vinegar. The important thing is that the rice remains solid, as opposed to the liquid alcohol used as the starting point throughout the rest of the vinegar-making world. The first step in making Zhenjiang vinegar, then, is to ferment the rice to alcohol, which is done with a starter named *qu* (similar to that used for making soy sauce). Then, once it has become alcoholic, a second vinegar starter (similar to the 'mother' in other methods) is added until it turns sour.

Finally, water is washed over the rice to extract the vinegar (this is repeated multiple times with fresh water; each iteration yields a lower quality). The final product is lower in acidity than balsamic or sherry vinegars, yet also more punchy – its dark colour would make it easy to compare with malt vinegar, but while there is a maltiness to it, the flavour is much more earthy and savoury. It's often used in Chinese cooking, but is also typically a table sauce for dipping dumplings. I've got some that I purchased from a rather magical five hundred-year-old pickle shop in Beijing, where it was decanted from a huge barrel into a plastic bottle which I was terrified would leak all over my luggage. In the UK, you'll most easily find the Hengshun brand, with its signature yellow label. If you're able to find three- or six-year aged vintages, grab them, as the price they're usually sold at represents tremendous value.

None of the above are really suitable for that most noble of vinegar appointments – being dashed liberally over fish and chips. Malt is very much the vinegar of the nation – as British as a phone box full of crumpets – and we once had dozens of brands. Now it's being edged out by an ersatz vinegar substitute that for legal reasons must be called 'non-brewed condiment', which is simply a mix of chemically derived acetic acid and flavourings. I think it is best avoided. In the search for actual malt vinegar, it's now rare to find anything apart from Sarson's, and even that's not a British company any more, as in 2012 it was bought out by the Japanese company Mizkan. (They must have a penchant for brown British condiments – they also own Branston.) If you have a scout about, though, you'll find a few newer producers popping up. Artisan Malt Vinegar, produced in an old nuclear bunker in Cornwall, is an excellent choice. Bottled unpasteurized, it's also useful as a starter for your own vinegars – particularly dark ones, like beer vinegar. (Or 'alegar', as it was known in the Middle Ages – a much more succinct and pleasing name.) As the creation of soured beer in England as an intentional product rather than a brewing mishap became a major industry, manufacturers moved out of beer breweries. Once vinegar was no longer a by-product, they discovered that removing the hops usually found in beer increased shelf life, and thus malt vinegar was born. Beer vinegar is now a vanishingly rare beast, superseded by the chippy's favourite. This is a shame because it can be absolutely delicious, is very easy to make, and, with the range of craft beers (particularly stouts) now available, almost endlessly varied. If you're going to make vinegar at home, starting with something that's near impossible to buy is naturally appealing, so buy an extra bottle of your favourite ale and get vinegaring.

VINEGAR IS A FERMENTATIVE ANOMALY. Every other ferment in this book wants to be starved of oxygen, whether it's cabbage packed beneath the brine in sauerkraut, or yogurt sealed up in a thermos. Fermentation, as we've explored it thus far, has been an anaerobic activity; the various microbes that help process our foods and drinks do not need oxygen, and so we've created 'selective' environments with lids and weights and other such devices that exclude air, and by extension the moulds that thrive in it. Vinegar is the opposite – it is aerobic. Like us, it loves oxygen.

The bacteria responsible for turning things into vinegar, being rather different to those in other ferments, are named quite distinctly as well. While you'll often hear (in fizz-positive food circles) about lacto-fermentation and LAB (lactic acid bacteria), vinegar is made by acetic fermentation using AAB (acetic acid bacteria). Instead of turning sugar in all its various forms (glucose, fructose and lactose in pineapples, cabbage or milk, for example) into lactic acid plus fizzy carbon dioxide, these AAB turn alcohol into acetic acid. As a neat quirk of nature, because AAB work on alcohol, which is hostile to most other bacteria and yeasts (hence why alcohol works as hand sanitizer), they don't have to worry much about competing with the plethora of aerobic moulds in the environment. Basic vinegar is pretty much a case of exposing alcohol to oxygen and waiting; the concept that vinegar is just old wine is not far from the truth. Any alcohol can be 'vinegared' this way, whether it's wine, sherry, stout or even whisky – the enormous range of alcohols available is what makes vinegar such a fecund ground for experimentation.

There's a single caveat before you merrily start acidifying your drinks cabinet – the booze can't be any stronger than 10%, or the AAB will die. The answer to this is simple: dilution. If your chosen tipple is too fierce, you just have to cut it with water until it's weak enough for our microbial barflies to tolerate. As long as it's below their limit of 10%, the higher the alcohol percentage, the higher the acidity of the finished vinegar will be – handily, the alcohol converts to acid at just below a 1:1 ratio, so a 7.5% cider should produce a 6.5% acidity vinegar. Wait – why are we suddenly talking about acidity percentages, when elsewhere in this book I've discussed sourness in pH values? Well, while pH is more generally used, acidity percentage is more accurate in the case of vinegars. Unfortunately there isn't a simple translation between pH and acidity. Suffice to say, when you buy vinegar it will list its 'acidity', not pH. Typically, vinegars fall in the range of 4.5–8% acidity, with malt and cider vinegars towards the bottom, and *Gran Reserva* sherry vinegar near the top. When you're making your own vinegar, as long as you know the starting alcohol percentage, you can estimate the final acidity as accurately as is needed to make sure it won't go mouldy. In short, as long as you start with alcohol that's between 5–10% ABV, you'll be fine.

The biggest drawback to making vinegar is that it's slow. Without even embarking on the multi-year ageing process that many vinegars like balsamic or sherry undergo, the basic 'vinegaring' process can take a while. To be fair to *acetobacter aceti* (the most common AAB), trying to breathe oxygen while submerged in a vat of wine is probably quite taxing. Vinegar makers have developed a clever trick, however, by way of a mother.

The 'mother' is a kind of starter – which is to say, a microbe-rich sample from the finished product used to kickstart fermentation. The idea of keeping a little of the dough for future batches will be familiar to anyone who has tried their hand at making sourdough bread (or yogurt, as we'll cover later). The vinegar 'mother' is quite a specific type of starter though. Similar to that used to make kombucha, the mother is a liferaft that the AAB make in order to support themselves at the surface of the liquid, by knitting themselves together with cellulose to form a gel which strengthens into a disc. This lets the bacteria access as much oxygen as they need from the top, while drawing more food (in the form of alcohol) from beneath. The 'mother' also provides further maternal care, protecting the top of the vinegar like a blanket to exclude intruders. This mother also works for us would-be vinegar-makers as a starter – and, thankfully, 'vinegar with mother' is now widely sold in health food shops, so it's easy to get hold of for kickstarting your own vinegars (cider vinegar is easiest to find, but the mother can be repurposed for other alcohols). You won't usually find vinegars sold with a fleshy disc at the top of the bottle, even when sold 'with mother', because consumers would find that weird and gross. Don't worry though, it's in there – the main layer (or 'pellicle') of the mother may have been strained out, but AAB will remain floating about in your purchased vinegar. Once exposed to food (in the form of fresh alcohol) these will rapidly wake up and start growing, bundling together to form a new 'mother' at the top of your now rapidly transforming vinegar. A bit like making sourdough bread, without a starter you *might* capture some of the wild yeasts eventually, but it could take months. With a bit of shop-bought vinegar 'with mother', I've seen wine turn to vinegar within three weeks.

It wouldn't be fair to make mother do all the work though. Since it adores oxygen, vinegar forms most easily in open air. So, you should always leave vinegar-in-waiting in an open jar. Unfortunately, fruit flies are inexorably drawn to vinegar, and will kamikaze themselves into your souring apple cider with abandon. In fact, fruit flies carry a lot of AAB about them, and so are probably critical to the evolution of vinegar in nature – ripe fruit falls, becomes alcoholic, attracts fruit flies carrying bacteria which turn the alcoholic juice into vinegar. Still, it's not ideal, as they also carry less welcome microbes and, quite frankly, straining flies out of one's vinegar somewhat diminishes its appeal. So – keep your open containers covered with muslin (or some other mesh-like fabric) strapped down with a rubber band.

Incidentally, vinegar's aerobic requirements also suit it to the vessels that we would shun for other ferments – the wide-mouthed, stout jars made for easily accommodating a pickle-groping hand, or, on a smaller scale, the shapely upwards-sloping ones that a certain French variety of jam comes in are perfect (that vinegar thrives in a jar labelled 'good mother' can be no coincidence). The more air that can get to our vinegar, the better. An open shelf would be an improvement on a small, airless kitchen cupboard (though keep them out of direct sun), unless you're brewing a sufficiently large batch that the smell begins to deter visitors. AAB operate best at around 25–30°C, so as I write this during an August heatwave I've been finding my test batches positively gallop along. In winter, you'll need to pick a warm corner of the kitchen.

If you *really* want to accelerate your vinegar production, you could deploy the Boerhaave Process. Invented by eighteenth-century French *vinaigriers* to increase oxygenation, this involves filling a container with 'packing' – a mass that's mildly porous like wood shavings or dried grape vine – and then pouring alcohol over it. Some of the alcohol will cling to the packing, and thus be exposed to oxygen, and start turning to vinegar. This process is then repeated, pouring the alcohol over the packing again. The more regular the wash cycles, the faster it works. It's kind of ingenious, if a little faffy at home – using this trick, you may be able to turn wine to vinegar in as little as ten days. If you're in a hurry then try it out using the vine left over from a bunch of grapes – it won't improve the final product though, only hasten its arrival. This process dominated the vinegar industry for about two hundred years, with only minor improvements like spraying the alcohol over the packing instead of pouring it, until it was finally superseded by the acetator. This Schwarzenegger-sounding device bubbles pure oxygen through the alcohol, like a massive vinegar bong.

Though the flies circling your nascent vinegar seem like a pest, their feet carry bacteria that cause it to ferment.

Once the vinegar tastes ready, it's important to stop it fermenting. If left for long enough, the bacteria, having consumed all the alcohol, will eventually start converting the acetic acid they just produced into water and carbon dioxide. It's easy enough to halt this process, though, as the other excellent implication of vinegar's unique aerobic fermentation is that we can stop it simply by putting a lid on it, cutting off its air supply. This is why vinegar (even living vinegar) doesn't need to be kept in the fridge – simply removing access to oxygen is enough to put it into stasis. By keeping the mother we can quickly get another batch started – ideally it should stay floating in a little vinegar. Vinegar manufacturers usually use a siphon or a low tap when removing their finished product, so the mother stays floating on top, but if you're careful you can just pour the vinegar out from under the mother (lifting it back on top if it sinks) – don't worry too much if it ends up submerged, though, as another will form soon enough when you add fresh alcohol. If you're not about to make more vinegar, make sure to store the mother and vinegar in a sealed jar – metal lids will rust quite quickly, but placing a layer of cling film between the jar and lid will prevent this.

Once you've completed your first batch, it is of course prudent to get to work immediately on another (and the mother won't be fussy if you switch to another alcohol). Meanwhile, your newly created vinegar can be used to dress salad, marinate meat or pickle vegetables; it can be infused with fruit, flowers or herbs; it can be the base of a sauce, or the finishing touch in a stew. The most common mistake when making vinegar is thus drinking too much wine, beer or cider, and leaving too little to be vinegared.

White Wine Vinegar (high alcohol)

I'm including two base recipes here – this first one works for wine, spirits and any alcohol over 9–10% ABV, and the other for beers, ciders and the like. Treat both as starting places – I've included a few suggestions for different alcohols, but I absolutely implore you to experiment here. The basic concept remains the same for all alcohols (barring anything with a particularly high sugar content – Bailey's vinegar is a fantasy probably best left unrealized), and since the process is so simple and unassuming, I like to try batches of vinegars at once, and then repeat my favourites (which will be ready faster, as they'll have mature mothers of their own).

Vinegar-making is a pretty simple process, and it applies equally to pretty much all alcohols. Acetobacter is not a fussy drinker, but it has its limits – around 8–10% ABV. Stronger tipples need dilution, but are well worth the potential they unlock – champagne vinegar, bourbon vinegar, martini vinegar, port vinegar. Hell, I haven't tried ginegar, but it must be considered on name alone. Here's a conversion table for the most common alcohol strengths, to make 250ml at roughly 8% ABV.

Alcohol strength	Alcohol amount	Water amount
12.5%	160ml	90ml
15%	130ml	120ml
20%	100ml	150ml
40%	50ml	200ml

You can then proceed to make vinegar with your diluted drink using the 'low alcohol' method below. The only other caveat is that if you're using wine and it contains sulphites, which are an antibacterial preservative (and you should presume it does), then just decant the wine and leave it to breathe for an hour, stirring occasionally (they will largely evaporate off).

Stout Vinegar (low alcohol)

*Beer vinegar is an excellent but 'forgotten' British condiment, and if you
want to sample it you'll probably have to make it yourself. Thankfully,
the process is very simple. The more complex the flavour of the beer you
use, the more interesting the final product will be. Stouts and porters
are fine candidates – their earthy maltiness converts to a deep vinegary
savouriness, which is unmentionably good sprinkled over roast spuds.
They can vary widely in strength (imperial stouts are especially strong),
though, so make sure they're under 10% ABV (6–8% is ideal), or
you'll need to dilute them, as in the recipe for wine and spirit vinegars.
This recipe also works just as well with cider or mead.*

TIME / 3–12 weeks
YIELD / ~270ml vinegar

KIT / Medium wide-mouthed
jar, thoroughly cleaned
Muslin or cheesecloth
Rubber band

INGREDIENTS
250ml 5–10% stout
(OR cider OR mead)
50ml vinegar 'with mother'

1/ Combine the stout and vinegar 'with mother' in a jar, then cover the jar
with muslin, and secure with a rubber band to keep insects out.

2/ Leave out of direct sunlight and ideally somewhere warm (24–30°C)
with some airflow. After a couple of weeks give it a sniff and look for
a solid rubbery layer on top of the liquid (it won't always be present, but
if it is it may be transparent or off-white, but you shouldn't see any mould
or fuzzy growth – if you do, chuck the batch). If it smells vinegary, or a
new mother has formed, you're on your way. Leave it for at least another
week to complete fermentation.

Recipe continues overleaf...

3/ A week after it's shown signs of life, delicately lift a corner of the mother (if one has formed), being careful not to sink it if possible, and spoon off a little liquid (or use a straw). Taste it – if the alcohol taste has gone and is entirely replaced with sourness, it's ready. Otherwise, leave for another week and repeat. In summer it could be ready in 3 weeks, but in winter it may need up to 3 months.

4/ Once it tastes fully of vinegar, you can pour it out from underneath the mother (lift it like you're peeking under the edge of a rug) into a bottle and lid it. Your vinegar will last almost indefinitely as long as you keep it sealed between uses. If you leave 50ml of vinegar behind with the mother and lid that jar as well, then the mother will go into stasis, and you can restart the whole process by topping up the alcohol as needed – future batches using the fully grown mother will be faster.

Ageing Vinegar:

If you want, you can now age your finished vinegar – just keep it in a sealed container filled to the top (so there's no space for a new mother to form) and leave it in a dark place (or brown bottle). Vinegar can age like this for anything from 3 months to 25 years. If you want to emulate the flavour of barrel-ageing, you can do so by adding a few oak chips (homebrewing suppliers stock them) – just boil them for 5 minutes first to remove some of the excess tannins, and taste the vinegar every few months to check how 'oaked' it is tasting.

TROUBLESHOOTING / If your Vinegar is...

Without a floating mother	The vinegar mother slipping under the surface is slightly annoying, and may slow things down, but it's not necessarily a sign that anything is wrong (it usually just happens if the vinegar is moved – so try not to move it). A new one will likely develop on the top.
Smelling like acetone	There is a chemical which creates this smell during normal vinegar production, but it disappears so quickly you wouldn't usually notice it. If you do detect it, it's probable that the process has stalled. Likely this is either due to lack of oxygen (remember not to lid your vinegar until it is finished fermenting) or the alcohol being too strong (make sure it's between 5–10% – preferably no higher than 8%).
Becoming less sour	Make sure that once your vinegar is ready you store it in a sealed container, otherwise once the AAB has converted all the alcohol to acid, it will get desperate and start eating the acid it just made. It can't do this if you starve it of oxygen in a lidded bottle.
Attracting loads of fruit flies	Fruit flies are genetically programmed to seek out vinegar, but the muslin or cheesecloth will keep them out.
Full of tiny worms	These are rare, but used to be a real problem for commercial vinegar manufacturers. Called 'vinegar eels', they are not harmful, but obviously unsightly. They can be filtered out and the vinegar heated to pasteurize it, but you'll need to sterilize all your equipment before any future batches.

Vinegar Transformed

Infusion is an incredibly simple method for adding an extra layer to your vinegar – most things will impart their aroma within a few days or weeks. It is also an excellent way of bottling the flavours of delicate herbs, flowers and fruits when they're in season. Here are some of my favourites:

Tarragon: To me, the finest of *fines herbes*. Around 3 sprigs added to 250ml of white wine or cider vinegar will be delicious after 2 weeks. Remove the tarragon and it will keep indefinitely.

Garlic/Chive Flowers: A great use of the pretty flowers if you grow them. Add 4–6 flowers to 250ml of white wine vinegar and remove after 2 weeks.

Blueberry/Raspberry: This is lovely for salads, seafood or simply as a drink with a little fizzy water. Add 80g of blueberries or raspberries to 250ml of white wine or cider vinegar and remove them after a week, then add 1 teaspoon of caster sugar (or more to taste).

Four Thieves: This, I assure you, does not involve the pickling of any fugitives. It is, rather, a popular French vinegar infusion which a gang of miscreants claimed protected them from the plague. An eighteenth-century recipe instructed readers to 'wash your mouth, and rub your loins and your temples every day' with it. I think it makes a nice vinaigrette (see page 137). Mix 250ml of white wine vinegar with 3 cloves of garlic, 1 sprig each of rosemary, thyme and lavender, plus a sage and bay leaf. If you happen to have any wormwood (e.g. from running a moonshine still), chuck it in. Leave for a month and then strain. Splashed over an oyster or roasted vegetables it is without parallel.

Oatmeal Stout Pickled Onions

If there was truly a reason vinegar was put on this here Earth, it was surely to make pickles – you can, with the right attitude, pickle almost anything, from eggs (see page 55) to pig's ears. The cornerstone of a ploughman's lunch, this puckeringly patriotic pickle is quintessential British pub fare, and so it seems only apt to dress it in the most British of pints. Stout vinegar gives such silky brown depth to the pickled onion that I would humbly suggest that it is impossible to eat just one.

Time / 3–4 weeks
Yield / 400g pickled onions
Kit / A large (~500ml) jar

Ingredients
400g shallots
30g salt
350ml oatmeal stout vinegar
 (malt also works well)
70g caster sugar
10 black peppercorns
1 teaspoon yellow mustard
 seeds
1 bay leaf

1/ Top and tail the shallots (removing the bare minimum), then put into a bowl and cover with boiling water. Leave for 30 seconds, then drain and rinse the shallots. The skins should now peel away easily.

2/ Pack the peeled shallots into your jar, then mix the salt with 400ml of water and pour over. Leave them to soak in the brine overnight, and up to 14 hours, then remove and rinse.

3/ Mix the vinegar with the sugar and stir till dissolved, then add the spices and bay leaf. Pack the shallots back into the jar tightly, then pour over spiced vinegar, making sure they're all covered. Seal the jar and store somewhere dark and cool for a month before tasting them. They should keep for at least 6 months, but fridge them once opened.

Persian Pickled Cucumbers

These puckering little delights are my go-to shop-pickle, sold as they are at the Turkish grocers down my high street. Their secret is simple – tarragon. It is the greatest herb, and it goes gloriously with vinegar. If you must, use dill instead, and have regular pickles – it's your pickle party – but I think you deserve the best. For maximum crispness, hunt out some short, stout, firm little cucumbers and be sure to trim off the blossom ends, as these contain enzymes which gradually cause softness. You can use regular long, English cucumbers and slice them, but the pickles will have less crunch.

TIME / 3 weeks
YIELD / 500g pickles
KIT / A 1-litre jar (or 2 tall 500ml jars)

INGREDIENTS
500g cucumbers (ideally small, warty variety, otherwise cut in half, then quarter lengthwise into spears)
20g + 1 tablespoon salt
170ml vinegar (minimum 5% acidity – white wine or cider work well)
½ tablespoon caster sugar
2 cloves of garlic, peeled and bruised
3 sprigs of tarragon
1 mild chilli (jalapeño or similar), halved
1 bay leaf
1 teaspoon coriander seeds

1/ Wash the cucumbers and trim 5mm from the 'blossom end' (that's the opposite end to the one that attached them to the plant).

2/ Combine 20g salt with 500ml water and mix till fully dissolved, then put the cucumbers into the jar and pour over the brine until they are covered (you may not need it all). Leave for at least 3 hours, and up to overnight, then drain, discarding the brine.

3/ Combine the vinegar with 200ml of water, the sugar and 1 tablespoon of salt. Put the garlic, tarragon, chilli, bay leaf and coriander seeds into the jar.

4/ Pack the cucumbers into the jar as tightly as possible – any that float will go mushy – and pour over the vinegar mix, making sure it covers them entirely (mix vinegar and water in an equal ratio if you need a little more liquid). Refrigerate for 3 weeks and they'll be ready. They should last at least 2 months in the fridge, if you somehow don't eat them all first.

Spicy Miso Pickled Pineapple

If you've just finished making a batch of tepache (see page 182) and are looking for something to do with the pineapple flesh, I entreat you to try this. While perhaps a little more outré than pickled onions or cucumbers, don't be surprised if this awakens something inside you and leads you down the path to pickled cherries, mango and peaches. With any fruit, aim for slightly underripe specimens as they'll soften during the process.

TIME / 1 hour

YIELD / 300g pickled pineapple

KIT / Large (~500ml) jar
Small saucepan

INGREDIENTS
300g pineapple, chopped into 2cm pieces
2 red bird's-eye chillies, finely chopped
2 tablespoons chopped coriander

260ml apple cider vinegar
30g caster sugar
3 tablespoons *aka* miso

1/ Put the pineapple, chilli and coriander into the jar.

2/ Combine the vinegar and sugar in a small saucepan and bring to a simmer over a medium heat, stirring until the sugar has dissolved. Remove from the heat and stir in the miso.

3/ Pour the vinegar mixture into the jar, using enough to cover the pineapple (you may have some left). Leave to cool. It will be ready to eat after an hour, and will keep for a couple of weeks in the fridge.

Béarnaise Sauce

By now it's surely clear that vinegar is endlessly adaptable, and that by increasing and infusing your arsenal of vinegars you can really customize and tweak your cooking. Vinegar, as a condiment, is more often seen in cameo roles than as a lead, but where it can really take the spotlight is in sauces, where it can provide balance to fatty and rich flavours.

Vinegar not only comes from a mother, it can go on to form a mother sauce. A neat bit of French culinary organization groups sauces under five 'mothers', each of which can diversify into its own daughter sauces. The best known of these is hollandaise – the backbone of eggs Benedict. It's a very fine sauce, but the best thing it's ever done is spawn Béarnaise. Classically paired with steak, it's also excellent over asparagus or in a sandwich.

TIME / 20 minutes

YIELD / 200ml (enough for 3–4 people)

KIT / A stick blender
A mug

INGREDIENTS

4 sprigs of tarragon (2 whole, 2 stripped and leaves finely chopped)

90ml white wine vinegar

1 shallot, minced

1 teaspoon peppercorns

1 egg yolk

80g unsalted butter

1/ Combine 2 whole sprigs of tarragon in a small pan with the vinegar, shallot and peppercorns, and bring to the boil. Then, reduce to the barest simmer until the vinegar has reduced by half.

2/ Strain the solids from the vinegar and discard, then combine the vinegar and egg yolk in a mug. Set aside. Heat the butter in a small pan until it's foaming, then remove.

3/ Start blending the vinegar reduction in the mug and slowly add the hot butter – in the very thinnest stream at first (once the sauce has come together and started to thicken you can add liquid a little faster). Once it's all combined, add the chopped tarragon and salt to taste. It's best used while still warm, but will keep 1–2 days in the fridge. It doesn't reheat very well, but can be used cold instead of mayonnaise in sandwiches.

Beurre Blanc

This simple sauce is a showcase for its ingredients, so good quality wine, butter and of course vinegar will elevate it. You can add chopped herbs such as dill, tarragon or chervil as it comes off the heat, to take it in different directions. It is superb with scallops, white fish or asparagus.

TIME / 15 minutes	INGREDIENTS	50ml white wine
YIELD / 280ml	2 tablespoons very finely	250g unsalted butter, cubed
KIT / A small saucepan	minced shallots	and fridge cold
	100ml white wine vinegar	

1/ Place the shallots, vinegar and wine in a small saucepan and bring to the boil, then simmer until just about 2 tablespoons are left.

2/ Strain out the shallot and discard, returning the liquid to the pan.

3/ Reduce the heat to the bare minimum and add a couple of cubes of butter while whisking. Replace them as they melt, and remove the pan from the heat to whisk in the last two. Season to taste and serve warm.

Blueberry Vinaigrette

The basic 3 parts oil to 1 part vinegar ratio holds true for almost any vinaigrette, but when applying it here I've gone a little sharper to balance the added fruit and honey.

Lightly bruise a handful of blueberries in a pestle and mortar. Separately, whisk 2 tablespoons of olive oil with 1 tablespoon of blueberry vinegar, ½ tablespoon of honey and a pinch of salt. Mix with the bruised blueberries, and spoon over your salad. Pairs well with goat's cheese.

North Carolina Barbecue Sauce

This is a very different beast to the sweet, ketchupy barbecue sauce most often found in supermarkets. There's at least a dozen regional takes on how to properly sauce whatever you're barbecuing, and I think that North Carolina's contribution is the most interesting. Mop sauce is made to be swabbed over meat as it slowly roasts on the smoker. It's excellent at doing that, but its sour, spicy savouriness doesn't need heat to work its magic – splashing it over at the table also works fine. Traditionally it's made with apple cider vinegar, but stout vinegar works really well too.

TIME / 5 minutes
YIELD / 130ml
   (enough for 3–4 people)
KIT / A small jar

INGREDIENTS
100ml apple cider vinegar
1 teaspoon freshly ground
   black pepper
1 teaspoon dark brown sugar

¼ teaspoon table salt
½–1 teaspoon hot sauce
   (not too chunky)
2 teaspoons ketchup

Mix all the ingredients and jar. The sauce will keep for at least a couple of weeks in the fridge.

Four Thieves Tahini

A unique and herbaceous sauce that works exceedingly well with broccoli or roasted butternut squash.

Simply mix equal parts of tahini paste, four thieves vinegar (page 132) and water thoroughly until creamy, and season to taste.

Moromi & Vinegar Mushrooms on Toast

Yeah, I know, mushrooms on toast. You don't need a recipe for mushrooms on toast. But, to really make it shine, I'm going to insist that you make your own stout vinegar (though balsamic or a good malt vinegar will work at a pinch). I can be slightly more relaxed about the miso, though I'm afraid to tell you that when I tested this using the leftover moromi *from making soy sauce (page 82), it was very good. The halloumi is absolutely unnecessary, which is why it's there. You can use whatever bread you like – I'm not a sourdough puritan, but its glutinous crunch : pillowiness ratio works well here. Ciabatta is also a delightful bedfellow.*

TIME / 15 minutes

YIELD / Lunch for 2

INGREDIENTS

2 tablespoons butter

2 portobello mushrooms, thick sliced

80g halloumi, thick sliced

2 cloves of garlic, finely chopped

1 tablespoon *moromi*
    OR ¾ tablespoon *aka* miso

1 tablespoon stout vinegar

2 slices of top-tier toast

1/ Heat a heavy pan over a medium-high heat and add 1 tablespoon of butter. Once the foaming subsides, add half the mushrooms and cook for 2–3 minutes, until they are nicely browned, then flip and repeat. Once cooked, put aside and repeat with the remaining mushrooms, adding more butter as required.

2/ Fry the halloumi in the same pan for two minutes each side and remove.

3/ Add 2 teaspoons of butter to the pan, followed by the garlic. Once fragrant, add the *moromi*/miso and vinegar, then drop the heat to low and return the mushrooms to the pan. Cook for a further 5 minutes, until they're nice and softened, and all the flavours have combined.

4/ Top your toast with the halloumi, followed by the mushrooms, then season generously with pepper and serve.

Chapter six
Kefir

KEFIR IS THE NEW KID ON THE DAIRY AISLE. It may seem, at first glance, to be merely yogurt with health benefits – but that would sell it very short. It's more of a distant cousin to that muesli mainstay, fermented using starter 'grains', with a thinner texture, distinct flavour, and yes, lots of probiotics. It tastes a bit like a yogurt drink, but with more going on – a little minerality and sometimes a touch of fizziness – the result of a covert alliance between Danone and San Pellegrino, perhaps. It's easier to make at home than yogurt, as the bacteria will happily get to work at room temperature, whereas yogurt requires some careful heating. The whole process of making kefir takes less active time than it does to boil the kettle, and it goes fantastically well with the sweetened oat clusters that I kid myself are a healthy breakfast option – as such it is a near-constant staple in my fridge.

Kefir is, in many ways, at the very vanguard of living foods. Its ascent in the UK has been meteoric – a decade ago it was sold only in health food and Eastern European speciality shops, and it's now not only available in all major supermarkets, but has had the honour of being the first living ferment to feature on *The Archers*. If Tom Archer can start a kefir business, it's truly reached the mainstream. But the long road to Ambridge began far, far away, on the northern slopes of the Caucasus Mountains – likely among a tribe called the Alans – where legend has it that Prophet Muhammed gave kefir grains to Orthodox Christian nomads, who could thus carry their milk with them without it going off. Mohammed instructed them to keep the grains secret or they would lose their magical power, and thus kefir was hidden from the rest of the world until the late nineteenth century. The Alans were an equestrian tribe who roamed from their native Persia to the Iberian peninsula from the first to the fourteenth centuries, peaking around the ninth century when they founded the state of Alania (roughly corresponding to modern North Ossetia and Kabardino-Balkaria, just north of Georgia).

The Alans' version of kefir probably resembled an old fermented dairy drink named *kumis* (a Russian kefir researcher concluded in 1883 that the microbes in both drinks were related). Not something Tesco are probably rushing to stock, but this fermented mare's milk has been a hit everywhere from China (where, under Kublai Khan in the thirteenth century, it almost replaced tea) to Russia (Chekhov and Tolstoy were fans). William of Rubruck noted in 1253 that in the Mongol Empire it was known as *cosmos*, and the Greek word for (cow's) milk is *galaktos*, so the dairy connection with the Milky Way runs deep. The Greek historian Herodotus, writing in 430 BC, describes the process of making *kumis* thus:

> *They [the Scythians] insert a tube made of bone and shaped like a flute into the mare's anus, and blow; and while one blows, another milks [...] They make the blind men [the slaves] stand around in a circle, and then pour the milk into wooden casks and stir it; the part which rises to the top is skimmed off, and considered the best; what remains is not supposed to be good.*

We might take Herodotus' account with a pinch of salt, though, since he also claimed that Egyptian cat owners shaved off their eyebrows when mourning the passing of their pet.

It was in Russia that kefir went from a secret of the steppe to a national drink. In 1881 Edward Kern returned to Germany from a summer visiting the Caucasus, reporting to the Moscow Imperial Society of Naturalists that he had been introduced (by 'the mountain people') to a drink which could cure 'various stomach and chest disorders (even consumption)'. He observed that the miracle drink had spread from the highest habitable parts of the mountains down into the cities of Pyatigorsk, Stavropol, Vladikavkaz and Tbilisi. A pair of cheesemaking brothers called the Blandovs, who had first brought the Dutch edam technique to Russia, read about kefir and saw its commercial potential. The cheese pioneers already had a factory in the Caucasus Mountains, but despite their local connections, they made little headway with buying kefir grains. They discovered the Karachay (another Turkic people, adjacent to the Alans, though Sunni Muslim) had kefir, which they made by leaving milk and kefir grains in a sheepskin bag and hanging it over an external door in the sun, where passers-by would tap it as they passed to agitate the grains. They had no luck in procuring any of the kefir grains themselves, however, so sent one of their employees – the award-winning butter-maker Irina Sakharova – to try and convince a Karachay prince to part with them. The prince held banquets and entertained Irina, but he refused to give her any of the precious grains either, and so she left. On her return trip,

she was allegedly kidnapped as his bride (the prince's great-grandson refutes this telling of events, though, claiming he happily gave her the kefir). The prince was arrested, and a judge ruled that Irina should have the kefir grains as recompense. He sent her 10 pounds of kefir grains, which she studied and used to recreate kefir production – first to supply hospital patients, and then in commercial manufacture in 1908.

In Russia, even in the face of post-Soviet foreign influence, kefir has yet remained more popular than yogurt. The country's dairy options have always been impressively diverse – by contrast to the four colours of milk bottle top available in the UK, the USSR in the late 1980s had as many as fifteen, including green for kefir, green and silver-striped for low-fat kefir, and pink for honey-kefir drink.

Kefir is known in Chile as 'yogurt of the little birds'.

Nowadays, kefir has since found its way far across the world. In Mexico, it's known as *búlgaros*, or 'Bulgarians' – likely in honour of the Bulgarian microbiologist Stamen Grigorov, who first analysed the microflora of yogurt. It does result in some rather strange translations though – one Mexican website on preparing kefir breezily states that, 'Those of us who have Bulgarians and take care of them know that they are multiplying rapidly.' In Chile kefir is rather sweetly named *yogurt de pajaritos*, or 'yogurt of the little birds' – the 'little birds' being the 'kefir grains'.

The name, in English, 'kefir', is borrowed from Russian, where it was adapted from a Karachay term. I've sometimes seen it called 'Tibetan mushrooms', which I thought odd at first, but it turns out that kefir also has a tradition in Tibet. The Alans were subjugated into the Mongol Empire in the thirteenth century, so it's possible that the secrets of kefir travelled back East with the Mongols. It may have arrived far earlier, though – recently, mummies from 1600 BC were unearthed in China's Taklamakan Desert (which borders Tibet) with blocks of cheese strung around their necks – and analysis indicated that the low-lactose cheese was fermented with kefir grains.

Unlike yogurt, kefir doesn't need to be heated in order to ferment, which makes the process much simpler. It isn't unique, however, but rather part of a global family of easy-fermenting dairy drinks. The majority of these are found in the Nordic countries, which are passionate about dairy; Finland routinely consumes more milk per capita than anywhere else in the world, and Sweden isn't far behind. It's no surprise, then, that they have such a range of crafty milk-loving microbial cultures (though it's a shame that more of them haven't taken off elsewhere). *Filmjölk*, from Sweden, is a kind of cross between yogurt and kefir, both in consistency (it's thinner than yogurt, but thicker than most kefir) and in method. It ferments at room temperature, like kefir, but instead of needing grains as a starter, you just need a bit of *filmjölk*. Variants on it include *långfil* (which has a 'long', elastic texture) and *fjällfil* (sometimes flavoured with birch sap). In Finland there's also *viili*, which stretches like honey, and *piimä* (similar to buttermilk). The root of *filmjölk* is very unexpected though – it comes from plants.

Carl Linnaeus, the Swedish botanist and zoologist, who would go on to create the binomial nomenclature system whereby every species gets a double name in Latin (e.g. *Lactobacillus acidophilus*), set out to survey the flora and fauna of Lapland in 1732, aged twenty-four. While on this six-month trip around the most northerly reaches of Scandinavia, Linnaeus became very interested in the culture of the reindeer-herding, nomadic Sami people. He noted in his journal that the Sami prepared reindeer milk eighteen different ways, including one in which the leaves of an insect-eating carnivorous plant called butterwort were used to make a yogurt-like drink. One Mrs Margareta Jonsson, born in 1877 in Hälsingland, wrote that as a child she would pick *tättgräs* (sundew – another carnivorous plant), with which her mother would thicken their milk. Recent research has shown that these plants do indeed harbour lactic acid bacteria, and are thus very possibly the microbial fountainhead for many (if not all) of these Nordic fermented milks.

In South Africa, a similar drink, *amasi*, which also ferments at room temperature, is made by leaving milk in a type of hollowed-out gourd called

Dried out calabashes are used to ferment amasi, *and also as musical instruments and money boxes.*

a calabash. There hasn't been a great deal of research into how this traditional Xhosa drink works, but it's likely that the bacteria that causes the milk to ferment comes from the calabash, rather like butterwort provides the starter for *filmjölk*. Nelson Mandela revealed how he was 'very fond of this sour milk' in his autobiography, *Long Walk to Freedom*, but also how it nearly gave away his hiding place when he was secretly living in a friend's apartment in a white suburb – a couple of Zulu men noticed that milk had been left out on the window ledge to ferment, and, recognizing it as *amasi*, thought it out of place in a segregated neighbourhood. Mandela left the next night.

One drink that has no relation at all to kefir, incidentally, is 'water kefir'. It's also known as *tibicos* in Mexico, and its starter grains as 'Japanese water crystals' or 'California bees', so it clearly has a bit of an identity crisis. Though it does have little grains like regular milk kefir, the grains cannot digest lactose in milk and will only ferment sugary liquids, so the resultant drink is far more similar to kombucha.

WHEN I DESCRIBE KEFIR, the first reaction I get is often, 'Isn't drinking sour milk a bit gross?' It's an interesting thing – warm milk that you leave out all day until it clumps up and goes sour is transformed into something palatable by its familiar name: yogurt. In terms of breaking our food taboos, milk that you leave out all day *without* warming it up (such as kefir) should really seem more palatable. It is only a case of familiarity, and I hope by explaining how exactly kefir works, it will seem more familiar and less weird – it is, after all, delicious, nutritious and laughably easy to make (drawing up a recipe for it almost feels like writing down how to make tea).

Kefir uses tiny colonies of microbes formed into gelatinous polysaccharide bundles called 'grains' or 'seeds' to kickstart the fermentation process, which are a bit like the starter that you'd use for sourdough bread. Unlike sourdough starter they're SCOBYs (or, symbiotic culture of bacteria and yeasts), so closer to the 'mother' in vinegar or kombucha. Kefir SCOBYs are the very cutest you'll come across, looking something akin to miniature cauliflower florets made out of ricotta. No other dairy ferments need a starter in this way – all the rest can replicate happily from any part of the finished product, a bit like The Thing (or Groot if we're being modern). To provide a regular supply of kefir you'll need to recover these tiny grains from each batch, and feed (or simply use) them regularly. As you feed them they'll slowly grow,

eventually enough that you can donate some to a kefir-curious friend. What's more, I promise, even for those that have struggled to provide for a colony of sea monkeys, these are incredibly low-maintenance pets – they'll happily snooze in the fridge, submerged in a covered shot glass of milk, as long as it's changed out once a week.

Kefir SCOBYs are the cutest-looking bundles of microbes you will ever get to ferment with.

In requiring the fishing out and retaining of the starter grains between batches, kefir may need slightly more care than yogurt, but it is infinitely easier to make. While yogurt is fermented with thermophilic bacteria, meaning that it needs to be heated up (then incubated at 42–46°C), the bacteria within kefir are mesophilic, meaning they'll happily get to work at room temperature (*meso* comes from the Greek for 'middle'). In practice, this means you can drop your kefir grains into a jar of milk before you head to work, and it'll be ready on your return. (It's so easy I'm sometimes surprised that commercial kefir is sold at all.)

Many of the strains of bacteria within these fluffy little bundles of potency had never been seen elsewhere before, and hence when discovered in kefir were given names like *Lactobacillus kefiranofaciens* and *Lactobacillus parakefiri*. So, alongside their flocks of sheep, ancient shepherds may have unknowingly been selectively breeding brand new microbes to ferment their milk as they made kefir over the centuries. As is the case with sourdough starter, scientists have also found that kefir grains from different regions possess their own unique collections of bacterial strains, so you could think of kefirs as being somewhat distinguished by their microbial terroir.

Most kefirs are quite complex, with a whole host of different bacteria and yeasts jostling and intermingling across the manifold surfaces of the squishy little grains. Apart from the kefir specialists mentioned above, *Lactobacillus brevis*, *Leuconostoc mesenteroides* and *Lactococcus lactis* are the most common. *L. brevis* is loved by our guts (it seems to improve immune response) but despised by brewers – at one point, it was accused of causing most beer spoilages in Germany. Along with *L. mesenteroides* its regular presence is welcome in kimchi, sauerkraut and many other ferments, as both bacterial strains help acidify their environment and produce bacteriocins (toxins which keep other unwanted microbes away). *Lactococcus lactis* is used in cheesemaking, as it helps to form curds – though in kefir it isn't usually dominant enough to separate the milk too much. (It was also voted to become the 'official state microbe' of Wisconsin by the state assembly, but the Senate sadly denied the motion.) Another common bacteria in kefir is *Lactobacillus acidophilus*, often included in probiotic supplements since it is one of the only strains of probiotic bacteria studied sufficiently to confirm a health benefit (it reduces lactose intolerance and decreases colon cancer risk).

The main job of the bacteria within kefir is to break down the milk sugar lactose into its component parts, galactose and glucose – for which reason it is often suitable for those who are lactose intolerant. Having said which, it doesn't necessarily remove all the lactose, so if dairy does trouble your gut then try kefir with care. The bacteria then consume most of the newly created glucose to turn it into lactic acid, but they also convert part of it into a substance called kefiran, an exopolysaccharide. Exopolysaccharides are substances produced by some bacteria which thicken liquids – in this case giving kefir its characteristic texture. One study has indicated that it could reduce cholesterol and blood pressure levels (at least, it does in rats), and another suggests it could help with asthma (again, currently just for mice), so scientists have been working on how they can make kefiran-rich kefir. A group at South Ural State University in Russia found in 2018 that ultrasound might boost kefiran production – you can also just let your kefir develop for longer (and without a lid – it needs air) to achieve similar effects, but if you're short on time then by all means try setting up a speaker next to your milk.

While the bacteria are hard at work, the yeasts that coexist beside them make use of any leftover sugars. These yeasts are mostly made up of various strains from the *Saccharomyces* genus, including the common-or-garden baker's or brewer's yeast, which is a bit of a jack-of-all-trades, ready to turn up anywhere, roll up its tiny sleeves and turn sugar into carbon dioxide. Of course, the moonlighting brewer's yeast also has a propensity to make alcohol, but in kefir it's polite enough to know that alcoholic milk is not really what anyone wants, so it keeps this activity to a minimum – you'd have to actively try to get above 0.5% ABV. (If you're keen, try a long second ferment – after the grains are removed – at room temperature without a lid.)

The other main yeast lurking in your kefir, *Kluyveromyces marxianus*, is the fastest-growing yeast on the planet, replicating quicker than any other plant, animal *or* yeast, in fact – it's used to create biofuels from whey, a by-product

of cheesemaking. Within kefir, however, *K. marxianus* creates chemicals called esters, which are responsible for giving the drink a slight fruity aroma. It also, incidentally, fulfils a similar role in the Mexican spirit mezcal.

For all the biochemical wranglings taking place beneath its opaque surface, the process of actually making kefir is wildly simple – once you've got hold of some grains, that is. Thankfully, due to the advent of the internet, obtaining them no longer requires stealing from or seducing a prince; eBay harbours plenty of fermenters with spare grains to sell, while enthusiasts will often give them away if you search on the usual social networks. Just make sure you're buying 'kefir grains', not 'powdered kefir', which can only be used a few times. Once you've found some, you'll be able to keep re-using them forever, as long as they are stored properly in milk. By the way, you may have read somewhere that stirring kefir with a metal spoon will destroy it, or rob your starter grains of their fermenting abilities. I'd avoid storing your kefir in a metal container long-term, but brief contact isn't a problem – I've never strained my grains with anything but a metal strainer, and they're doing just fine.

One advantage of making your own kefir is that you can choose how you like it. A lot of the control you have comes from its fermentation taking place in two distinct 'stages' – the first, when the milk is left at room temperature with the kefir grains, gives an initial sourness and the baseline kefir flavour, which is something like a thin, tangy yogurt with a hint of mineral complexity. Interestingly, kefir will work both aerobically or anaerobically, meaning you can just cover it with muslin to allow airflow, or a tight lid to restrict it. Air will allow yeast to dominate, leading to more bready flavours, whereas a sealed environment is conducive to lactic acid bacteria, so it will have more of a sour tang – I usually go for the latter, which is also better for preventing contamination. This initial stage of fermentation usually takes around 8–12 hours, but can be longer if it's cold, or quicker if you're using a lot of grains (more than 1 teaspoon per 300ml of milk). If you prefer your kefir sourer, extend this primary ferment. However, do note that if you over-ferment your kefir (especially easy to do in hotter weather) it will eventually split into curds and whey. If this is only slight then you can recombine by shaking – but after a point it can get quite difficult to strain the kefir grains from the curds.

After this, the kefir is ready to drink, but I like to do a secondary ferment. This takes place after the grains have been strained out and the kefir (if previously only covered) has been moved to a sealed container. I usually do this in the fridge, where it will take a day or two, but you could also do it at room temperature to speed things up. This stage is where you get a bit of fizziness, and you'll also find the kefir thickens some more, the flavours round out and the sourness reduces a bit, displaying a bit more creaminess and mellow, earthy butter notes. You can also add other flavourings at this point without needing to worry about them contaminating your kefir grains. A pinch of cinnamon or a couple of dried rose petals with a teaspoon of honey is really nice, or a little lemon zest or half a banana blended in. Note that if you choose to sweeten the kefir, you may find that the second fermentation gets a bit more vigorous, and the sweetness may fade away again after a day or two, as the sugars get consumed by hungry kefir microbes (sometimes I'll add a little honey at the beginning of the secondary ferment, and then a little more to taste when I drink it). The longer you leave it during this stage, the fizzier and thicker it should get (to really increase the fizz, add half a plum during the second ferment – the extra yeast from its skin should get things going).

The only time you'll need new grains is if your kefir goes off. In case you're worried about how to tell the difference between 'good' and 'bad' kefir, let me assure you that if it happens you won't be in any doubt. The flavour of kefir covers a gamut, and it changes over time and with temperature, but the one absolute certainty is that you'll know when it's off. Much like milk itself, 'off' kefir is immediately obvious – it's not something 'you're not into' or 'a bit funky' – it is totally, unquestionably going straight down the sink. If you are planning not to use your kefir grains for a while, you can freeze them – simply rinse the milk off, leave them to dry uncovered overnight in the fridge and then freeze them in a sealed bag. They should last at least 2 months like this, and possibly a year or more, though you may need to cycle them through milk a couple of times after they've defrosted to revive them.

Kefir

It's incredible the range of flavours kefir can extract from milk, from buttery to earthy and fruity to sour. Whether you want to make healthier smoothies, a tastier bowl of cereal, or merely a refreshing summer drink, kefir demands your attention. It's quick and easy to make, with the only real risk being that you forget about it and it over-ferments (in which case, you can make kefir cheese – just follow the recipe for labneh on page 230, substituting kefir for yogurt). It's versatile too – it will work happily with whatever fat content of milk you prefer, though whole milk will result in the thickest final product.

TIME / 8–12 hours
YIELD / 300ml kefir

KIT / A glass OR jar
A small bottle
Strainer

INGREDIENTS
300ml milk (whole, skimmed or semi-skimmed)
~1 teaspoon kefir grains

1/ Pour the milk into a glass or jar, add the kefir grains and stir. Seal the container and leave for 8 hours (or 12 if it's cooler than 21°C).

2/ Taste the kefir and see if it tastes sour enough for your liking. When it does, strain the kefir into your bottle and lid it, then (optionally) keep in the fridge for another 24–72 hours for secondary fermentation – this can also be done at room temperature but will complete much faster. This is also when other flavourings can be added – see below. The finished kefir will last about a week in the fridge.

3/ Put the leftover kefir grains into a small container for storage and pour over just enough milk to cover them. If you make kefir less than once a week, rinse the milk off the grains weekly and replace it.

Kefir Smoothies

Kefir is delicious on its own, of course, but it's also a superb vehicle for carrying other flavours. However, to prevent contaminating the grains, these should be added during the secondary ferment, after the grains have been removed.

Cinnamon & Honey: Add ½ teaspoon of ground cinnamon to 300ml of kefir straight after you've removed the grains, then lid and refrigerate for 24 hours to give the kefir a secondary ferment, shaking occasionally to mix in the cinnamon. Add 1½ teaspoons of honey just before you drink it (if you add it earlier, the honey will feed the kefir and it will become more sour).

Malt & Blueberry: After removing the grains, lid and refrigerate 300ml of kefir for 24 hours, then add 3½ tablespoons of malt drink powder (e.g. Ovaltine) and 60g of blueberries and blend for a few seconds.

Peanut Butter & Banana: After removing the grains, lid and refrigerate 300ml of kefir for 24 hours, then add 3 tablespoons of peanut butter and half a banana and blend for a few seconds.

TROUBLESHOOTING / If your Kefir is...

Not thick/fizzy	This is fine – as long as it tastes sour it has worked. If you'd like to have more sourness or fizz, do a longer 'secondary ferment' after the grains have been removed in a sealed bottle in the fridge.
Splitting/too sour	Use fewer grains, or more milk, and put it somewhere cooler.
Tasting off (like fish or something else untoward)	Kefir should taste like sour milk, with a hint of cheesiness sometimes, but should not have 'off milk' flavours. If it does, it's time to replace your kefir grains. If you look after them by refreshing the milk they're in regularly, they can last indefinitely.
Sticky (grains)	The grains can become gummy or sticky after they've been stored for a week or so in the fridge without being used. This is normal, but you can safely rinse them in cold water without causing harm.

Lacto-fermented Oats

I love porridge, but it sits in a kind of breakfast/brunch twilight zone, too time-consuming when I'm in a rush, but not quite indulgent enough when I have time to luxuriate over my morning meal. 'Overnight oats' (also known as Bircher muesli) is a neat process whereby instead of cooking your porridge oats you simply let them rehydrate in water or milk overnight. By replacing the liquid with kefir, we can add heaps more flavour – the oats ferment slightly, and some of the starches break down, making for a more complex end product. You can increase the fermentation to a couple of days for added tang – it'll bring it closer to an old Scots dish of fermented oats called sowans *or* virpa *(which is made without any kefir though).*

TIME / Overnight
YIELD / Porridge for 2
KIT / A medium or large jar

INGREDIENTS
100g oats
70ml kefir
Fruit (optional)

½ teaspoon ground cinnamon
(optional)
80ml milk (optional)
1 tablespoon honey (optional)

1/ Put the oats and kefir into a clean jar, top up with 150ml water and seal. The oats should be fully submerged (add a little more water if necessary).

2/ Leave to ferment overnight.

3/ By the morning it should taste nicely sour. It's delicious hot or cold, with fruit and/or cinnamon, honey or demerara sugar, and a splash of milk. Medjool dates and sliced almonds are a lovely combination here too.

Kefir Panna Cotta with Mandarin & Thyme

*Panna cotta is simply creaminess embodied – a total comfort food –
and in this simplicity, it's the perfect place for the subtle flavour of kefir to
come through. Thymol is one of the main flavour compounds in mandarins,
so by adding thyme, it's possible to accentuate this flavour in the fruit.
When combined with orange blossom, the syrup is reminiscent of orange
jelly cubes eaten whole. Sorry Mum. Together with the kefir, it's like
ice cream and jelly in pinstripe, with a splash of perfume. You should
find orange blossom water in any Middle Eastern grocers.*

TIME / 5 hours	**FOR THE PANNA COTTA**	**FOR THE SYRUP**
YIELD / Dessert for 4	2 sheets of gelatine	2 mandarins/clementines
KIT / 4 small silicone moulds	250ml double cream	40g caster sugar
or ramekins	50g caster sugar	1½ teaspoons orange blossom
	200ml kefir	water
		4 sprigs of thyme

1/ Soak the gelatine in cold water for a few minutes to bloom, then
squeeze dry.

2/ Put the cream and 50g of sugar into a small pan and warm on a medium-
low heat until the sugar has dissolved. Bring to a low simmer, then remove
from the heat.

3/ Add the softened gelatine to the hot cream and stir until completely
dissolved. Pour through a fine sieve into a small jug. Leave to cool till
just warm, then stir in the kefir.

4/ Lightly grease your moulds or ramekins with a little vegetable oil,
then pour the mixture evenly between them. Refrigerate for 4–5 hours
(and up to overnight).

5/ Meanwhile, make the syrup. Zest the mandarins/clementines and then juice them, reserving the zest for serving. Heat the juice, along with the sugar, orange blossom water, thyme and 2 tablespoons of water in a small saucepan on a low heat, until the sugar is all dissolved and the syrup begins to thicken (approx. 5–10 minutes). Remove from the heat, pass through a sieve and set aside to cool.

6/ To serve, invert the moulds on to small plates (if they resist, try a firm shake or put them in hot water for a few seconds, and try again), and then pour over a little of the syrup (you won't quite need it all for 4 people), and top with the reserved zest.

Kefir Soda Bread with Kefir Cultured Butter

Cultured butter is the hot thing in modern British restaurants, and I hate them for it because I will inevitably keep on eating bread until it's all gone, and then find I'm no longer hungry when the main course turns up. The solution: make it at home. Doing so creates buttermilk as a by-product, which you can then upcycle into a loaf of soda bread. Make the butter ahead of time, and you can knock up the soda bread in under an hour. If you have kids at a loose end you can direct them to shake the cream in a jar instead of using a mixer/whisk, but it will take about 20 minutes!

TIME / 24 hours for butter
+ 1 hour for breads
YIELD / 350g butter
+ 1 medium loaf
KIT / A stand mixer OR
electric whisk
A baking tray
A strainer

FOR THE BUTTER
600ml double cream
(best you can find)
2 tablespoons kefir
¾ teaspoon flaky sea salt
(optional)

FOR THE BREAD
175g plain flour
220g wholemeal flour
1½ teaspoons bicarbonate
of soda
1 teaspoon salt
2 teaspoons honey
150ml buttermilk
(from butter recipe)
150ml kefir

Butter:

1/ Mix the cream and kefir in a jar. Leave it lidded on the counter to culture for 24 hours, or until it thickens to the consistency of sour cream.

2/ Once thickened, place in the fridge for at least 4 hours. (You can use this, should you wish, as a delicious sour cream.)

3/ Transfer the chilled sour cream to the stand mixer, or a tall jug if using an electric whisk. Mix it at medium-high speed. It will first turn to whipped cream, and then become a little 'grainy' before beginning to separate – drop the speed at this point, and be careful as it is liable to splash. Have another bowl on hand with a sieve over it – pour the liquid out into here, and then whisk the butter again. Once all the liquid has fallen out, strain the butter to get the last of it out, then whisk once more to check, and refrigerate the liquid buttermilk for later use when baking the bread.

4/ From this point, a rubber or silicone spatula will be very helpful in moving the butter between bowls without getting your hands very buttery. To remove the last of the buttermilk, put the butter into a bowl of cold water and knead it, replacing the water until it is no longer milky (this will stop it going off). Put the butter in a clean cloth and squeeze the cloth until the butter is dry. Flatten the butter to around 1cm, and sprinkle over the salt evenly (if using – it will help preserve), then knead it a couple more times to mix before flattening it again and rolling it up into a log. Wrap this in greaseproof paper and refrigerate.

Bread:

1/ Preheat the oven to 200°C. Mix the flours, bicarb and salt together in a bowl. Next, combine the honey, buttermilk and kefir thoroughly before adding to the dry ingredients and mixing until it's all just combined (don't overmix). If you're short on buttermilk, add more kefir.

2/ Scrape the dough out on to a greased baking sheet and, with wet hands, shape the dough into a thick disc. Then, using a wet knife, slash a deep cross from the centre out to the edges.

3/ Bake for around 35 minutes, until the crust is golden brown and the loaf sounds 'hollow' when tapped. Leave to cool on a wire rack, and serve with the kefir butter.

Kefir Pancakes (*Olaydi*)

These delicious little morsels are the hidden, secret Russian pancake, to be hastily scoffed while the rest of the world is distracted by blinis. If blinis resemble mini-crêpes – skinny little layers of batter – olaydi are more like puffy American-style hotcakes, only improved by the inclusion of kefir, the acid in which powers the bicarbonate of soda to turn them into little clouds. They're traditionally served with smetana *(sour cream), but the sour cream from the kefir cultured butter recipe works superbly (as, for that matter, does adding mashed banana to the batter, or studding the pancakes with blueberries while they cook, somewhat less traditionally).*

TIME / 15 minutes
YIELD / 12 small pancakes
KIT / A heavy frying pan

INGREDIENTS
200g plain flour
1 tablespoon caster sugar
½ teaspoon salt
½ teaspoon baking powder
½ teaspoon bicarbonate
   of soda

1 egg, beaten
1 tablespoon butter, melted
   + 1–2 tablespoons for frying
190ml kefir

1/ Put the flour, sugar, salt, baking powder and soda into a large bowl and mix well.

2/ Separately, mix the egg, butter and kefir, then make a well in the top of the flour mix and pour the liquid into it. Stir briefly, until everything is just combined, and leave for 8–10 minutes to rest.

3/ Heat your pan over a medium heat and brush with a little butter. Working in batches, scoop small ladles of batter into the pan, leaving room between them for flipping. Cook them until their bottoms are golden brown and bubbles form on top (~3 minutes). Flip and cook for about 1–2 minutes more, until golden brown. Serve immediately, or keep in a warm oven until you've finished batching them.

Kefir Fried Chicken

Using boneless chicken is not just a concession to the fussy eater – it means that the chicken pieces will cook through faster without risking the outside over-browning. Adding a bit of rice flour or potato starch to the flour lends crunch, but the real trick is letting it sit once it's floured, which prevents the crispy bits from detaching during cooking. Serve it with any home-brewed hot sauces you may have at your disposal.

TIME / 40 minutes
  (+ 6 hours marinating)
YIELD / Dinner for 2
KIT / A heavy frying pan
  (preferably straight-sided)

INGREDIENTS
140ml kefir
450g chicken thighs, deboned,
  skin removed (halve if large)
80g flour
2 tablespoons rice flour
  OR potato starch

½ teaspoon baking powder
½ teaspoon paprika
½ tablespoon fresh ground
  white pepper
1 teaspoon garlic powder
½ teaspoon mustard powder
Vegetable oil for deep-frying

1/ Combine the kefir with ½ teaspoon of salt. Marinate the chicken in the mixture for at least 6 hours and up to overnight.

2/ In a large bowl, mix the flour, rice flour/potato starch, baking powder, paprika, white pepper, ½ teaspoon of salt, the garlic and mustard powder.

3/ Remove the chicken from the kefir and allow most of it to drip off, then toss it in the seasoned flour until thoroughly coated – get it into any nooks. Dip it briefly back into the kefir and flour it a second time. Leave the floured chicken to rest in the fridge for at least 20 minutes, and up to 2 hours.

4/ Put 2cm of vegetable oil into a heavy pan and heat until very hot: a cube of bread should brown in 40 seconds.

5/ Gently drop half the chicken into the hot oil, or less depending on pan size, making sure not to crowd it – you'll need to do it in at least two batches. Fry for 4–6 minutes until golden, then flip and fry for 4–6 minutes more. It should be deep golden brown.

Raspberry, Almond & Kefir Crumb Cake

The crumb cake (or streuselkuchen, *as it's known in its native Germany) is a wonderful invention, replacing icing – which I'm sure you'll agree is largely an irritating barrier between you and cake – with delicious buttery crumbs. The almond flakes spearing through the crumbs provide contrast, and the kefir and raspberries form a sweet-sour double-team in the cake below. Kefir works well in all sorts of bakes and cakes – even if its acidity weren't helpful for activating the bicarbonate of soda, its subtle flavour is always welcome.*

TIME / 1 hour
YIELD / Cake for 8
KIT / 23cm springform pan
Electric whisk

FOR THE CAKE
180g plain flour
1 teaspoon baking powder
¼ teaspoon bicarbonate
   of soda
¼ teaspoon salt
120g unsalted butter (slightly
   softened), cut into cubes
150g caster sugar
2 eggs
120ml kefir (better after
   a longer second ferment)
½ teaspoon almond extract

FOR THE CRUMB TOPPING
35g plain flour
55g light brown sugar
¼ teaspoon ground cinnamon
30g unsalted butter, melted
150g raspberries
40g sliced almonds

1/ First, to make the cake, preheat the oven to 180°C, then mix the flour along with the baking powder, soda and salt in a small bowl.

2/ Next, mix the butter and sugar together with an electric whisk for a couple of minutes on high speed until it's all coming together in a single creamy mass. Add the eggs, kefir and almond extract and whisk briefly until combined. Then add the flour mixture bit by bit, whisking until it's all just combined – it should be quite thick. Set aside.

3/ To make the crumb topping, mix the flour, sugar and cinnamon together, then add the butter and rub it together with your fingertips into crumbs.

4/ Lightly grease the springform pan, then scrape the cake batter into it and smooth it out. Dot the raspberries through it (half facing up, half down – the upward-turned ones will float), then sprinkle over the sliced almonds and finally the crumbs.

5/ Bake for 40 minutes, then check it's fully baked – if a skewer stuck into the centre comes out clean, it's done. Leave to cool, then remove from the tin and serve.

White Caucasian Cocktail

The White Russian – a drink almost entirely known due to its prominence in The Big Lebowski. *But what if the featured cocktail wasn't a White Russian at all? Jeff Bridges calls his milky libation a 'Caucasian' more than once, which I imagine might go something more like this. Kefir that's gone through a secondary ferment in the fridge works best on this occasion.*

TIME / 5 minutes
YIELD / A single cocktail
KIT / A cocktail shaker

INGREDIENTS
60ml vodka
30ml Kahlua
45ml chilled kefir
A pinch of cinnamon

Shake the vodka and Kahlua over ice, and strain into an ice-filled glass. Slowly pour the kefir down the side of the glass and serve with a sprinkle of cinnamon over the top.

Chapter seven

Kvass

KVASS IS SUCH AN INTRIGUING IDEA – somehow making a fermented drink out of bread seems so wonderfully unexpected and deviant. Kvass is extremely popular across Russia (hence the proverb: 'We have bread and kvass, and it's all we need') and much of Eastern Europe, but almost unheard of elsewhere. It's baffling to me that, here in the West, it has never achieved the popularity of other low-alcohol fermented drinks like kombucha, since the latter requires you to source a starter, while kvass merely needs a couple of slices of rye bread to be toasted then fermented with water and honey. Kvass's low alcohol content is often surprising to people – I think perhaps because they expect it to taste a bit like a pint of Guinness. It does not. It's closer to a root beer, with some of the maltiness of a good pilsner, but with more yeast and occasionally some notes of peach, depending on microbial caprice. In common with the other fermented soft drinks in this book, it makes a superb alcohol-free option if you fancy something less sweet than the usual offerings, but where tepache and kombucha lend themselves best to hot summer days, kvass has a more autumnal feel.

The word 'kvass' comes from the Proto-Slavic for 'fermented drink', and its etymological roots reach back six thousand years to the Proto-Indo-European *kwat* meaning 'to ferment'. The first record of kvass is found in a manuscript at the Russian National Library, 'The Tale of Bygone Years', which dates from 1113. The venerable text recalls that, in 987, Prince Vladimir the Great of Kiev was considering a new religion for his people. Having rejected Islam because, he declared, 'drinking is the joy of the Rus', he converted to Christianity, giving kvass to his subjects to help them celebrate – although we don't know how alcoholic it might have been, as the term 'kvass' has, at various points, encompassed a whole range of sour beverages. It's only more recently that 'kvass' has come to mean specifically 'fermented rye bread drink' – and even this can be made in more or less alcoholic styles.

In 1632 Tsar Mikhail Fedorovich imposed sanctions on Lithuanian hops after Russian spies 'discovered' that a sorceress in Vilnius had cursed the hops in order to spread a plague in Russian cities (as if Lithuanian witches

have nothing better to do). Through a bit of metaphorical thinking, I suppose you could see beer as a kind of curse, and it's possible that the disease it was spreading was simply everyone being pissed all the time. Better that they drink kvass, the drink on which, as British Lieutenant Colonel Howard Vincent bitterly complained in a 1877 lecture on Russian military might in East Thrace: 'the Russian soldier flourishes, and so flourishes that he can endure almost anything'.

A Russian tsar banned the import of Lithuanian hops, believing them cursed.

The popularity of kvass in Russia throughout the Middle Ages mirrors that of 'small' (low alcohol) beer in Europe. There's a persistent myth that peasants consumed low-alcohol brews in such quantities due to the scarcity of clean water. This doesn't make a lot of sense, since London, for example, had the Great Conduit running from Tyburn Springs (modern-day Bond Street station) to Cheapside as early as the thirteenth century, and even if pathogens and disease weren't properly understood, no one wanted to drink water that smelt like a stagnant ditch. The real reason that weak beer, kvass and other fermented drinks were so popular with the peasants and proletariat was their high nutritional value and low cost – a drink that's filling and tasty will always win out when work is hard and calories are hard to come by. For a while, the Russian Society for Public Health even took to brewing their own 'hospital kvass' to assist with the convalescence of their patients.

I like to imagine there's an alternate dimension out there where kvass, not IPA, monopolizes the taps of craft pubs the world over. On this side of the time-kvass continuum, though, it remained locked away in the Slavic kitchen until the late nineteenth century, when mass migration to cities created a niche for the enterprising kvass brewer to make huge batches which they would sell directly from the barrel.

Kvass can be considered to be part of the very fabric of Russian culture. It's mentioned by Tolstoy in *War and Peace*, while to Pushkin's villagers in *Eugene Onegin* it is 'as needful as air'. It's often used as a signifier for rustic honesty and peasant hospitality – Tolstoy's semi-autobiographical landowner Lëvin is overcome with gratitude when an elderly farmworker shares a 'rag-stoppered jug' with him in *Anna Karenina*, and Dostoevsky has a monk greet one of the Brothers Karamazov with a meal of 'three kinds of well-baked bread, two bottles of wine, two of excellent mead, and a large jug of kvass'. In a very different pocket of pop culture, high-alcohol kvass is also included in the lore-rich tabletop game Warhammer, where it's carried by Kislevite troops into battle (or so I'm told – it's been a long time since I've played).

The kvass jug, so evidently familiar to Russian literature, is formed at the juncture at which the utilitarian transcends to the exquisite. The classic form is a ring with a flattened base, somewhat like a hollow, clay bagel, and this shape meant that these were some of the most challenging objects a potter could create. They were therefore regarded as the signature of a master artisan, and the most beautiful, ornate '*kvasniks*' (as they're called) now reside in the cabinets of Moscow's museums, covered with paintings of animals, ships and soldiers. One of my favourite examples casts the empty circle in the centre of the jug as a tearoom in which a couple of porcelain figures sit across a table sipping kvass poured from a smaller *kvasnik* while a cat curls about their legs.

Over the years the modest libation adapted, much like the little bacteria within, to suit its environment. While researching in the British Library, I found a pocket guide to kvass published in Moscow in 1967 which details dozens of recipes using all sorts of ingredients. (The author went on to register a patent in Austria, Great Britain and the USA for a method of kvass production, so I wonder whether he planned to open an international factory?) Flavours in his recipe collection included mint, oregano, caraway, horseradish, calamus root (which is actually toxic), ginger, blackcurrant leaves, lemon, juniper and cinnamon with Borodinsky bread (a dark brown sourdough rye). He makes special mention of Moldovan oat kvass, observing that 'even in the distant past, people noticed that kvass made from oats is the most delicious and invigorating'. Interestingly, he also gives recipes that don't contain any bread or cereals at all – instead fermenting cranberries, carrots, strawberries, raspberries, honey, pine needles and even milk (made with sugar and yeast, so much thinner than yogurt or kefir). Of all of these, the one

Traditional kvass jugs have a large hole in the middle, a bit like a bagel.

that flourished in the intervening decades was beetroot kvass – searching for kvass online you're now as likely to come across this episcopal purple variety as the bready stuff, as it is the very backbone of a certain beetroot soup.

Much like the bread in kvass, beetroot is far from integral to borscht – in fact, its original ingredient and namesake is a herb called *borshchivnyk* in Ukrainian, known in English as hogweed (you'll have seen it on road verges). Beetroot is, however, very good in borscht, especially when it's fermented first (of course) – any shortcuts involving vinegar should be disregarded. The kvass base gives the soup a sour note to contrast with the sweetness of the additional,

Beetroot kvass has eclipsed all other varieties in popularity.

unfermented beets, and the richness of the stock. Some versions of beet kvass use rye bread, and some omit it – especially those of Jewish origin, so that the borscht may be served during Passover (when leavened bread is forbidden).

In the late-1960s, with sales of Coca-Cola booming in America, the Russian government saw an opportunity to strengthen the cultural capital of kvass – which was already being consumed in around twice the volume that Americans consumed all non-alcoholic drinks. A 'GOST' (Governmental Standard) was developed for the recipe, so that it could be consistently produced, bottled and distributed across the country. Slowly it became more like an American soda – the microbes were pasteurized, and the sour flavour largely offset by sugar. As industrialization took hold and moved production from folk tradition to factory lines, all those esoteric types of kvass from that little 1967 book began to vanish. The Russian chemist Mendeleev, inventor of the periodic table, had already complained in 1892 that 'the art of home manufacture of kvass has begun to disappear' and this was the final death knell. This conglomeration of kvass production into massive factories undermined the humble street seller, and as shelf-life increased and quality dropped it could have been curtains for decent kvass.

The first billboard for Coca-Cola in Moscow was erected in 1989, two years before the Soviet Union collapsed, and so it seemed the soft drink would continue its march to world domination. By 2005, though, kvass was beginning to stage a commercial fightback. An advert for the Russian kvass brand 'Nikola' ('no cola') shows a cola-swigging man entering an apartment dressed as Gene Simmons and flicking his tongue, provoking tears from his family, until a beige-suited gent gives the spandex-and-chain-clad father a glass of kvass, and normalcy is restored. In another ad, a Michael Jackson impersonator moonwalks into a sauna with a huge cup of cola, clearly baffling the other occupants. The adverts worked – one market research company in Moscow estimated that bottled kvass sales had tripled between 2005 and 2008.

Seeing an opportunity, Coca-Cola launched its own version of kvass in Russia in May 2008. The company then decided to mark the occasion of a visit from President Medvedev in 2010 by trialling it in the USA. Promotion for Kruzhka & Bochka (translation: 'Mug & Barrel' – lazy hipster names are the same in all languages) involved performances from Cossack dancers and free samples in the New York metro area. The reaction is unrecorded, but as of writing Coca-Cola does not have a kvass brand in America.

Despite the increase in sales in Russia, it's hard to find something that resembles the kvass of yore. In 2019 one kvass-seller disparagingly told a Moscow magazine, if you buy bottled kvass at a shop it is almost certainly a pasteurized 'kvass drink'. Even if we discount the clear vested interests of someone with a barrel of authentic kvass to sell, her point certainly holds true in the UK. Finding kvass in shops is hard – Polish, Russian and Lithuanian shops are your best bet – and finding anything that doesn't taste like the mutant cousin of New Coke from the Cola Wars of the 1980s is harder still, since there isn't currently a market for a 'craft' kvass with a short shelf-life. Perhaps surprisingly, the best efforts have come from beer brewers, like the excellent Welsh microbrewery Tiny Rebel, who occasionally rustle up an alcoholic crossbreed kvass with strawberry and mint called (somewhat distastefully) AK-47. I've heard that the head of Chicago's Goose Island brewery has a passion for kvass, but while their IPAs can often be found in British supermarkets, I don't know if the kvass ever made it out of the taproom. On the whole though, the easiest way to try kvass is to take a couple of slices of rye bread and get fermenting.

KVASS IS RELATIVELY UNUSUAL among the ferments in this book, as it is fermented twice – once in the making of its ingredient, bread, and then once more as it's being converted into its liquid form. This doubled process gives it a rich complexity. Within the bread, the rye has a malty, caramel flavour – the Maillard reaction that occurs as the crust browns produces hundreds of flavour compounds. When thinking of amber-coloured, grain-powered, yeast-started and mildly alcoholic fermented drinks, beer is always going to spring to mind, and one might be forgiven for assuming that kvass has a similar microflora – which is why we need microscopes. The microbial makeup of even commercially produced kvass has been found to contain equal amounts of bacteria and yeast (whereas in beer, anything but yeast is usually undesirable), with many of the familiar friends that you'd also find in sauerkraut, kefir and cheese. While yeast may be expected to dominate, given its role in helping bread dough to rise, all this is killed off in the oven. The yeast that *is* present in kvass is thus likely to come either from baker's yeast if it has been added as a starter, or to be naturally present on raisin skins added for the same purpose. This most common species of yeast (*Saccharomyces cerevisiae*) is used in beer too (though it is a different strain – baker's yeast produces more carbon dioxide, whereas brewer's yeast produces more alcohol), and can be combined with lactic acid bacteria to make sour wheat beers like Berliner Weisse. It is also the official state microbe of Oregon.

The bacteria-yeast tagteam in kefir is far from unique within the world of fermented drinks – the grains in kefir and the pellicle in kombucha are both generational SCOBYs (symbiotic culture of bacteria and yeasts), passed down between batches. But, unlike with these, in kvass no such starter SCOBY develops, and instead the souring is dependent on wild fermentation (unless baker's yeast is added), with yeasts and lactic acid bacteria working in a kind of unwitting and spontaneous microbial harmony. The lactic acid bacteria (LAB) create a slightly acidic environment that suits the yeasts, while yeasts produce amino acids and vitamins that feed the LAB. Both microbes compete for the same food (sugar), but higher temperatures favour yeast, whereas higher acidity favours the bacteria, so we can tip the scales towards one or the other while we're fermenting. Since baker's yeast is a bit of a fermenting powerhouse it can easily overshadow any other cultures, though I'll sometimes add it to kvass in small quantities to get it going if it's being a bit stubborn. If you were to use it, letting the kvass sit for a couple of days before adding any supplemental yeast should give the LAB a head-start in getting established.

Wild fermentation is quite magical, but can also be erratic at times – and in kvass particularly so. It relies on capturing the strains of yeast and LAB that are drifting around us every day, just waiting to settle on something microbes consider nutritious and homely like a flask of kvass. The nature of this technique doesn't strongly preclude other strains of eager bread and sugar water-loving bacteria in our kitchens, and as such is a bit like luring microbial Pokémon – you can't predict exactly what you'll catch or when. I've made a few batches of kvass which have never really shown signs of life, and so if you struggle it can be helpful to use a starter motor. To give the desirable microbes a bit of an edge, raisins are often added, as they often have a profusion of naturally occurring yeast on their surface (hence the desire of grapes to turn to wine). What's neat about these yeasts is that because they're not uniform superstrains which have been intensively cultured towards a specific end (producing carbon dioxide in the case of baker's yeast, and alcohol with brewer's yeast) the range and complexity of metabolic by-products and thus flavours they can produce is much greater – in a similar way that sourdough is a different, more nuanced loaf than regular white bread. Also, since they're not regular barflies these wild yeasts can't tolerate alcohol very well, and will die off before making your kvass too alcoholic. The only downside is that they're a bit unreliable. Not all raisins are created equal, and certainly a good number of them are treated to remove anything that might risk reanimation on shop shelves – any that are marked as being sulphite- or sulphur dioxide-free will be better able to help you here. In lieu of raisins, there are many other fruits, dried or fresh, which can stand in. Plums are often covered in yeast – that's the white powderiness you see on their skin.

Adding baker's yeast to your kvass will invariably supercharge it. In either instant or active dry forms, baker's yeast (*Saccharomyces cerevisiae*) has been developed, cultured and refined to rise bread as quickly and reliably as possible. It is violently efficient, as you'll witness when adding it to kvass. It will transform your sedentary bottle into a volcano of fizz – so much so that I would very much recommend opening it over the sink.

One more option for getting your kvass going is to add some from your last batch. I'm afraid this is going to be frustrating advice if you're attempting to get your first bottle going, but once you've tasted success it'll be all the easier next time. The process, which is known somewhat unpleasantly as 'backslopping', is used in everything from sausage-curing to *idli* (South Indian fermented lentil and rice cake) production, and you'll also deploy it when repeating the yogurt recipe (page 226). It is a kind of alternative to using a pure 'starter' – instead of maintaining a separate culture, as with kefir or sourdough, you simply take some of the end product and add it back to your next batch. One advantage is that the microbes should be very lively, as they never really stop feeding (and are simply moved from one slightly exhausted food source to fresh pastures), which can reduce fermentation times quite drastically. However, if your ferment ever goes wrong, you won't have a 'sample culture' (as with a separately stored starter) to fall back on.

The third yeast that will find itself at home in your kvass is, I'm afraid, an unwelcome one. You may go over to check on your ferments in the morning and find a milky white film spread across the surface. It doesn't look like mould – it's too translucent, and it doesn't 'clump' or vary in the same way. Sometimes you'll see bubbles caught in it, frozen ejecta from better behaved yeasts trapped below. The surface of any ferment is, of course, a border between worlds. Like many borders, it's a busy place, full of exchanges, tensions and conflict. For aerobic microbes, it is a place where they can take oxygen from above, and nutrients from below. The yeast that is useful to us, however, can happily grow under the surface, without oxygen. We therefore remove the nutritious chunks of bread after they've had a good soak in the kvass, so they can't float to the surface and provide alms for other, aerobic microbes.

These unwanted surface microbes are often known as 'kahm yeast' (a term with origins in sixteenth-century German beer-brewing), though the name actually refers to a collection of different strains (mostly from the genera *Pichia*, *Debaryomyces* and *Candida*). Thankfully these unwanted microbial visitors generally aren't dangerous. They are irritating, however, as they're unsightly and can cause a bitter taste, so it's best to scoop them off if they appear (and, if your kvass is sufficiently fermented, bottle it up and put it in the fridge, which will arrest further growth).

Since these 'kahm yeasts' need oxygen to survive, and none of our ferments do (bar vinegar, in which it won't appear), the best tactic is to limit their access to it. The main ways to do this are to make sure all food sources (fruit, veg, bread) are submerged, and to minimize opening jars as much as possible, unless we already know them to be very fizzy (in which case they'll also be robust enough to fight off undesirables).

Whatever their source, the yeasts in kvass mean that your end product, much like tepache or kombucha, may be slightly alcoholic, as yeast can convert sugar into carbon dioxide and ethanol. You'd have to really put the effort in to get drunk by using my recipe, but do be aware of this if you can't consume any alcohol. The typical alcohol by volume of kvass ranges from around 0.1% (for commercial kvass, where alcohol can be controlled and removed) to around 1–2%, but in my experience tends to be lower than the

You can make prison wine similarly to kvass, but you'd need to add so much sugar that it's unlikely to happen by accident. Still, it's not a bad life skill to have.

drinks in the tepache chapter. If you work at it you might achieve a 3–4% 'hard kvass', but this is dependent on how much sugar or honey you add (since this fuels the yeast) and how long you let it ferment. Incidentally, the method for making pruno, or prison wine (using oranges, apples, bread or crushed-up sweets), isn't too dissimilar from making kvass, but you'll need to use a lot more sugar, and to hide it in your toilet cistern (it's part of the ceremony). As with all your ferments, it's a good idea to taste along the way in order that you can have them at the stage that suits you, and then refrigerate at the right moment to arrest fermentation.

Some say that kvass tastes better when made with softer water, on the grounds that the extra minerals within the hard water can make it taste bitter and interfere with the fermentation process. I've only ever made it with London tap water, though, which is harder than diamonds, and never had a problem, so I wouldn't worry too much. However, as with all ferments, if you're struggling to find signs of life make sure your water supplier doesn't add chlorine – in the UK, levels tend to be very low, thankfully, but if you're concerned then simply leave a jug of water out for an hour before using to allow any chlorine to evaporate off.

Kvass

Rye bread comes in many forms – from heavy, dark and cakey German pumpernickel to the Danish sourdough style. Across many batches of kvass, I've found more success with the paler, 20–30% rye varieties than the darker, 100% rye ones. Ukrainian 'Borodinsky' bread, made with molasses, coriander and caraway seeds, is traditional if you can find it.

TIME / 3–14 days
YIELD / 1.3 litres kvass
KIT / A large jar (sufficient
    to hold 1.5 litres)
A 1.5 litre bottle

INGREDIENTS
2–3 slices (120–150g)
    rye bread (see above)
50g honey
1½ tablespoons raisins

1/ Chop the bread roughly into chunks and put them on a baking tray in the oven on 140°C for about 1–1½ hours till they're beginning to darken and are dry like croutons, then remove (or keep it baking till it's blackened if you prefer darker kvass).

2/ Allow the croutons to cool, then boil a kettle and pour 200ml of boiling water into your jar with the honey. Stir until it is fully dissolved, then add 1.1 litres of cold tap water followed by the raisins and bread (don't add them directly to hot water). Try and pack the bread in so it doesn't float if you can, adding a weight if needed.

3/ Leave the jar in a warm place (around 22–24°C) for 36–48 hours, then strain out the bread and raisins and discard – they've done their job and are only likely to float and foster yeasts or moulds. You can now bottle up the kvass and leave at room temperature.

4/ Check the bottle once a day for fizz. In 2 or 3 days, you may notice signs of fermentation, though it could take 2 weeks. Sometimes it sours without fizzing (it depends on exactly which microbes you catch), so it's worth tasting it every few days.

5/ Once it's tasting good and sour, refrigerate it. If it's very fizzy, make sure to loosen the lid occasionally to reduce pressure!

TROUBLESHOOTING / If your Kvass is...

Not fizzing	Being a wild ferment, sometimes kvass just isn't very fizzy, though it should be sour. If it's neither fizzy nor sour, it hasn't fermented. Try leaving it for a little longer, and if this doesn't work, try adding something to get it started (a little old kvass, or 2 teaspoons of sourdough starter, or ½ teaspoon of dried yeast).
Going white on the surface	This is probably kahm yeast growth (see page 170). For the next batch, remove the bread earlier, and remove the raisins if they're still floating after 48 hours (if they sink then start floating again, it's a sign your kvass is ready).
Doesn't taste of much or just tastes like bread-water	Likely it hasn't fermented yet – kvass can be slow (see above)! If it has fermented (and tastes sour) but you'd prefer something more malty, bake your croutons for a bit longer next time.

Cherry & Rye Cocktail

Rather than rye whisky, it's rye bread in this bourbon-based cocktail, which sits somewhere between a Manhattan and a Jack & Coke.

TIME / 5 minutes
YIELD / A single cocktail

INGREDIENTS
100ml kvass
50ml bourbon
30ml cherry Heering

Mix all the ingredients over ice for a minute, until thoroughly chilled, and strain into an old fashioned glass.

Beetroot Kvass

This earthy, sour brew is often touted as a health tonic – irrespective of which, it certainly makes a tasty drink, like tomato juice but more refreshing and rich. Where it really shines, though, is in borscht, for which I think it is really an essential component. You can also use it as a savoury substitute for lemon juice in all sorts of things, from salad dressings to sauces (try mixing a little with mayo and horseradish), and you can also substitute it for kimchi brine when pickling eggs (see page 55).

TIME / 5–14 days
YIELD / 600ml beetroot kvass

KIT / A large jar (sufficient to hold 750ml)
Fermentation weight or small cup (see page 9)

INGREDIENTS
15g salt
1 beetroot (100g), peeled and finely chopped

1/ Combine the salt with 600ml of water in the jar and stir until dissolved. Add the beetroot, and a weight to keep it all submerged if necessary.

2/ Leave at room temperature to ferment. This may take as little as 5 days or up to 2 weeks. It doesn't tend to get very fizzy, so taste it now and then to check how it's doing. It may brown just at the surface as the beetroot oxidizes a little. Don't worry, it'll return to a normal hue once it's stirred. Once it's sour enough, strain and refrigerate it – it will keep for a month.

Chilled Beetroot & Kefir Soup (*Šaltibarščiai*)

Niki Segnit drew my attention to a chilled Lithuanian version of borscht in The Flavour Thesaurus, which, with its addition of kefir, turns an amazing shade of hot pink that can't help but conjure images of Miami, rollerblading and open-top Cadillacs. Summer in a bowl. If you buy the beetroot raw, then roasting it in large chunks brings out the flavour nicely, but pre-cooked beetroot works perfectly well in a rush (or if it's too hot to have the oven on).

TIME / 5 minutes
 (+ 30 minutes refrigeration)
YIELD / Lunch or light dinner
 for 2

INGREDIENTS
2 beetroots, peeled and cooked
½ a cucumber
1 hard-boiled egg, peeled
A small bunch of fresh dill
 (~20g)

2 spring onions, greens only
400ml kefir (page 150)
 OR yogurt
100ml beetroot kvass

1/ Finely dice the beetroots, cucumber, egg and dill, and slice the spring onion greens into 1cm pieces. Mix all in a bowl.

2/ Combine the kefir and beetroot kvass with the veg mixture, mix well, season to taste and chill for at least 30 minutes (and up to overnight) before serving.

Ukrainian Oxtail Borscht

This – the classic, hearty form of the beetroot soup – was born in Ukraine, and there's dozens of variants from there. It is, however, also beloved all across Eastern Europe, with versions in Eastern Orthodox, Greek Catholic, Roman Catholic and Jewish meals. You'd think for all that it might taste a bit more ascetic, but it can be turned into something very indulgent – Olia Hercules, while translating a study on the history of borscht, came across one prepared for a nineteenth-century tsar using a triptych of stocks, 'one of veal, another of morel mushrooms, and a third of goose and dried prune'. This recipe dials that back down just a fraction, for those without access to the Winter Palace's kitchen (and brigade de cuisine*).*

TIME / 5 hours
YIELD / Dinner for 6–8 (serve with *pampushky*, below)
KIT / A large pot

INGREDIENTS
1.5kg oxtail (a little more if they're small pieces)
2 carrots, 1 roughly chopped, 1 grated
2 onions, 1 halved, 1 finely diced
3 cloves of garlic, minced
4 beetroots, peeled and finely diced (wash and chop greens separately if they come with them)
2 bay leaves
2 Maris Piper potatoes, peeled and chopped into 1cm chunks
½ a small cabbage, shredded
3 sprigs of thyme
400ml beetroot kvass
Horseradish (to serve)

1/ Heat 1 tablespoon of vegetable oil in a large pot over a medium-high heat and cook the oxtail, turning until it's browned on all sides. Cover with 3 litres of water, add the chopped carrot and halved onion and bring to the boil, then reduce to a simmer, skim any foam and leave to cook for around 4 hours until the meat is easily coming away from the bone, but before it starts to disintegrate.

2/ Lift the oxtail out, leave it to cool slightly, then remove the meat and set aside. Strain out the rest of the veg and discard, skim excess fat off the stock and reserve, and set the stock aside.

3/ Heat 1 tablespoon of the oxtail fat over medium-low heat. Add the diced onion, reduce to low and cook for 10–15 minutes until softened but not browned.

4/ Next, increase the heat to medium, add the minced garlic and cook for around 30 seconds, then add the grated carrot and continue to cook another couple of minutes, stirring frequently to prevent browning. Add the diced beets and bay leaves and cook for a few more minutes.

5/ Add the stock, oxtail, potatoes, cabbage, thyme and beet greens (if using) and bring to the boil. Once boiling, reduce to a simmer for 20 minutes, until the vegetables are tender.

6/ Remove from the heat, pick out the bay leaves and thyme, add the kvass and season with salt and pepper, adding more kvass if desired. Serve with a dollop of horseradish.

Garlic Pampushky

A Ukrainian soup befits a Ukrainian accompaniment, and there can be none better than pampushky *– competing for the title of 'Most Onomatopoeically Satisfying Bread', these garlicky little rolls are perfect dipped in your borscht. They're best consumed warm, once the oil has had a few minutes to sink in and the garlic has mellowed slightly from the heat. You can also serve them sweet in more of a doughnut style by omitting the garlic oil and instead stuffing them with boiled, ground poppy seeds combined with sugar and cinnamon.*

TIME / 2½ hours
  (20 minutes active)
YIELD / 8 small rolls
KIT / Stand mixer
  OR large bowl
Round ovenproof dish

FOR THE DOUGH
350g strong white flour
1 teaspoon instant yeast
2 teaspoons sugar
200ml warm water
½ tablespoon olive oil
1 teaspoon salt

FOR THE DRESSING
  (WITH LEFTOVERS)
150ml olive oil
10 cloves of garlic, peeled

1/ For the dough, you can use either a large bowl or stand mixer with a dough hook attachment. Add all the dry ingredients, bar the salt, and stir briefly. Then add the water while mixing slowly, until you have a soft dough. If it is still a little dry add a tablespoon or two more water. Next mix the oil and salt in slowly, then knead for 5 minutes. Cover the bowl with a damp cloth and leave to proof in a warm spot until doubled in size (about 1–1½ hours, depending on kitchen temp).

2/ Meanwhile, combine 150ml olive oil with the garlic cloves in your smallest saucepan, making sure all the garlic is covered (you may need to use a little more oil), cook over the lowest possible heat until soft and just slightly bronzed (20–30 minutes), then remove from the heat and leave to cool. You won't need all of this, but it will keep for a week in the fridge, as long as you keep the cloves covered in oil. It's great over roast veg.

3/ After it's risen, divide the dough into 8 pieces and roll into round balls. Nestle them side by side in a small-ish oiled, round ovenproof dish. Leave to rise once more until doubled again (about 60 minutes). Preheat the oven to 190°C.

4/ When the bread rolls have risen and pressed against each other like a litter of doughy pups, put them on the middle shelf of the oven and bake for around 15–16 minutes, until nicely golden on top.

5/ As soon as they come out of the oven, pour around 4 tablespoons of the garlic oil over them and allow to cool slightly, then serve with borscht and spread with confit garlic to taste.

Chapter eight
Tepache & Ginger Beer

TEPACHE IS A MEXICAN FERMENTED pineapple drink, flavoured with cinnamon and slightly sweetened with *piloncillo* (unrefined cane sugar) or brown sugar. I can't tell you how much I love it. It is the perfect, refreshing soft drink, and what's more it uses up leftovers otherwise destined for compost. Like cooking parmesan rinds into tomato sauce, adding coriander roots to curry paste or pickling eggs in kimchi brine, there's something utterly satisfying about using the leftover skin and core of a pineapple to make tepache.

Although the situation is improving, it can be hard to find good, alcohol-free alternatives to water and fruit juice. I can only suspect this is due to a longstanding international conspiracy of measuring errors, but it seems like most commercially produced soft drinks are impossibly sugary, or anyway taste like they are (due to a multitude of synthetic workarounds). Fermented fruit drinks, like tepache (as well as kvass and kombucha), address this really well, as they transform sugars into acids, bringing a far more balanced flavour. Even putting health considerations aside, I think that a market-driven society such as ours should surely allow for a breadth of options to include non-alcoholic drinks that don't taste like a melted Calippo. All I ask for is choice. But perhaps I should step off my milk crate and make one myself.

The precise origins of tepache are difficult to trace, but it dates back at least to the Pre-Columbian era – which narrows it down to somewhere between 1519 AD and the moment, forty thousand-ish years ago, that ancient humans first left preservable footprints in the Valley of Mexico. It's not even clear how long Mexico has been in possession of pineapples, although some clues exist. In the late 1990s, a stone slab slightly taller than an A4 sheet of paper was discovered in a heap of debris by construction workers building a road in a village between two bends of the Coatzacoalcos River in south-east Mexico. This slab, which became known as the Cascajal Block and dates to around 1,000 BC, depicted an alphabet that had never been seen before, representing the earliest writing system west of Egypt. Among the sixty-two glyphs on the Block is a shape that strongly resembles a pineapple. So we can surmise that the fruit has probably been around for a while.

While Mexico didn't possess cane sugar before it was brought to the Americas by Europeans, the Mayans certainly had honey (and even a honey god), which would have worked perfectly well to ferment something akin to tepache. Indeed, pre-Columbian Mexicans had another source of sugar which they used to ferment a drink called *pulque*. The syrup of the agave (a spiny plant with a heart that doesn't look too dissimilar from a pineapple) is the same stuff that the Spanish *conquistadores* would later distil into tequila and mezcal, but before that it was simply fermented into a milky-coloured, beer-like drink called *pulque*. A mythical Aztec opossum was thought to have discovered it after using its opposable thumbs to dig into the plant and get to its sweet, self-fermenting juice. The creator god Quetzalcoatl was then said to have become so utterly whiffled on the stuff that he slept with his sister; on emerging from his hungover shame cave the next day, he apparently went down to the beach and set himself on fire, his ashes becoming the planet Venus. A cautionary tale if ever there was one.

While the Aztecs controlled access to the drink, thus limiting intoxication, the Spanish invasion brought European leniency to alcohol consumption, and quickly *pulquerías* began to spring up. These booze-serving street stalls developed into taverns with seating and music (and wonderful names like *El Templo del Amor*), forming the backbone of Mexican drinking culture. By the early nineteenth century, Mexico City was home to roughly one bar for every fifty people of drinking age – and besides the legal *pulquerías*, many of these were unlicensed *casas de pulque*, awash with adulterated and ill-gotten agave juice. The drink thrived until a prohibitionist anti-*pulque* government campaign in the 1930s, coupled with the introduction of beer (whose producers started a rumour that *pulque* fermentation was accelerated with human faeces) finally saw its decline in popularity.

Pulque is said to have been discovered by a mythical Aztec opossum, using its thumbs to dig out the plant's juice.

Pulque wasn't the only fermented drink to emerge from Mexico though. The word 'tepache' is thought to have origins in the central Mexican Nahuatl language (which is a font of culinary loanwords like 'avocado', 'chilli', 'chocolate' and 'tomato'). In Nahuatl, the original word is *tepiātl*, meaning 'corn drink', so it seems likely that the first iterations of tepache were maize-based, and would have been made without sugar. The Spanish brought sugar cane, and this was soon added to tepache to accelerate fermentation. Alongside *pulquerías*, tepache drinking establishments (*tepacherías*) proliferated in Mexico City through the early twentieth century. In the less salubrious *cantinas*, the tepache they were making was often alcoholic, and derived from mixing fruit with unsold *pulque* which had become too sour. At some point, among the citrus fruit, apples and guava that were being thrown into the pot, someone realized that otherwise useless pineapple peels could be used, and tepache as it is best known today was born.

Tepache remains a small-scale industry on the whole, with sellers setting up market stalls and tiny shops in the cities of Mexico, and pulling out awnings from the side of trucks along the highways. The *tepacheros* make barrels of tepache in batches calculated to meet daily demand and scheduled by the weather – since tepache ferments quickly, especially in the tropical sun.

It seems like pineapple-flavoured tepache first emerged in Jalisco, the west coast state that is also responsible for tequila, sombreros and mariachi – unsurprising, then, that 'Jalisco is Mexico' is the state motto. Perhaps because Jalisco already had a corn-based fermented drink (called *tejuino*), tepache became more firmly associated with pineapple rather than maize. Corn tepache is still popular in many parts of Mexico, though, such as Veracruz, where toasted corn and sugar are steeped in water gently heated

In Veracruz, tepache is made from toasted corn and sugar steeped in water heated by the last embers of a fire.

with the last embers of a fire to speed up fermentation. In fact, throughout the country there are still dozens of regional pockets of tepache which vary enormously in style. In Hidalgo and Puebla they make it with *pulque*, honey and anise, whereas in Michoacán they keep the pineapple skin, but also add banana peel, toasted corn leaves and tamarind (the last of which is definitely worth trying). In Oaxaca there's an alternative riff on tepache made with water kefir grains, called *tepache de tibicos*, which confusingly has no relation to regular milk kefir, even if the grains (which are gathered from the pads of the prickly pear cactus) do look remarkably similar.

Though 'tepache' usually refers to the most popular pineapple version (especially outside of Mexico), the huge range of drinks that fall under the name shows the versatility of the same basic process – something which has not gone undiscovered elsewhere in the world. I have picked out some of my favourite fermented fruit drinks and included them here, alongside tepache, not only because the basic method for making them is (on the whole) similar, but because I reach for them on similar occasions.

Every year in Finland, the coming of spring is celebrated during the May festival of *Vappu* with a glass of *sima* and some piped doughnuts called *tippaleipä* or *munkki* (classic doughnuts with a hole – I'm guessing the name may relate to a monk's traditional tonsure). *Sima* is a fermented lemonade, which much like tepache has its origins in something more alcoholic (mead), but which is now predominantly served as a refreshing soft drink. It was sufficiently known in the 1750s to be included in a very popular Swedish cookbook of the era, written by a woman called Cajsa Warg. The slow fermentation process, and the inclusion of the lemon's rind, makes this incredibly lemony lemonade a unique take on a familiar drink. A smart Scandinavian fermenting innovation is to add a couple of raisins to the bottle as it brews – when they float, you know it's ready (organic raisins may also provide some extra yeast too). It's usually made with the addition of dried yeast to kickstart it, but it can be made with wild fermentation too – or, more reliably, by using a starter from ginger beer or similar.

To the south, in Poland, there's a similar drink with a sylvan twist. *Piwo jałowcowe*, or 'juniper beer', has its nineteenth-century origins in the Kurpie Forest, a once isolated and self-sufficient place where the people wore shoes of braided tree bark, and the wooden, thatched houses were decorated with colourful paper-cutout art. As the forest was slowly felled, the Kurpies

In Finland, sima *is served with piped doughnuts called* tippaleipä.

dispersed and much of their culture faded away. One of their traditions was this simple, fermented drink made from just juniper berries, sugar, hops and water. It has an absolutely unique and gloriously fresh flavour. It was all but eliminated from Polish memory until it was made for a tourist folklore event in 1990, and the response from this shindig started a *piwo jałowcowe* revival. Similar drinks can be found in Albania (where it's known as *hardiç*) and Bosnia (as *smreka*), and in more alcoholic forms in Finland, Sweden and Estonia.

In the UK, ginger beer was originally popular as a fermented drink. I apologize for introducing another layer of ambiguity to a drink that already has a divided identity through its dual incarnations as an 'ale' and a 'beer'. Anyway, making fermented ginger beer originally involved a starter, which was known as a 'ginger beer plant', despite not being a plant at all (quite fitting really, for a beer that's not really a beer at all). This 'ginger beer plant' resembles milk kefir grains (though it is somewhat squishier), and was known up and down the shires of England. If you speak to anyone who grew up in the 1950s or '60s, they'll likely remember it (as my Essex mother-in-law and New Zealander aunt both do) as a pantry staple. Where it originally came from isn't clear, but it seems to have first emerged around the mid-1700s, and was soon being exported to the various British colonies and outposts across the globe in rather beautiful (and now very collectable) stoneware bottles to contain the fizziness while in transit. When Corfu fell under the flag of the United States of the Ionian Islands – a short-lived British protectorate (with no relation to any other United States) – the English imported a few traditions from home, including cricket and ginger beer. The drink became popular enough with the locals that it stayed after the Brits ceded control back to Greece in 1864, and even today you can find unpasteurized, fermented *tsitsimbira* for sale on the island. As the 'ginger beer plant' is now far less prevalent, the drink is now more commonly wild-fermented (using 'ginger bug'), and this method works very well too.

A 'WILD' FERMENT HAS NO STARTER, and thus the particular path that it takes is somewhat dependent on the winds of fate, and the microbes that they blow into your kitchen. Half the ferments in this book are made in this manner, including tepache, and while I've made every effort to ensure consistency, they can be rather prone to variation. Every time I make a batch of kvass, for instance, it is a bit of an adventure – even if I take exactly the same ingredients and split them into two jars, sister-batches are likely to taste a little different. On the other hand, tepache rarely deviates from its standard form (which, thankfully, is totally delicious). Because of this, combined with how simple it is to make, it is always top of my list when recommending recipes to those who are new to fermenting.

What makes tepache so reliable? Well, the skins of pineapples (like living things in general actually) harbour many bacteria and other microbial flora. We need these for fermentation, so while rinsing a pineapple intended for tepache is fine, do not scrub its skin, since among these microbes lie those that excel at fermenting the flesh within these skins – having evolved to seek out and snuggle into the crevices and cracks of the fruit and veg that they're later planning on feasting upon. But, without our help, these desirable strains would represent only a handful of the microbial fruit fans among millions of competing species trying to get a piece of the proverbial pie. It is our duty, as fermenters, to encourage the good and weed out the bad.

Our assistance comes through creating the perfect conditions for these yeast and bacteria to thrive – a selective environment – with sugar, salt, temperature, pH and oxygen (or the lack of it). In the case of tepache, by stepping in and steeping the rind and core of the pineapple in sugar solution, we're starving the surface of oxygen (as long as we make sure all the fruit is fully submerged). Meanwhile the sugar will also inhibit the amount of water some microbes can access, and the acidity of the pineapple itself will begin to reduce the pH of the liquid.

With this help, the first microbes to wake will likely be yeasts. *Saccharomyces cerevisiae* – from the Latin 'sugar fungus of beer', and better known as baker's or brewer's yeast – is incredibly abundant in nature. It exists everywhere from oak bark to soil to insects' feet, and of course fruit skins. It's likely your tepache will include some too, carried in on the pineapple peel. Other species of yeast may be present as well, though not always together – *Candida boidinii*, which was for a time thought to have been first discovered in tepache, before someone realized it was the same stuff that had previously been found in a leather tanning workshop in France twenty years prior; and *Pichia membranaefaciens*, a species very commonly found on strawberries and in tequila production, which makes a toxin that specifically kills off *C. boidinii*. These yeasts, or some of them, are responsible for creating most of the fizz in your tepache, and the small amount of alcohol too.

On alcohol – tepache fermented for two to three days is typically below 1–2% ABV, and so is very unlikely to get anyone drunk (though do please try it yourself before letting your child loose on a couple of litres). If left to ferment for a week or longer it may reach up to 5% (if you happen to capture exactly the right yeast strains), but it's unlikely to happen by accident. If you want alcoholic tepache, you'll have a much easier time simply cutting it with beer for a delicious Mexican shandy (see page 198).

Meanwhile, the bacteria in tepache are primarily responsible for making it sour. Though lactic acid bacteria (LAB) are known to be heavily present in tepache, the exact species have not, to my knowledge, been fully identified. They do, however, include at least one interesting candidate – *Lactobacillus pentosus*. This bacteria is rare among the many microbes in fermented food, as it has been shown to survive its journey into the gut, which is a major stumbling block for many bacteria with probiotic potential. Studies to find out whether this particular bacteria could be helpful in the gut are still ongoing, but there's potential for it to tackle lactose intolerance (as *L. pentosus* can break down lactose), reduce inflammation from psoriasis and even shrink colon cancer.

The 'fuel' traditionally used in tepache is *piloncillo*, which is a kind of minimally processed sugar set in conical moulds (*piloncillo* means 'little pylon' in Spanish). It has a lot more to it than brown sugar, but it can be tricky to track down in the UK, where there's a paucity of Mexican grocers. If you have access to a Latin American shop, they may carry it under the name *panela*, but otherwise Indian *jaggery* is quite similar and makes a good substitute – failing that, simple brown sugar is absolutely fine.

Ginger beer has a rather more studied history than tepache. The science behind it was first described by Harry Marshall Ward – a man with a fearsome walrus moustache – who in 1892 wrote of a 'curious substance' which he had obtained from his friend and tutor, the Assistant Director at Kew Gardens. He identified the primary microbes to be *Lactobacillus hilgardii* and a yeast called *Saccharomyces florentinus* (meaning that, much like kefir grains and kombucha mother, ginger beer plant is a type of SCOBY, or 'symbiotic culture of bacteria and yeasts'). His seventy page paper on the ginger beer plant, ending endearingly with an apology that he has not had time to experiment further, warns us that 'if the lumps [of ginger beer plant] are vigorous and the conditions favourable, there is serious danger of the bottle bursting, and I have had one or two nasty experiences with such fermentations'. *Plus ça change* . . . While a bit of ginger beer plant would've once been the kind of thing you could beg a neighbour for, it has passed from ubiquity to obscurity over the last half century. You can still buy it online, but thankfully making ginger beer doesn't strictly require this starter at all. You can create something which tastes very similar simply by making a 'quick' starter called 'ginger bug' from grated unpeeled ginger, sugar and water. This has become much more popular in recent years, and is often used to start other, non-ginger ferments – rhubarb, grapefruit and hibiscus flower all make refreshing drinks. You can make almost any flavour combination you like, as long as you stay within the basic parameters of sweetness, to fuel fermentation. I would wholeheartedly encourage you to experiment (and please share your successes with me).

One thing universal to all fermented drinks of this nature is that they can be quite explosive. Their fizziness is without peer, and it would be remiss of me not to warn you of this, so – open any fermented beverage *carefully*. You should use bottles that can handle the pressures of fermentation – swing-top glass bottles work well, but plastic bottles that previously held a fizzy drink are good too (and you can squeeze them to check pressure without needing to open them). I've never had a bottle explode myself, since I am quite vigilant about checking ferments-in-progress, but I have heard of others creating inadvertent bottle bombs. Refrigerating bottles before opening them (again, carefully) will also slightly reduce pressure. If you are worried, stick to plastic bottles, as at least they won't be of any danger to you if they ferment too fiercely and rupture. Either way, avoid square glass bottles – they are pretty but weak. If, conversely, you want to increase fizziness, give your drinks a little time out of the fridge (overnight, say) once they are bottled up. You can boost this 'secondary fermentation' even further by adding a little (e.g. 1 teaspoon) sugar to the bottle as it sits out.

Left unattended, fermented drinks can turn into bottle bombs.

Pineapple & Cinnamon Tepache

Every time I have a bottle of tepache ready, I become a little sad, as I know I'll drink it all before I realize I must start making another bottle, and then I'll have to wait for it to be ready. Cutting it with beer (see page 198) makes it last twice as long, but maybe you should just make a double batch. You can make a banana version by substituting the cinnamon and cloves with a tablespoon of dried tamarind pulp (mash this in with the sugar water while it's warm) and a thoroughly washed ripe banana skin (without the stem).

Time / 3–7 days
Yield / 1.25 litres tepache

Kit / A large (minimum 1.5 litre) jar
A large (minimum 1.5 litre) bottle

Ingredients
100g *panela/piloncillo*
(or dark brown sugar)
1 ripe pineapple
4 cloves
1 cinnamon stick

1/ Heat 1.2 litres of water in a pan with the sugar until it's dissolved, then leave it to cool until it's just lukewarm.

2/ Remove the leaves and base from the pineapple, then peel it, keeping its rind in long strips, and remove the core. Wedge the core and strips of rind into the jar so they'll stay submerged – arranging them in horizontal stripes around the sides of the jar works well. (Keep the pineapple for another use.) Add the spices, then pour over the sugar water, making sure all the fruit is fully covered in liquid, and seal the jar.

3/ Leave to ferment in a warm spot (around 22°C) for 2–6 days, checking once a day until you see evidence of fizzing (be careful on opening, it can be very vigorous). Once fermentation is under way, try the tepache daily until it is to your liking (it's likely to take around 3–4 days total unless it's <18°C), and then strain into the bottle, being sure to leave a couple of centimetres at the top, and refrigerate. It will keep in the fridge for a week or so, but open it every so often (over a sink!) to stop it getting too fizzy.

TROUBLESHOOTING / If your Tepache is...

Not fermenting	If your tepache doesn't taste sour at all after a week, something hasn't worked. First check that your sugar water isn't too hot when adding to the pineapple (this will kill the bacteria and yeasts). Otherwise, I've heard reports of some pineapple growers using chemicals which may kill off the surface yeasts, so try buying your pineapple elsewhere, and consider an organic option if available.
Foamy at the top	This is the result of a type of yeast called 'top-fermenting'. It's not a problem at all, despite being a little less attractive.
Going mouldy	Likely the fruit became exposed to air. Start again and make sure you keep it submerged under the liquid, either by wedging the pieces or using a weight.
Smelling like acetone	This can happen occasionally when fermenting at higher temperatures – find a cooler spot if you can.
Too fizzy	Tepache (and the other ferments in this chapter) can be wildly, violently fizzy. Do take care when opening bottles (and indeed storing them before they go into the fridge). Try fermenting in a cooler spot for less time before refrigerating, and opening bottles very gently over the sink.

Chipotle Glazed Ham in Tepache with Beans

*While burrowing through a pile of esoteric cookbooks, I stumbled upon
the Mexican edition of Jules Gouffé's colossal nineteenth-century tome on
French cooking, Le Livre de Cuisine. It includes a number of local recipes,
including one for a ham cooked in tepache. Though one may have guessed
Nigella's famous Ham in Coca-Cola was inspired by an earlier tradition
from across the pond, tepache did seem an unexpected precursor. But
then, pineapple with ham is a pairing as old as the hills, so it should be
no surprise that it works so well. The beans are my addition, though I feel
Gouffé would approve, given that it brings the whole affair a bit closer
to cassoulet.*

TIME / 2½ hours

YIELD / Dinner for 6–8

KIT / One lidded saucepan
just wide enough for the
ham and another medium
saucepan

Baking tray

Immersion blender OR masher

INGREDIENTS

400g pinto beans, dried

2kg smoked boneless gammon

1.5 litres tepache

1 onion, peeled and halved

1 carrot, roughly chopped

1 cinnamon stick

2 bay leaves

4 whole allspice berries

70g *piloncillo* OR brown sugar

1 dried chipotle chilli, seeds
and stem removed

A dozen or so cloves

½ teaspoon ground cinnamon

3 tablespoons maple syrup

1/ Soak the beans in ample water overnight.

2/ Place the gammon and tepache in the pan (adding water as necessary
to cover it). Add the onion, carrot, cinnamon stick, bay leaves, allspice
and sugar.

3/ Bring to the boil, then reduce to a simmer and cover for 2 hours, topping
up with water if necessary to keep it covered. 15 minutes before it's done,
remove about 50ml and use it to soak the chipotle.

4/ Meanwhile, drain the beans and place in a medium saucepan with enough
water to cover amply.

5/ Bring the beans to the boil and skim any foam which rises to the surface, then reduce the heat and simmer, uncovered, for 45 minutes. Check they're soft enough to easily crush (if not, cook for another 5–10 minutes), and then drain (retaining about 250ml of cooking liquid).

6/ Preheat the oven to 200°C, then lift the ham out of the tepache and leave it to cool slightly.

7/ Carefully trim the rind (if present) off the ham with a sharp knife, leaving the fat on. Score the fat all over in a criss-cross pattern, and stud cloves into the intersections.

8/ Remove the chipotle from its soaking liquid and blend it, along with the cinnamon and maple syrup. Place the ham on a baking sheet and pour the mixture over the ham, concentrating on the fat on top.

9/ Put the ham in the oven for around 20 minutes, until the surface is caramelized and slightly crispy.

10/ Meanwhile, using either an immersion blender or a masher, smash the beans and reserved liquid into a loose, chunky mash and cook in the pan for 5 minutes further on a low heat, then season to taste.

11/ Cut the ham into thick slices and serve over the beans.

Ginger Beer (made with plant starter)

While there seems to be a period between the 1980s and 2000s when this starter almost entirely disappeared, it is now quite possible to find and order it online. It is a specific combination of a single strain of bacteria and species of yeast, and its flavour will thus differ from the more variable, wild fermented 'ginger bug'. After using, keep the ginger beer plant submerged in a little of the ginger beer in the fridge until you need it again (it can rest for up to a month).

TIME / 3–7 days
YIELD / 850ml ginger beer

KIT / A large
(minimum 1 litre) jar
Muslin OR cheesecloth
Sieve

INGREDIENTS
80g caster sugar
2 tablespoons ginger beer
plant grains
50g (~5cm) ginger (more
if you want it spicier)

1/ Mix the caster sugar with 850ml of water in a large jar, and stir until the sugar has dissolved. Rinse the ginger beer plant grains in a sieve, then add to the sugar solution.

2/ Grate or finely chop the ginger (unpeeled) and tie up in a piece of muslin, then drop it into the jar. Cover the top of the jar with another piece of muslin, secured with a rubber band.

3/ Leave to ferment out of the sun for 3–7 days (depending on temperature), until you witness a bit of fizzing to indicate fermentation. Try it, and if it is to your liking, remove the ginger and discard, then strain the liquid into a bottle with 1 teaspoon more sugar, making sure to leave at least a couple of centimetres headspace at the top.

4/ Leave out overnight for a secondary ferment to make it fizzy, then refrigerate. The ginger beer should keep for at least a week, but make sure to open it regularly to prevent explosions.

Ginger Bug Starter

This wild fermented starter seems to have appeared in the absence of easily available ginger beer plant. Not only can it be used to make a regular supply of ginger beer, it can also be used to ferment a load of other drinks as well. It only requires ginger, sugar and water to establish and sustain it (and is very resilient when you forget to feed it too).

Time / 5 days
Yield / 250ml ginger bug starter

Kit / A jar
Muslin or cheesecloth

Ingredients
~9cm ginger
40g caster sugar

1/ Mix 250ml of water with 1 tablespoon of sugar in a jar, and stir until dissolved.

2/ Grate 1½ tablespoons of ginger (leave it unpeeled) and add to the jar.

3/ Cover with a piece of muslin and secure with a rubber band, then leave overnight.

4/ The next day, feed it 1 teaspoon of sugar and 1 teaspoon of grated ginger. Continue to do this for 4 more days. It should now be very active and fizzy, and can be used to make ginger beer (or other drinks). Keep it refrigerated while not using it (for up to a month), and give it a feed (1 teaspoon of sugar and ginger) a day before using next time to wake it up, and replenish it with the same volume of water to replace what you use.

Ginger Beer (from ginger bug)

Since ginger bug tends to balance towards yeast (as it's such an omnipresent microbe), it will likely fizz a little faster than ginger beer plant, but can also be slightly less predictable.

TIME / 3–6 days
YIELD / 850ml ginger beer

KIT / A jar
A large (minimum 1 litre) bottle

INGREDIENTS
75g caster sugar
5–10cm grated ginger (to taste)
50ml ginger bug

1/ Bring 800ml of water to the boil, add the sugar and ginger, then leave to cool.

2/ Strain the cooled ginger tea and the ginger bug to remove the ginger, then bottle them up together, leaving at least a couple of centimetres of space at the top.

3/ Leave to ferment in a warm spot (around 22°C) for 2–6 days, checking once a day until you see evidence of fizzing (be careful on opening, it can be very vigorous). Once fermentation is properly under way, try the ginger beer daily until it is to your liking (it's likely to take around 4 days in total unless it's quite cold), then refrigerate. It will keep in the fridge for a week or so – make sure to open it occasionally to relieve pressure.

More Fermented Soft Drinks

Ginger bug works very well as a starter for other fermented drinks – they won't taste particularly of ginger (unless you choose to add more ginger), but should develop a nice sourness and fizz. Once you've got the hang of it, you can add other flavours simply by experimenting with other fruit juices (or even aromatic rhizomes such as galangal or turmeric).

Hibiscus Soda: Agua de Jamaica is a cold tea made from dried hibiscus flowers which is popular in Mexico. It has a refreshing sourness – a little like cranberry juice, but without the bitter astringency. To make a fizzy, fermented version, simply repeat the recipe for Ginger Beer (from ginger bug), substituting the ginger with 4 tablespoons of dried hibiscus flowers.

Rhubarb Soda: A deliciously English libation, and it comes out a lovely shade to boot. Repeat the recipe for Ginger Beer (from ginger bug), substituting half the ginger with 2 stems of chopped rhubarb and adding an extra 100ml of water (to account for evaporation), and simmer for 20 minutes with a lid before allowing to cool.

Juniper Beer (*Piwo jałowcowe*): This drink almost entirely disappeared around the 1920s, and when revived it was made with instant yeast for reliability and speed. This version, using ginger bug as a starter, is a bit more interesting. It makes an alcohol-free alternative to white wine that I think is really without peer – it tastes something like a pinot grigio with a nod to retsina. Repeat the recipe for Ginger Beer (from ginger bug), substituting the ginger with 2 tablespoons (~10g) of dried juniper berries, cracked open slightly with a pestle and mortar, and the sugar with 50g of honey (the berries have a lot of sugar in them already, but this will speed things up), and do not strain the juniper out of the liquid when you bottle it. It can be very slow to ferment – possibly because juniper has some antibacterial properties – but leave it to do its thing until it tastes good and sour.

Cedar Box Cocktail

Green chartreuse makes up half of one my favourite cocktails – the Last Word. By mixing the French liqueur with the crisp herbaceousness of white vermouth, and adding juniper beer, you end up with a long drink that has all the dry complexity, but without the knockout.

TIME / 5 minutes
YIELD / A single cocktail

INGREDIENTS
150ml juniper beer
50ml white vermouth
40ml green chartreuse

Mix all the ingredients over ice for a minute, until thoroughly chilled, and strain into an old fashioned glass.

Tepachelada

This Mexican iteration of the shandy is a wonderfully refreshing way to drink-without-drinking (but if you'd rather something a shade stronger, a dash of mezcal rounds it out nicely).

TIME / 5 minutes
YIELD / A single cocktail

INGREDIENTS
150ml pilsner or other lager, chilled

150ml tepache, chilled
15ml mezcal (optional)

Fill a stemmed beer glass or highball glass halfway with ice, then pour over the ingredients. Stir and taste, adjusting the tepache/beer ratio as necessary.

Fermented Lemonade (*Sima*)

While the culture wars between carbonated and cloudy lemonade rage on, the Finns have found a middle way – lemonade with fizz AND flavour.

TIME / 3–6 days
YIELD / 900ml lemonade

KIT / A large (minimum 1 litre) bottle

INGREDIENTS
3 lemons
60g caster sugar
30ml ginger bug starter

1/ Carefully peel one of the lemons, removing as little of the white pith as possible, as it will make it bitter. Reserve the peel and juice all 3 lemons.

2/ Combine the sugar with 800ml of water and stir until dissolved, then pour into a bottle along with the lemon juice, peel and ginger bug, making sure to leave at least a couple of centimetres of headspace at the top.

3/ Leave to ferment in a warm spot (around 22°C) for 3–6 days, checking once a day until you see evidence of fizzing (be careful on opening, it can be very vigorous). Once fermentation is properly under way, try the lemonade daily until it is to your liking (it's likely to take around 4 days in total unless it's quite cold), then refrigerate. Make sure to keep opening it regularly (over the sink) even once chilled, to prevent it getting explosively fizzy. It will keep in the fridge for a week or so.

Grapefruit Soda

In Japan, through my ardent patronage of vending machines, I found a type of incredibly quenching grapefruit soda. This is my attempt to replicate it.

Repeat the recipe for Fermented Lemonade (above), substituting the lemons with 2 grapefruits (using the peel of just half of one) and ½ teaspoon of salt.

Chapter nine
Kombucha

KOMBUCHA, BREWED FROM SWEET TEA mixed with myriad flavours, is probably the most popular non-alcoholic fermented drink in the world. And yet, trying to get a handle on its nebulous identity is as clear as reading tea leaves. Flavoured with everything from rooibos to rosemary and galangal to gooseberries – it's sometimes tricky to even think of it as a single drink.

To start with, we can't even be sure of where kombucha (or, even more basically, its name) came from. 'Kombucha' is likely a loanword from Japanese, but in that language it means 'kelp tea', which doesn't quite fit – the starter required to make kombucha can have a bit of a seaweed-like texture, but, given that kelp tea is an *actual* Japanese drink, these are muddied waters. Kombucha isn't its only name, just its most common – it goes by more than 160 different labels around the world, ranging from the promissory *champignon de longue vie* ('mushroom of long life') in France, to the perfunctory *Japanischer Pilz* ('Japanese mushroom') and the frankly fanciful *Wolgameduse* ('Volga jellyfish', referencing the Russian river), both in Germany.

Gathering all these names gives us a little data set to analyse. What first jumps out is that over half the names are split between German (which has forty-nine) and English (forty-two). Discounting English (global dominance), why are there so many ways to say 'kombucha' in German? It became popular in Germany after the First World War, when returning soldiers and prisoners of war brought it back from Russia. So did it start in Russia? Maybe – looking again at our list we can see that Russia-related words crop up fifteen times (like the German *Kargasoktee*, referencing a town in Siberia). But, hold on, Japan is namechecked in sixteen – almost equal. China and India get mentions too, so there's no real consensus here. The use of multiple places in names is often indicative of origin confusion – much like how a turkey is called *misirka* ('Egypt') in Macedonian, *ayam belanda* ('Dutch bird') in Malay, *peru* in Portuguese and *hindi* ('from India') in Turkish. You can go on a wild turkey chase around almost the entire globe, but let's return to kombucha, and to English. One etymological explanation dating back to the year 414 has it named after a physician called Kombu from the kingdom of Silla on the

Kombucha has more than 160 names around the world, ranging from 'Japanese mushroom' to 'Volga jellyfish'.

Korean Peninsula, who gave the drink to Japanese Emperor Ingyō as a health treatment – but the only contemporary source I can find has the medic's name as Kon Mu (*kind of* like kombu) and says nothing of a curative tea.

It seems like we may never conclusively determine the true birthplace of kombucha – though it seems likely to have been somewhere in East Asia – but we can at least plot its path through modern history. In 1835 a Russian government official who had been sent out to Irkutsk reported that:

Irkutsk is an amazing city. Here tea is drunk not only hot, as is customary for us, but also cold, infused with a slippery cake, like a mushroom that grows on rotten stumps. However, the drink is quite tasty, similar to our Vyazma kvass.

Aha! Tastes like kvass, but has some kind of mushroom growing on top of it? Sounds like kombucha. For a while, all's quiet on the kombucha front, until the 1910s, when there's a sudden flurry of interest as it pops up in Poland, with newspaper articles and classified ads mentioning a 'Japanese mushroom'.

One of my favourite anecdotes is from Germany – Dr H. Waldeck writes to report his discovery of kombucha while stationed in Russian Poland during the First World War. His 'heavy field diet' had given him constipation, so he went to his pharmacist landlord for some castor oil. Short on supplies, the pharmacist instead dug out 'a rather unclean teapot', from which he dispensed a vial of liquid. Upon enquiring what the potion was, the man only told him '*Wunderpilz*' (miracle mushrooms) – Waldeck reports that he 'bravely choked down half a cup' and found it quite effective. Some days later, he learned that Austrian soldiers were trying to take his landlord's last remaining cow (a chemist with a cow? I suppose he had a smallholding on the side). Waldeck stands up for him, and in exchange manages to get hold of a bit of the kombucha mother, which he takes back to Germany.

This 'new' drink soon acquired a reputation across Europe for being 'blood-cleansing', 'detoxifying', and a remedy for everything from gout to anxiety to 'intestinal sluggishness'. Early medical reports were translated by newspapers into cure-all sensationalism (adding a tantalizing dab of mysticism along the way). Kombucha saw a surge of popularity in Italy in 1954, with the 5th December edition of *La Stampa* asking, in classic tabloid rhetoric, 'Does it heal all ailments and restore youth?' before going on to report that 'a lady from Turin brought it from South America'. With no small amount of confused Orientalism, it is dubbed the *fungo Cinese* or 'Chinese mushroom', due to the 'mystery that surrounds it'.

It was around this time that a bit of folklore (still perpetuated to this day) began to appear about kombucha, claiming that the mother must be given freely – if it were bought or sold, it would at best lose all its power, and at worst curse all involved. A couple of weeks after the *La Stampa* headlines, 'mushroom mania' reached fever pitch across the country, dominating the public consciousness. A weekly paper ran a full-colour front page illustration showing a frankly pretty racist 'cunning sage' depiction of a Chinese man, hands clasped around a flask filled with a murky liquid replete with the mother floating on top. A few months later, Neapolitan superstar crooner Renato Carosone even wrote a song about it – 'Stu Fungo Cinese' begins, 'It came from Beijing / in a vase / a mysterious thing / No more medicines / said a Mandarin / who brought her here'. Is this the moment where the Italian kombucha craze jumped the shark?

A year later, as quickly as it exploded in Italy, kombucha all but disappeared. Somewhat a victim of its own success, the fable requiring the rapidly replicating mother to be given away freely ends up generating a kind of unsustainable fermenting 'chain letter', whereby essentially everyone in Italy ends up with their own jar of kombucha starter. The nation collectively got a bit bored, and moved on.

Fermented tea rumbles along through the 1950s, '60s and '70s, popping up here and there without ever really catching the imagination in the same way as during its Italian holiday. There are rumours that one of Stalin's doctors, Vladimir Vinogradov, prescribed it to him in 1952 as an anticarcinogen (Stalin had regular nightmares about dying of cancer) and then got caught up in a KGB plot where Vinogradov was accused of trying to poison the leader. Stalin went on to die the next year, but similar wild tales of kombucha therapy later emerged about Reagan, who'd allegedly begun drinking buckets of it in the wake of his colon cancer diagnosis.

The 1990s were a strange and turbulent time for fizzy drinks. In the wake of the great cola war between Pepsi and Coca-Cola, innovators like Red Bull entered the soft drink market, and Tango's Orange Man first appeared on our screens (voiced by none other than Gil Scott-Heron). Among the sea of sugary soda, though, some were looking for a healthier alternative. One evening in 1992, after a class at the Brahma Kumaris Meditation Centre in Hollywood, a graphic designer named Betsy Pryor was offered a drink with a mushroom floating in it by a German instructor who claimed it would 'heal the planet'. Betsy took it, and soon started a mail order business from her home in Venice, Los Angeles (named Laurel Farms, despite the squarely urban location). With her partner, Norman, she started posting kombucha mothers across the country for $50 a piece – with 70% off for the sick. Each was labelled with a promise that the recipient could 'Expect a Miracle'. By 1994 Betsy was sending out kombucha to one hundred new converts a week; meanwhile, Norman was fiercely fanning the mythos, singing in tongues to his growing SCOBYs (see YouTube for videos), and claiming each of them to be 'probably as intelligent as a dolphin'. This message of sentience found footholds, with one credulous kombuchaphile telling the *New York Times* that, 'throwing out a baby kombucha would be like throwing out a little puppy'. I still hold out hope that if I make enough kombucha my SCOBY will eventually sign up for law school and start contributing to the bills.

Through the 1990s and 2000s, kombucha pushed further and further into the US mainstream, segueing from hippy mail order to Whole Foods; at the same time, its reputation began to shift from alternative medicine to soda alternative – which is where, paradoxically, kombucha really came into its own in terms of improving people's health. In 1998, Americans were drinking a colossal 200 litres of soda each per year, but by 2014 this had fallen by a

An early American kombucha salesman claimed that his SCOBY was 'probably as intelligent as a dolphin'. Whether this wisdom could be conferred through consumption is unclear.

quarter, as people became more conscious of the 'empty calories' in soft drinks. Kombucha arrived at just the right time to give people a potentially low-sugar alternative – Coca Cola has 10.6g of sugar per 100ml, whereas kombucha has between 1 and 4g/100ml (4g is about the same as tea with one sugar, and most kombucha is well below this).

Unfortunately, in 2010, just as kombucha seemed to be reaching its fizzy zenith, the Department of Agriculture did a spot check on some bottles and found that they contained alcohol – anywhere between 0.5% and 2.5%. Perhaps due to its enormous popularity, it had begun to attract new start-up brands either not attentive enough in their manufacturing, or simply unaware of the risks; in any case, many retailers yanked it from their shelves. Producers reworked their recipes to ensure the alcohol content was below the required minimum, but not before Lindsay Lohan allegedly claimed a probation-breaking positive test from her alcohol-monitoring ankle bracelet was simply the result of drinking too much kombucha. For some producers, the booze scare sent them in the other direction, goading their SCOBYs into higher alcohol production to create 'hard' kombuchas, with one even distilling it into a 40% ABV kombucha fernet.

Over the last few years, having shaken off its status as marginal alt-medicine, kombucha has become much more popular in the UK, with more than a dozen varieties available at one major supermarket alone, and increasing numbers of restaurants and pubs stocking it as well. It's now being pitched at the new, young market for alcohol-free drinks – with nearly a quarter of 16- to 24-year-olds identifying as teetotal in 2018, it's no surprise that kombucha brands are focusing more on positioning themselves as wine-and-beer alternatives. It's not too difficult to see kombucha microbreweries following in the footsteps of craft beers – one brand already sells itself under the tagline of 'champagne reinvented' – and, given that you can find it on the menu at the Fat Duck, they might be on to something.

MAKING KOMBUCHA IS RELATIVELY straightforward. You take some previously made kombucha, along with a kombucha mother (the jelly-like pellicle that forms at the top), add these to some sweetened tea cooled to room temperature, then leave it to ferment before optionally adding flavourings. Underneath the surface, though, the science of kombucha is just as tangled as its history.

In many ways kombucha is a 'superferment'. At its heart it's powered by a SCOBY (symbiotic culture of bacteria and yeasts), in the same way as kefir, ginger beer and soy sauce. However, these other ferments host two, four, or at most maybe a dozen different microbes, whereas scientists have found around thirty-five unique species of bacteria and yeasts in kombucha (though not all at the same time). To top it all off (quite literally), unlike any of these other symbiotic brews, it has a pellicle much like vinegar.

So, who are these thirty-five different microbes calling kombucha their home? In broad categories, there's species of lactic acid bacteria (LAB), which are the varieties present in most non-vinegar ferments, but there's also vinegar's acetic acid bacteria (AAB); not forgetting the yeasts that make the whole thing fizz. It's a regular Lilliputian hotel. This kind of diversity within one drink is quite staggering, as you'd usually expect a ferment to perform best as a niche for a select few species to monopolize, and to see these reappear consistently each time – especially since kombucha is a starter-based ferment, meaning that the same microbes are being introduced across consecutive batches and transported between different producers.

The reason for this multiplicity of microbes is that, instead of acting as a gladiatorial arena, kombucha is a microbial soup of cooperation, built around developing sweet tea into a welcoming home to a number of palatable species, while building fortifications and obstacles against toxic invaders. A high degree of hierarchy prevails within the kombucha alliance, as each of the many microbes disembarks from the SCOBY to the tea like a seed ship full of terraforming specialists landing on a new planet.

One of the first chemical reactions to take place after the SCOBY is added to your sweetened tea is that yeasts (primarily *S. cerevisiae* – brewer's/baker's yeast) create an enzyme called 'invertase'. This splits (or 'inverts') the sugar that you've added into glucose and fructose. Inverted sugar has many uses – it's in jam (where it's produced when sugar is heated with acid), golden syrup and the centre of Cadbury's Creme Eggs. Bees also produce invertase in order to convert flower nectar into honey, but here it's going to be eaten by far smaller beasts than bee larvae. The now inverted sugar is much easier for both the yeasts and bacteria to consume.

Next up, yeasts perform another public service by converting some of this sugar into alcohol, which serves a dual purpose. It acts as an antiseptic, repelling many otherwise eager colonizers of your deliciously tempting sweet

Over the course of many batches, kombucha will begin to form new layers, which are often called 'babies'.

tea; and it provides food for the acetic acid bacteria (in much the same way as in vinegar), who then convert it into acetic acid. As this acetic acid builds up, it eventually discourages the yeast from making more alcohol (which is partly why kombucha isn't usually particularly alcoholic). As you might guess, acetic acid is *also* an antiseptic, so the yeast and AAB have a hostile environment tag team going on. Acetic acid, which kombucha shares with vinegar, is usually its greatest sour component, but it's far from the only acid at the party. Due to its enormous microbial diversity, it also has varying amounts of gluconic, glucuronic, malic, lactic, tartaric, citric, amino and oxalic acids (tongue-twisting as well as mouth-puckering). Glucuronic acid is used in our livers to bind with and excrete toxins from the blood, so it's the focus of much research into kombucha's potential health benefits.

Lastly, the bacteria (and in particular a strain called *Komagataeibacter xylinus*) start decorating the place with a bit of knitting. Using nanocellulose as their yarn, these unique AAB not only produce acetic acid, but also weave a mesh which becomes a floating island atop the sea of sweet tea. This allows them to better access the oxygen which they need to breathe, while simultaneously creating a barrier to any pathogens which might be in the air, protecting the colonies already present in the kombucha. By the way, when making kombucha you'll find that this pellicle will float much more sturdily than the ones that are created when making vinegar (which, if jostled, will easily sink and are near-impossible to 're-float'). They are so robust that they will (over multiple batches of kombucha) begin to form new, thin layers, which are often called 'babies'. These can be removed and stored in mature kombucha, either to give to a friend or as a backup in case anything goes wrong with your brew.

Because of all this symbiotic behaviour, kombucha has been proposed as a 'model system' for cooperation, suggesting that it could be used in further research experimentation to determine how and whether microbes will work together in certain circumstances (e.g. under stress, or with abundant resources).

The first thing I thought about when trying to make kombucha was how its microbial diversity might be mirrored by the variety of teas it could be fed with. It turns out that others have leapfrogged past me and successfully made kombucha with everything from coffee to wine, cactus pear juice, cola, Jerusalem artichoke extract and even milk. Its success surely comes through the sheer variety of microbes that are involved in a kombucha SCOBY, since there's likely to be a strain of something that'll be happy to munch down on whatever you throw at it.

Unfortunately, though, kombucha will not really thrive long-term on anything but tea. It's well-adapted to the medium of sweetened black or green tea (jasmine is fine too), but other teas like rooibos and peppermint may not be able to provide exactly the right environment to sustain kombucha and, worse, may even contain antiseptic oils (e.g. bergamot in Earl Grey) or flavours that could damage it. This doesn't mean you can't incorporate flavours from these other teas, but that you should do so during secondary fermentation, once the SCOBY has been safely removed so as to avoid weakening future batches. For primary fermentation, even keeping within the parameters of black and green tea, many options exist when it comes to customizing your kombucha. The standard black tea varieties of Darjeeling, Assam and Ceylon all work interchangeably, as do green teas like gunpowder, matcha or sencha – any teas, essentially, that don't contain additives. On the weirder side, I've really enjoyed using a blend with around 25% pu'er tea, which is already fermented during its curing process, and has a lovely vegetal flavour which is somehow both smoothed out and complicated by making kombucha with it – though the subtleties of a twenty- or thirty-year aged tea may not come through enough to justify the cost, so try a young vintage first.

Kombucha mothers are so hardy that material scientists and fashion designers have begun to find novel uses for them. When Suzanne Lee, a former senior research fellow at Central Saint Martins, started investigating 'living materials' in 2003, she came across kombucha and was intrigued by its ability to synthesize a sturdy, rubbery substance from tea, sugar and water. She began creating batches in her bathtub (maximizing the surface area, since she was more interested in culling the cellulose than the liquid beneath it), and drying them. Once cured, it became a material that resembled leather; what's more, if it was draped over an object (like a mannequin) while it dried, it would hold its contours, effectively meaning she could create seamless garments. The fabric has since been seized upon by many other designers who've started labels like Kombucha Couture and ScobyTec, and has been used to develop catwalk creations including shoes, handbags and jackets. It

Suzanne Lee created huge kombucha pellicles in her bath and cured them into a kind of vegan leather. As she put it, 'I grow frocks'.

may have some way to go before you see it on the high street, but biofabricated clothes have a bright future in sustainable fashion.

Meanwhile, the European Space Agency, as part of its astrobiology research, has sent kombucha up into the heavens. The eighteen-month mission began in summer 2014 and aimed to test the resilience of kombucha's cellulose pellicles in the face of a vacuum environment and huge temperature changes, with a background of cosmic and unfiltered solar radiation. The SCOBY was launched aboard the Progress 56P cargo spacecraft bound for the International Space Station, where it was externally mounted alongside more than six hundred other biological samples in a kind of extraterrestrial endurance deathmatch, to see which would survive the ravages of space. Anything that is discovered to be able to replicate and grow beyond our atmosphere would be incredibly valuable, not least because the enormous costs involved in sending anything into orbit are currently a major barrier to further space travel. When it was brought back down to earth ten weeks later, Ukrainian researchers discovered that the kombucha seemed to have survived its celestial voyage intact, recovering to a state very similar to that of its cousin, which had remained on Earth as a control. Meanwhile, at Imperial College in London, a team of synthetic biology students engineered a super-productive strain of kombucha's *Komagataeibacter* that would create cellulose in stressful environments (like space) in order to fabricate construction materials (such as on Mars). Together, these studies paint a clear picture of fermented tea's future potential as we travel beyond our pale blue dot, furnishing offworld settlers with both a delectable brew as well as a roof over their heads.

Kombucha (primary fermentation)

This process will give you a blank canvas of unflavoured kombucha – but even if you want it simply 'tea-flavoured', it's the secondary fermentation afterwards that will get it fizzy. If this is your first time making kombucha, you'll need to buy a SCOBY online (it will come with some starter liquid which can be used in place of the kombucha from a previous batch).

TIME / 6–9 days
YIELD / 1.5 litres kombucha
KIT / A wide-mouthed jar
  OR jug
Muslin/cheesecloth
Rubber band

INGREDIENTS
3 tea bags of black tea
  (e.g. Yorkshire Tea)
  OR 2 tea bags of black tea
  plus 1 green
80g caster sugar

200ml kombucha
  (from a previous batch)
1 kombucha pellicle/SCOBY

1/ Pour 450ml of boiling water over your tea, and leave to steep for 15 minutes, before removing the tea bags.

2/ Add the sugar and stir until fully dissolved.

3/ Fill your jug or jar with 1 litre of cold water, and pour the sugary tea into it. It should now be room temperature or just slightly warmer (20–30°C).

4/ Add 200ml of previous kombucha and the SCOBY to your diluted tea, then cover with the muslin and a rubber band. Leave for 5 days at room temperature (ideally at 26–27°C – it will be very slow below 18°C, but you'll get too much alcohol north of 30°C), then taste to see if it's beginning to sour slightly (it should still be slightly sweet) – it may need 1–3 days more.

5/ Once ready, remove 200ml of your kombucha to a small jar, and add the SCOBY to this and seal it (if it has divided you can give your 'baby' SCOBY to a friend, or keep it as backup). It can be stored at room temperature for 1–2 months (or until you want to make more kombucha) but after this it may lose potency. The remaining kombucha can proceed to secondary fermentation.

Kombucha (secondary fermentation)

Now to flavouring your kombucha. With the 'starter' SCOBY removed, you can be as experimental as you like without fear of tainting it. Until you find your favourite flavours, I'd recommend multiple, smaller bottles for secondary fermentation, so that you can try different recipes. Be aware – this is also the stage where you run the risk of exploding bottles if you leave them out for days, so do check the bottles regularly for pressure (especially in hot weather).

To make any of the following, add the flavourings to a 500ml capacity bottle and top up with kombucha, leaving about 2cm of airspace at the top. Leave at room temperature for 2–6 days, making sure not to let it overcarbonate (at the same time, if you fully open them all the time they'll never get a chance to build up any gas – just open the lid by a crack once or twice a day to check). Once your kombucha is nicely fizzy, refrigerate it for at least a few hours before drinking (you can strain out the flavourings and rebottle it if you like, but it will be less fizzy, so best to strain it as you serve).

Rosemary & Grapefruit: Add the juice from half a grapefruit (~80ml) along with a sprig of rosemary (~10cm).

Galangal, Lemongrass & *Makrut* Lime: Add 1 tablespoon of chopped galangal (~5cm), a third of a stalk of lemongrass and 3–4 *makrut* lime leaves.

Fig & Fennel Seed: Add half a fig, slightly mashed, with a heaped ¼ teaspoon of fennel seeds. Watch out, the sugars in the fig makes this particularly fizzy.

Thyme & Honey: Add two sprigs of fresh thyme and 1 teaspoon of honey.

Peach & Maple: Finely chop half a peach and add along with ½ tablespoon of maple syrup.

Mint & Lime : Add 10 mint leaves along with the juice of half a lime, and ½ teaspoon of brown sugar.

Chamomile & Lavender: Add ½ teaspoon of sugar with ½ teaspoon of chamomile (you can empty from a tea bag) and ¼ teaspoon of dried lavender.

TROUBLESHOOTING / If your Kombucha is...

Not fermenting	If it still just tastes like sweet tea after 9 days of primary fermentation and the pellicle is still sitting at the bottom of the liquid, then your kombucha is not alive. I'm afraid you'll need to start again, making sure that you're not adding it directly to hot tea, or using tea with any flavours or oils in it.
Very acidic and vinegary	It's over-fermented. For your next batch, try reducing the primary and secondary fermentation by a day or two.
Not fizzy	During secondary fermentation, make sure that you provide enough sugar for the yeasts to feed on (this can be in the form of fruit or honey). If this doesn't do it, try putting the bottles in a warmer spot (up to 28°C), or otherwise save the kombucha from the bottom of your primary fermentation to start your next batch (this should contain more yeasts).
Populated by brown stringy bits	These are little offshoot yeast colonies, and are nothing to worry about. Strain them out before secondary fermentation to prevent your kombucha from getting too fizzy.
Alcoholic (or you're worried about this)	This is caused by excess yeasts, so just as you can warm it up to make it fizzier, keeping your fermenting kombucha in a cooler spot will reduce alcohol (as well as fizz). In addition, strain out any brown stringy bits, and take leftover kombucha from the top of the bottle for the next batch, as the yeast usually hangs out at the bottom. Don't go too far though, as at least a little yeast is necessary for kombucha.

Baked Quince

Consider the quince – the flirtatious, perfumed cousin of the cooking apple – which is rock-hard and almost inedible raw, yet sliceable with a spoon when cooked. Sometimes served sweet and sometimes savoury. Go ahead and use whatever kombucha you have on hand for this, but I think the fig works very nicely.

TIME / 1 hour
YIELD / Dessert for 2
KIT / A small baking dish
A small pan

INGREDIENTS
400ml kombucha
45g caster sugar
2 cloves
½ a cinnamon stick

1 large or 2 small quince
   (~300g)
4 teaspoons honey
Cream OR ice cream to serve
   (optional)

1/ Combine the kombucha with the sugar and spices in a small pan.

2/ Peel then quarter the quince (or halve if using 2 small ones) lengthways and core it. Place each piece in the kombucha as it's ready, to minimize browning.

3/ Bring to the boil, then drop the heat and reduce to a simmer for 25 minutes. Preheat your oven to 160°C.

4/ Once ready, remove the quince pieces and arrange, cored side up, in a snug baking dish. Pour over half the cooking liquid, minus the spices. Dot a teaspoon of honey in the hollow of each piece and bake for 40–45 minutes until tender.

5/ Serve with cream or ice cream and a drizzle of the reduced cooking syrup.

Chapter ten
Yogurt

HOW DID WARM MILK MIXED with old milk and wrapped in a jumper overnight until it sours become the world's most popular living ferment? Starting with the obvious, its creamy deliciousness is curiously versatile – what other foods are equally at home in a Keralan curry and atop a Swiss breakfast? Yogurt has the kind of casual ubiquity that most ferments could only dream of, and yet yogurt-making has remained one of the rare vestiges of the 1970s thus far unrecovered by the long arms of nostalgia. But you and me, we're going to change all that. Listen, I'm at my core a lazy man, but I can assure you that once you've rattled through it a couple of times, making yogurt is *easier* than going to the shops.

The name yogurt is Turkish in origin, from the root *yoğ* meaning 'thicken'. Beyond that, we can't really agree on how to spell it – should it be yogurt or yoghurt? The fickle 'h' originally comes from the 'ğ' in Turkish being transliterated as 'gh', which is actually pronounced a lot more like the French word, *yaourt*. This is also a close approximation of how the English word sounds when spoken with a mouthful of yogurt.

It didn't originate in Turkey though. A Hindu collection of Sanskrit hymns called the Rigveda, which dates back about 3,500 years, espouses the health benefits of fermented milk products. *Dahi*, which is similar to yogurt, is one of the most ancient Indian foods. The technique for making *dahi* is just a little less prescriptive than yogurt, as it sometimes uses freshly caught lactobacillus instead of specific strains retained from a previous batch. A common technique uses chilli stalks as a source of bacteria – you can make it at home by simply subbing in a dozen or so instead of using old yogurt in the recipe below. Researchers now believe that bacteria that we use for yogurt may also have originated from the surface of plants, and that it was unintentionally transferred to milk, perhaps passing from a leaf to a milkmaid's hand and then into the pail of milk, and the rest is history.

Yogurt in the Vedic period (~1500–600 BCE) was used in divine offerings (as it still is today), often combined with a plant called 'soma' to create a particularly potent mystic food, referred to in the Rigveda as 'Creator of the

Gods'. It isn't known exactly which plant or plants this 'soma' was – it's a hot topic of debate in the budding science of entheology (the study of psychoactive substances in religious contexts) – but the strongest case is for *Ephedra sinica*, which contains the chemicals ephedrine and pseudoephedrine. These compounds are used today in decongestants, weight loss drugs and methamphetamine production. 'Meth yogurt' may not seem the likeliest of divine foods, but there you go.

Northern Europe is the archetypal homeland of dairy. It's no coincidence that these countries also have populations remarkably adept at digesting milk – a genetic skill called 'lactase persistence', meaning the possession beyond childhood of an enzyme able to break down lactose. One of the theories as to why certain people might carry this enzyme into adulthood (and there are a few) is that that those with the ability to digest lactose-rich milk more easily would have been at an advantage in the cold, dark northern winters, when vitamin D deficiency is widespread, as lactose is thought to perform a similar function in making calcium easier to absorb.

In contrast to this, the development of soured milk products (such as yogurt) generally originates from Mediterranean and Middle Eastern countries, where lactase persistence is less prevalent. Although many of these cultures were similarly dairy-dependent, at these latitudes it didn't make as much sense to breed livestock for higher milk production, which would not suit the nomadic life of mountain shepherds and goatherds, nor the scrubby grazing lands. Instead, microbes were employed that could reduce the lactose in milk by fermentation, while at the same time creating a product that would

Northern Europe, home to Friesian cows, Jersey butter and holey cheese, is also where people are genetically most likely to be able to digest milk beyond infancy.

spoil less quickly in the heat. In this way, yogurt is the perfect example of the confluence between human, microbial and cultural evolution.

The ancient Greeks had a food which sounds similar to yogurt – *oxygala*, meaning soured milk – that was often eaten with honey. Its deployment in savoury dishes dates back centuries, with Islamic Golden Age cookbooks including meat dishes cooked with yogurt at least as far back as the early 1200s. In a tenth-century Iranian cookbook (*Annals of the Caliphs' Kitchens*), the author includes a poem dedicated to yogurt in all its various forms, describing his joy at being presented with a table of eight different types of yogurt, including one 'drizzled with olive oil, easily mistaken for a net of gold'.

The adoption of yogurt into Western Europe was slow. King François I of France (who reigned 1515–47) was beset by terrible, chronic indigestion and diarrhoea. His ally, Sultan Soleiman the Magnificent, sent over a physician from the Ottoman Empire with a herd of sheep, who prescribed the king a diet of sheep's milk yogurt, which cured him of his stomach upset. The sheep were unfortunately unable to adapt to Parisian life and died soon after, while the doctor returned to Constantinople, taking the secret of yogurt with him. (Or perhaps King François kept the recipe, but inadvertently ate all the yogurt, leaving himself with nothing to use as starter for the next batch.)

It would take almost three hundred years before another migrant worker returned yogurt to Paris. In Odessa a Russian professor of zoology had twice attempted to take his own life. The first time, after his tuberculotic bride (who had been stretchered to the altar in her sickness) died, Ilya Mechnikov took an overdose of opium. He survived, and years later married one of his young students named Olga. When Olga contracted typhoid fever a decade

Boran, a dairy-loving seventh-century queen of Iran, is the likely namesake of borani, *an aubergine and yogurt stew.*

later, Ilya was certain she too would die, and in his depression took another deleterious substance. This time he purposely infected himself with relapsing fever (once a major worldwide epidemic disease), in order to investigate whether it could be transmitted by blood (it could). Both he and his wife recovered from their illnesses, and, with a renewed interest in the body's defence mechanisms, he moved to France to work at the Pasteur Institute.

Alongside winning a Nobel Prize for his work on immunity and cellular response to disease, Mechnikov started a yogurt craze in Paris. He developed a new hypothesis that, while pathogenic bacteria could harm the body, certain intestinal flora could heal it, and that these may be the key to longer life. While researching this, he was impressed by 'the number of centenarians to be found in Bulgaria', where he came across the work of Stamen Grigorov, a young Bulgarian student who had just discovered the bacteria responsible for fermenting yogurt. He wrote, 'As lactic fermentation serves so well to arrest putrefaction in general, why should it not be used for the same purpose within the digestive tube?' He investigated sauerkraut, kvass and kefir as well, but it was yogurt that he was to champion – dismissing kefir due to its (low) alcohol content, which he felt would accumulate in the body to deleterious effect. He also prefigured a lot of the research into probiotics and the microbiome that would only begin in earnest a century later, noting that children are born without gut flora, but quickly acquire it, and laying the foundation for study into faecal transplantation (whereby faecal bacteria are transferred from a healthy donor to a patient suffering from recurrent *C. difficile* colitis). His (slightly wilder) conclusion on yogurt, though, that 'agents which arrest intestinal putrefaction must at the same time postpone and ameliorate old age', caused a worldwide sensation. The idea that milk could be transformed into a health-giving elixir through the addition of bacteria was exciting, and pharmacies across Europe began stocking starter cultures and tablets. A cartoon in 1908 depicted the professor dispensing yogurt via a pump to an eager room full of elderly supplicants hooked up to a series of tubes, under the banner '*Manufacture de centenaires*'.

After Mechnikov turned yogurt into a European health sensation, John Harvey Kellogg took up the cause in America, but with an odd twist. The cereal inventor, nutritionist and anti-masturbation activist had some very concerning views on sexual health and eugenics, but an aptitude for healthy breakfasts. He digested Mechnikov's research and merged it with his own theories, to form a hypothesis in his 'Itinerary of Breakfast' that while meat 'putrefies' in the intestine, 'fruits and milk . . . ferment'. As proof of this, Kellogg claimed that he had 'in his possession a beefsteak' which had been kept 'in a state of perfect preservation for twelve years by immersion in buttermilk'. He believed that protective 'buttermilk germs' (what we'd now know as probiotics) should be planted in the gut, and so, at his enormous thirty-building sanatarium (sic), patients were only permitted to eat half their serving of yogurt, with the remainder being administered by enema to 'where [the germs] are most needed'. While yogurt became steadily popular as an American health food, its sour flavour didn't catch on. It was the addition of sugar that took it truly mainstream, taming its tartness and launching it on a trajectory to become the most widely consumed living ferment in the world. By 1973 barely 10% of yogurt sold in the United States was plain. First fruit compote took off, as 'sundae-style' yogurt, followed by frozen yogurt, as a wholehearted commitment to turning a health food into something which is frankly ice cream in all but name.

Despite the towering amounts of sugar, yogurt continued to be marketed as the key to long life. A late-'70s American TV commercial for Danone (or Dannon as it is in the States), with echoes of Ilya Mechnikov, showed elderly farmers toiling in the fields, while the announcer declared that in 'Soviet Georgia, where they eat a lot of yogurt, a lot of people live past 100'. As the first US TV commercial to be shot in the Soviet Union during the Cold War, the ad was a risky proposition, but Americans were won over by the Georgian

SOME MORE WORDS FOR YOGURT

Armenia	*katyk*
Azerbaijan	*dovga*
Brazil	*iogurte*
Egypt	*zabadi*
India	*dahi*
Iran	*mast*
Lebanon	*laban/leben raib*
Portugal	*coalhada*
Spain	*cuajada*
Sudan	*roba*

geriatrics, and by 1982 yogurt sales were growing by nearly 20% a year. In 2014, after a state senate debate, New York even pronounced yogurt its official 'state snack' – questions included whether it was inconsiderate to the lactose-intolerant, whether a pretzel dipped in yogurt would qualify the pretzel as a state snack, and if yogurt even *was* a snack, being eaten at breakfast (the bill's sponsor opined 'it is a snack, time doesn't matter. You are eating the state snack of yogurt at breakfast'). Regardless, yogurt doesn't need to be lobbied for; it's a fabulous ferment which is essential to cuisines the world over – indeed it is so omnipresent that it almost eclipses the category of living foods. I think everyone should be reminded of its microbial essence by, at least once in their lives, making yogurt themselves.

To UNDERSTAND THE CHEMISTRY of yogurt, it's easiest to look at how it differs from milk – which is to say, it's sour and it's thick. The acidity, as with other ferments, comes from bacteria converting sugars (lactose in the case of milk) into lactic acid. The change in texture, however, is peculiar to dairy. The thickness of yogurt is determined by its 'milk solids' – a term you may have seen on chocolate bar ingredients. This is the protein in the milk, primarily in the form of casein but also (in a small part) whey, and it is by denaturing these proteins that yogurt thickens. 'Denaturing' is when proteins unravel and lose their shape (or 'nature'). A lot of the textural changes in cooking happen because of denaturation through heat, as when liquid egg in cake batter turns into sliceable sponge as it bakes. In yogurt, it's primarily acid that causes the milk proteins to denature and thicken. (If you've ever wondered why low or zero-fat yogurt can be just as thick, it's because it still has as much protein as full-fat yogurt.) Heat does assist this process too though – quite apart from ensuring that the milk is a 'clean slate', free of any other microbes, when you heat milk beyond 85°C to make yogurt you also kickstart the denaturation process, and you'll notice the milk thickens slightly.

There are so many types of yogurt around the world, in myriad styles, from countless different cultures (in both senses of the word). Some are truly divergent, others merely renamed. To simplify things – there are, to my mind, two factors which can be used to describe the eating experience of almost any yogurt, disregarding other ingredients like fruit or sugar. There's acidity, ranging from the mild and creamy to the puckeringly sharp; and there's texture, anywhere from a thick shake to sliceable tofu-like firmness.

Even for similarly thick and sour styles of yogurt, the route they take to arrive on the acidity/firmness graph may differ. Letting your yogurt culture for a longer period will (like with most fermented things) make it more acidic, but added time also has the effect of firming it up. So, what if you want a thick yogurt that *isn't* sour? You could deploy a different bacterial combination, or you could also strain it, thus removing some of the liquid, as with traditional Greek yogurt. You could culture it in its final storage vessel, in the 'French style', rather than decanting it, to avoid disturbing it as it thickens. Or you could do what many manufacturers do, and add milk powder. Even simply leaving it overnight in the fridge will help.

Because yogurt is such a popular food in so many different cultures, distinct bacterial strains have had the opportunity to evolve to suit their environments, with more of one bacteria or another, or a greater diversity of different species. The bacteria most common to yogurt are *Lactobacillus delbrueckii* subsp. *bulgaricus* (formerly known as *Lactobacillus bulgaricus*) and *Streptococcus thermophilus*. Both these bacteria thrive at around body temperature, which is why you need to keep your milk warm – *S. thermophilus* prefers to be at 35–42°C while *Lactobacillus* works best at 43–46°C. As in other multi-microbial ferments, like kombucha, kimchi and kefir, the bacterial duo operate symbiotically. First, *S. thermophilus* reduces the pH and amount of oxygen to levels more manageable for the *Lactobacillus*, which in turn produces nutrients that *S. thermophilus* can consume, and then as the yogurt gets really sour, only the *Lactobacillus* can handle the high acidity. Even within this elaborate dance, there's room for variations, and if you're buying a starter culture (rather than using shop-bought yogurt as a seed) you can pick a strain to provide the kind of yogurt you prefer. A higher ratio of

Beijing yogurt contains microbial strains which induce the thickness necessary to create the yogurt drink nai lao.

S. thermophilus, for example, will typically produce a less sour final product, as it's less acid-tolerant. Getting more specific, Beijing yogurt starter contains particular Chinese strains of *S. thermophilus* which have been discovered to produce high numbers of exopolysaccharides – long-chain sugars – which produce a milkshake-like thickness typical of the delicious Beijing yogurt drink *nai lao*. Other starter cultures, marketed as Greek or Bulgarian, are usually thick in the more traditional, cleavable sense.

When you're buying a yogurt starter I'd advise seeking one labelled as 'heirloom', which means it can be used many times, similarly to a sourdough starter or vinegar mother. The alternative to heirloom cultures are 'direct-set', which allow for specifically selected and balanced bacterial combinations, but tediously these starters are unstable and tend to break down within a couple of batches as the various strains fall out of proportion to each other. All starters need to be used at least once a week or so – the more often you make yogurt, the more often you're feeding your bacteria, and the more often you feed them, the stronger they'll get.

One really neat thing about yogurt, though, is that you don't need a starter at all. You can just use a tablespoon of your favourite shop-bought yogurt (as long as it says 'live cultures' in the ingredients). Personally, I've found that 'proper starters' don't necessarily work any better than a really good commercial yogurt, and it's always nice to be able to taste the end product before you start. (Plus, there's the illicit thrill of dairy piracy.)

Yogurt is made up of solid 'curds' and liquid 'whey'. You'll often notice the whey at the top of yogurt, or find it rushing in to fill the gap as soon as you dig your spoon in – unless it's been removed or 'stabilized' through some industrial process. The solid parts – the curds – result from milk proteins (casein) clumping together, and separating out from the whey. We can push that separating process further by straining yogurt – simply wrapping it up in a cloth that's fine enough to hold the curds, while allowing the whey to drip through. This is one of the most traditional methods for a thicker final product, which you'll often find sold as Greek yogurt, though it's also found in Denmark (*ymer*, sprinkled with rye breadcrumbs and brown sugar, is named after a Norse god whose eyebrows were shaped into the realm of man), as an Indian dessert (*shrikhand*) flavoured with cardamom and saffron, and in the Netherlands, where it goes by the quintessentially Dutch name of *hangop* (because, you know, you hang it up). My favourite version, though, is

Yogurt consists of clumped casein proteins called curds, and liquid proteins called whey.

the super-strained iteration found all over the Levant in the form of little balls called *labneh*. These delicious morsels can be so firm that they fall somewhere between being yogurt and fresh cheese, and are particularly delicious rolled in crushed pistachios, sesame seeds, rose petals or za'atar. In their undressed form they are often stored covered in olive oil, where they can keep for months, though I've never managed to let them survive more than a few days before they get eaten.

Making a batch of labneh leaves behind about half the starting weight in whey, though, so what to do with it all? Commercial yogurt producers end up with hundreds of litres of whey, and for them it's a real environmental hazard. It's damaging if it gets into waterways, because its nutrients lead to algal blooms which kill fish. Producers are therefore finding ever more creative ways to upcycle the serum (Latin for whey, by the way), from animal feed to vodka production, but by making your own yogurt instead of buying it, you can put it to good use yourself. If you'll forgive the pun, one of the benefits of making yogurt is that you can grow your own whey.

Whey makes a decent drink on its own, especially taken on a tuffet (sorry). It tastes quite a lot like thin, sour yogurt – an enterprising small yogurt company in New York sells it as a 'probiotic tonic'. I try to save it for cooking if my wife doesn't drink it all – it's a superb buttermilk substitute in anything from pancakes to bread, makes an excellent acid brine for meats, and works really well as a sour element for sauces and dips like raita. I've even seen a few enthusiasts suggest it as a starter for other ferments like sauerkraut and kvass, which seems on a waste-not-want-not level like a great idea – but there's a catch. Look at the bacteria that we'd expect to find in yogurt (*L. delbrueckii* and *S. thermophilus*) and those which should turn up in sauerkraut (*L. mesenteroides*, *L. brevis* and *L. plantarum*). There's no crossover. One set is adapted for fermenting yogurt (at high temperatures), and the other is adapted for fermenting vegetables (at room temperature). Thinking about the idea of creating a 'selective environment', where you create conditions that favour specific bacteria, this is not it. It's a bit like putting a pair of penguins in the savannah because they have a glancing resemblance to zebras, and hoping for the best. However, there is one ferment that whey is really great as a starter for – more yogurt! If you remove it and stick it in the fridge you won't have to worry about making sure the last of the yogurt isn't eaten, leaving you with nothing to start the next batch.

After you've made yogurt a couple of times you may notice that it often looks really solid in your fermenting vessel (for which you can use anything that will retain heat for many hours – a Thermos flask works very well), only to split a bit as you pour it into its final, fridge-friendly container. When you transfer the yogurt, you break some of the delicate protein bonds that have formed. Instead of the usual industrial method of incubating yogurt in huge vats before redistributing it, French or 'set' yogurts are fermented in their final pots from the start – usually small glass jars – to take advantage of this curd quirk. Most manufacturers do this by placing the small jars in walk-in low-temperature ovens, though I have read of a Japanese plant which attaches each jar to a harness, which very slowly moves them on a conveyor through a heated room over 8 hours, before they arrive in a chiller, thus avoiding clumsy human contact almost entirely. You can emulate this at home rather more simply, either by using towels and foil to very (very!) thoroughly insulate glass jars which can later go into the fridge, or by using the style of yogurt maker that accommodates multiple small containers, so that they never need to be decanted between heating, incubation, refrigeration and consumption.

A more recent trend in yogurt making is to incubate it at lower temperatures for a longer time – at 32°C for 12–14 hours for example. While I'm attracted to this – since I have found cooler/slower fermentation to improve other ferments like kimchi – the risk with yogurt is that with a minimum fermentation temperature of 22°C, there's a possibility that your yogurt could cool too much during incubation unless you take care to insulate it very well, or keep it somewhere very warm.

A very common method for firming up your homemade yogurt is to use additives, the most common of which is milk powder (around 60g/litre), which is literally just adding more milk to milk. However, you can approach this another way; instead of increasing the solid content of your milk by adding more milk, you can reduce the water content by heating the milk for longer so that it evaporates. A yogurt scientist discovered through thorough experimentation that heating your milk to 82°C for 30 minutes, stirring all the while, will make for the thickest yogurt. Thirty minutes of stirring and temperature-monitoring is a bit of a chore, but I've found even keeping the yogurt at heat for 5 minutes makes a noticeable difference.

Ever keen to cut corners, I've also experimented with adding evaporated milk, which tends to be more readily available than powdered. Mixed 50/50 with semi-skimmed milk, this makes a rather excellent yogurt with a custard-like texture and a hint of caramel flavour. There are other thickeners you can use if you're questing for the very thickest possible yogurt – add 1 tablespoon of gelatine (first stirred into a small amount of cold milk) or 2 tablespoons of tapioca flour per litre of milk as the milk is cooling (tapioca should be added at 60–65°C for best results).

Saving the simplest solution till last, just leaving your yogurt overnight in the fridge will usually thicken it quite substantially, so don't be disappointed if it's slightly runnier than you'd like at first.

I haven't mentioned fat content here, as that doesn't actually do so much to determine thickness. It does affect yogurt in other ways, though, particularly texture – higher fat yogurts tend to be perceived as having a creamier and smoother mouthfeel and, curiously, also taste less sharp. It's certainly worth experimenting yourself to see what you prefer (and if you want to really go for luxury, augment your milk with cream), but in the interests of fridge space I usually use whatever milk I have on hand (and can thus testify that you can make very good yogurt with semi-skimmed).

Yogurt

You can really get creative with insulating your fermenting yogurt. I've employed foil, padded envelopes, tea towels, oven gloves and cool boxes, but it's important to check they can keep a liquid within 8–10°C of the starting temperature for the 8-hour duration. If you want a very tidy, simple solution, then a good-quality wide-mouthed (sometimes called 'food jar') thermos works very well. You can buy a yogurt maker of course, which will do all the heating and insulating for you, but I try to keep my 'single-use' kitchen appliances to a minimum, so would always recommend a thermos and instant-read thermometer instead.

If you don't have a thermometer, the first temperature (82°C) is just below a simmer, and you should see thin wisps of steam as the milk begins to thicken. The second (46°C) is harder to estimate, but it's probably about 5–10°C cooler than your hot water tap.

TIME / 6–8 hours
YIELD / 500g yogurt
KIT / Thermos (minimum
   500ml capacity)
Digital thermometer

INGREDIENTS
550ml milk (whole, skimmed
   or semi-skimmed)
1 tablespoon yogurt (store-
   bought 'live'/cultured or

from a previous batch)
OR 1 packet of yogurt starter
(available online)

1/ Pour your milk out into a small pan and warm over a medium heat, stirring regularly, until it reaches at least 82°C (but no higher than 93°C). Reduce the heat to low, and keep the milk at this temperature for 5 minutes, now stirring and scraping all the time. The more you stir, the smoother the final product.

2/ Turn off the heat, and stir occasionally as the milk cools to 42–46°C (about 30–45 minutes).

3/ While the milk is cooling, boil a kettle and pour it into your thermos to preheat it.

4/ Once the milk has cooled to 42–46°C, quickly empty the thermos and pour in half the warm milk without letting it cool further, followed by the yogurt or starter, and then the remaining half. Seal the thermos.

5/ After 6–8 hours, you can open your thermos and try your yogurt. If it hasn't set yet, seal it back up quickly and leave for another hour before checking again. Once it is ready, gently decant into a jar or similar, and put it in the fridge overnight.

Extra Thick Yogurt: To get an even thicker, more custardy yogurt (even without straining it), simply substitute 200ml of the milk in the above recipe for evaporated milk, and proceed as normal.

TROUBLESHOOTING / If your Yogurt is...

Grainy	Heat the milk more slowly, and stir it more often.
Lumpy and split	Strain it to remove the whey, then whisk the remaining curds. For your next batch, try fermenting for less time, or at a lower temperature.
Too thin	Keep it at 82–93°C for longer, stirring continuously. Ferment it for longer (up to 8–10 hours), and if that doesn't work, try adding some evaporated milk (as above) or use a different starter.
Too sour	Reduce the fermenting time first, and then the temperature slightly (it should be at least 42°C though).

Aubergine Borani

Boran, a seventh-century queen of Iran, was the first woman to ascend to the throne of the Sasanian empire and, though she reigned for only two years, she was a benevolent and just ruler, now largely remembered for minting some very nice coins. She also really loved yogurt, and created a trend for dishes which combined it with cooked vegetables, called borani. *Borani* banjan, *or aubergine* borani, *is often served as an appetizer with flatbread, but by layering the aubergine you can turn it into a main course in its own right, a bit like an aubergine parmigiana with yogurt in place of the cheese. (Incidentally I've borrowed Kenji López-Alt's microwave technique for wilting the aubergine, as it works fabulously in his parmigiana recipe, and reduces the amount of salt and oil needed.) We could call the golden aubergine rounds 'coins', but this dish is far too delicious to require the support of such a crass food metaphor.*

TIME / 2 hours 10 minutes
YIELD / Dinner for 2–3 (served with flatbread)
KIT / Mid-sized heavy lidded saucepan
22cm x 30cm baking dish

INGREDIENTS
2 tablespoons olive oil
2 medium onions, chopped
3½ cloves of garlic, minced
2 teaspoons ground coriander
½ teaspoon ground turmeric
¼ teaspoon mild red chilli powder (double if you like spicy food)
½ teaspoon ground cinnamon
2 x 400g tins of chopped tomatoes
2 large aubergines
Vegetable oil for frying
250g yogurt
½ teaspoon salt
1 tablespoon fresh coriander, chopped

1/ Heat 2 tablespoons of olive oil in a heavy lidded saucepan over medium heat, and cook the onions for around 4–5 minutes until they are softened but not browned. Add 3 of the cloves of garlic, and all the ground coriander, turmeric, chilli powder and cinnamon. Cook for a minute more until fragrant. Add the tomatoes and increase the heat to bring them to a simmer, then reduce the heat to a minimum, set a lid on ajar and cook for an hour, then purée until smooth.

2/ Meanwhile, cut the aubergine into 5mm discs, salt lightly and lay out on a piece of kitchen roll on a plate, then cover with another piece of kitchen roll, plate, then repeat with another layer and finally a third plate. You may not manage to squeeze in all the aubergine. Microwave for about 2½ minutes on high, or until the aubergine slices easily bend in half, then repeat with the remaining slices. Alternately, you can bake the kitchen-roll-interleaved aubergine slices squashed between two rimmed baking trays at 190°C for 30 minutes.

3/ Preheat the oven to 180°C. Add enough vegetable oil to cover the bottom of a large frying pan and heat on medium for a minute or two, then fry the aubergine slices in batches for a couple of minutes a side until they're golden and set aside on a piece of kitchen roll to remove excess oil.

4/ Cover the base of a 22cm x 30cm baking dish with a couple of tablespoons of your prepared tomato sauce, followed by a layer of aubergine, and repeat, finishing with tomato sauce. Bake for 25 minutes.

5/ While the aubergine is cooking, mix the yogurt with the remaining ½ garlic clove and ½ teaspoon of salt. Once the aubergine is done, remove from the oven and top with the seasoned yogurt. Garnish with the chopped coriander and serve with flatbread to mop up the sauce.

Labneh

In terms of beauty-to-effort ratio, these little morsels are gems beyond value. By straining it thoroughly, your lovely home-made yogurt can be rolled up into balls and coated in all sorts of things to make a beautiful little starter to be spread on bread. They are excellent vehicles for a whole host of creative claddings – I think a combination of labneh balls covered in red chilli flakes, crushed pistachios and dried mint looks and tastes particularly excellent, without any ingredient being too onerous to source, but you can also try sumac, lavender, rose petals or cumin seeds.

The same method works for making other styles of strained yogurt, depending on how much whey you remove – just reduce the straining time if you want to go elsewhere on the spectrum from Greek yogurt through to these, which are closer in firmness to feta. Make sure you start with a relatively thick yogurt though, or it'll be a bit of an uphill struggle.

TIME / 24 hours
YIELD / 9 balls (starter/side for 2–3 with bread)
KIT / 30cm square of fine muslin/cheesecloth
Wooden spoon, chopstick or similar

INGREDIENTS
500g thick yogurt (store-bought or using recipe above)
1 tablespoon mild red chilli flakes (Aleppo, *gochugaru* or Kashmiri are good)
1 tablespoon pistachios, finely chopped
1 tablespoon dried mint

1/ Spoon the yogurt into the centre of the muslin, then bring the corners together and tie around your chopstick or the shaft of the spoon. Leave to hang over a bowl in the fridge for 24 hours.

2/ Squeeze the yogurt to get the last of the whey out. (You can retain the whey for baking or other uses.) Untie your strained yogurt and season to taste.

3/ Shape the labneh into spheres slightly smaller than golf balls, and roll 3 of them in each of the different coatings. Serve with flatbread.

Flatbreads

One of the fastest routes to fresh-baked bread with nary a worry about crumb, crust or having a hot enough oven. The yogurt gives them a soft texture and lovely sour tang. They are best cooked on a barbecue, but indoors you can do them on a cast-iron griddle pan or under the grill.

TIME / 2 hours 15 minutes
YIELD / 6 flatbreads
KIT / Cast-iron griddle pan
  OR barbecue OR grill

INGREDIENTS
280g bread flour (OR 00 flour)
½ teaspoon salt
1 teaspoon sugar

1 teaspoon instant yeast
200g yogurt

1/ Mix the flour, salt, sugar and yeast in a large bowl. Add the yogurt and knead the dough for about 8 minutes on a well-floured surface (or in a mixer with a dough hook) until it is no longer sticky and springs back when pressed.

2/ Transfer the dough to a clean bowl, cover with cling film or a damp tea towel and allow to rise at room temperature for 1–2 hours, until nearly doubled in volume.

3/ Split the dough into 6 balls, then flatten each out with a rolling pin on a well-floured surface until they're about half the size of an A4 sheet, and cook as below.

To barbecue: Once the coals are white-hot, place the flatbreads on the grill. Resist the temptation to move them until bubbles form (about 1–2 minutes), then flip and repeat to cook the other side. Remove with tongs and keep warm under a tea towel until the rest are ready (the short rest will soften them).

To griddle: Preheat a cast-iron griddle pan over a medium-high heat until it's smoking hot (5–10 minutes), then cook the flatbreads, flipping them after 2–3 minutes when they're golden brown and blackened in spots. Rest as above.

To grill: Set the grill to medium and preheat for 10 minutes, then cook the flatbreads for 2–3 minutes a side, watching them vigilantly and flipping them when they are golden brown. Rest as above.

Yogurt Cinnamon Rolls

I bloody love cinnamon. It is one of those bewitchingly powerful food smells with the ability to make me hungry no matter how recently I ate – I adore it in both sweet and savoury forms, but without question it is most at home in that quintessential Scandi-breakfast, the cinnamon roll. Being well established that breakfast is the meal most befitting a pot of yogurt, it seems only sensible to fling some dairy into (and over) the dough, where it deftly offsets the sweet seams of cinnamon threaded through these puffy little joy clouds.

TIME / 2½ hours
YIELD / 7 rolls
KIT / 22.5cm round cake tin

FOR THE DOUGH
6 cardamom pods
450g bread flour
7g fast action yeast (1 packet)
½ teaspoon salt
60g caster sugar
70g unsalted butter, roughly
    cut into 1cm cubes
250g yogurt
1 egg, lightly beaten

FOR THE FILLING
75g unsalted butter, softened
    slightly
135g dark brown sugar
2½ tablespoons ground
    cinnamon

FOR THE ICING
60g icing sugar
3 tablespoons thick yogurt
½ teaspoon vanilla extract

1/ Break open the cardamom pods using a pestle and mortar, discard the husks, then grind the seeds to a powder. Mix them with all the dry dough ingredients in a large bowl. Rub the butter through the mix with your fingers, then make a well in the centre, add the yogurt and egg and stir until you have a soft dough without lumps.

2/ Scrape the dough out on to a lightly floured surface and knead for 6 minutes (or knead in a mixer with dough hook) until springy and smooth.

3/ Transfer the dough ball to a lightly oiled bowl, and cover with cling film or a damp tea towel. Leave in a warm place until well risen (about 1–1½ hours).

4/ Meanwhile, to make the filling, simply beat together all the ingredients until they are completely combined into a soft, smooth paste.

5/ Roll the dough out on a lightly floured surface into a rectangle approximately 25cm x 35cm. Use your hands to spread the filling mixture over the dough. Next, tightly roll up the dough, starting from a shorter edge. Place seam side down to help seal the edges, then, using a sharp or serrated knife, cut into 7 rolls.

6/ Preheat the oven to 200°C. Pop the buns, cut side up, into a lightly buttered 22.5cm cake tin and leave to rise once more for about 30 minutes, covering them again.

7/ While you wait, mix together the icing by sifting the icing sugar into a bowl with the yogurt and vanilla and whisking together until glossy.

8/ Bake the rolls for 20–25 minutes, until slightly golden brown. By underbaking them ever so slightly, they will stay soft in the middle. As soon as the buns come out of the oven, spoon over the icing and leave to cool for a couple of minutes before serving warm.

Acknowledgements

I learned so much in writing this book, and was encouraged, enabled, assisted and advised by a number of magnificent individuals. I could not have completed this journey alone, and I would like to humbly offer my thanks to the following:

CJ, my wife, first reader and recipe tester, and Carole, my mum, ever patient and supportive. Wondrous women both, who kept me going while tolerating all manner of bubbling jars and boisterous smells.

Richard Atkinson, Amandeep Singh, Sam Fulton, Imogen Scott, Shauna Lacy, Matt Hutchinson and everyone else at Penguin, for their knowledge, insight and invaluable guidance. As an inveterate tinkerer, working with such a scrupulous bunch was wildly reassuring. I really couldn't ask for a better team.

Zoë Waldie, my brilliant agent, for championing this project. When I first sat in her office and we went through my nascent scribblings together, her faith in me as a (then) stranger was enormously empowering.

Marija Tiurina, for her glorious artwork which has brought this book to life. I spent weeks coming up with a shortlist of illustrators for this project, and in the end, hers was the only name on it.

Matt Cox, for his beautiful design, which has tied it all together. Thank you for aligning, kerning, bubbling and brewing the words from a screen into this lovely book.

David Craigie, Harry Yeatman and everyone else who helped keep the kimchi flowing while I was writing. It is a joy to have the privilege of working with friends, especially faced with such large piles of cabbage.

Jane Burridge, for her advice and insight on turning ideas into books. Sorry for making you work while we were on holiday.

Robin Sherriff and all my fellow weirdos at the Fermenters Guild. There's more microbial knowledge in this group than fungi filaments in a gram of *koji*.

Alexa von Hirschberg, for sowing the seeds that started this endeavour.

Index

Reading List

I owe a great debt to a great many fermenters, folklorists and food scientists. Here's a very abridged list of texts that shaped my thinking. They're all in English – but some of the best books can be found in other languages, if you have the patience to translate them.

Handbook of Food and Beverage Fermentation Technology, edited by Y. H. Hui (Taylor & Francis, 2004) A well-referenced and technical nine hundred pages spanning from cheese and salami to *tempeh* and *meigan cai*. It can be elusive, but try your local university library.

The Art of Fermentation, by Sandor Katz (Chelsea Green, 2012) The bible of fermentation, covering everything from chewed potato beer to fermented eggs.

The Noma Guide to Fermentation, by René Redzepi and David Zilber (Artisan, 2018) A book of serious fermenting ambition, which prompted me to realize that more complex ferments like soy sauce were possible at home.

Cabbage: A Global History by Meg Muckenhoupt (Reaktion, 2018) Rarely has a monograph on a single vegetable been so surprisingly and entirely engrossing. It made me fall in love with cabbage all over again.

Humanistic Understanding of Kimchi and Kimjang Culture, compiled by World Institute of Kimchi (2014) A brilliant and freely available collection of essays addressing all manner of kimchi-adjacent topics.

The Queer History of Kombucha, by Mayukh Sen (on Food52.com) This incisive article cuts through much of the misinformation about kombucha, exploring its rise in America and its role as a purported AIDS cure.

Immunity: How Elie Metchnikoff Changed the Course of Modern Medicine, by Luba Vikhanski (Chicago Review Press, 2016) The superb biography of a figure central to early immunology research and responsible for yogurt's ascent to global popularity.

Soyinfo Center (www.soyinfocenter.com) This website, library and database enshrines the sum of human knowledge concerning the soy bean, including a 2,500-page book on soy sauce.

Vinegar, the Eternal Condiment, by Reginald Smith (Spikehorn Press, 2020) Reginald is a wonderfully, deeply knowledgeable vinegar nerd. His book shares enough vinegar expertise that I'm worried the balsamic mafia may come after him.

For Lilith:
you were bubbling
into being while I wrote this

PARTICULAR BOOKS

UK | USA | Canada | Ireland | Australia
India | New Zealand | South Africa

Particular Books is part of the Penguin Random House group of companies
whose addresses can be found at global.penguinrandomhouse.com

Penguin
Random House
UK

First published 2023

003

Copyright © James Read, 2023
Illustrations © Marija Tiurina, 2023

The moral right of the author has been asserted

Book design and layout: Matt Cox, Newman+Eastwood

Set in Garamond Premier Pro 10/12pt by Matt Cox
Printed in Latvia by Livonia Print

The authorized representative in the EEA is Penguin Random House Ireland,
Morrison Chambers, 32 Nassau Street, Dublin D02 YH68

A CIP catalogue record for this book is available from the British Library

ISBN: 978–0–241–45500–5

www.greenpenguin.co.uk

Young, Phineas Howe. Phineas H. Young Diary, April 1856–May 1857. CHL.

PUBLIC DOCUMENTS

1830 United States Federal Census (online database hosted by Ancestry.com, 2010). https://www.ancestry.com/search/collections/1830usfedcenancestry/.

1840 United States Federal Census (online database hosted by Ancestry.com, 2010). https://www.ancestry.com/search/collections/1840usfedcenancestry/.

1850 United States Federal Census (online database hosted by Ancestry.com, 2009). https://www.ancestry.com/search/collections/1850usfedcenancestry/.

1860 United States Federal Census (online database hosted by Ancestry.com, 2009). https://www.ancestry.com/search/collections/1860usfedcenancestry/.

1870 United States Federal Census (online database hosted by Ancestry.com, 2009). https://www.ancestry.com/search/collections/1870usfedcen/.

1880 United States Federal Census (online database hosted by Ancestry.com, 2010). https://www.ancestry.com/search/collections/1880usfedcen/. 1880 US Census Index provided by The Church of Jesus Christ of Latter-day Saints.

1890 United States Federal Census Fragment (online database hosted by Ancestry.com, 2009). https://www.ancestry.com/search/collections/1890orgcen/.

1900 United States Federal Census (online database hosted by Ancestry.com, 2004). https://www.ancestry.com/search/collections/1900usfedcen/.

Alabama, Texas and Virginia, Confederate Pensions, 1884–1958 (online database hosted by Ancestry.com, 2010). https://www.ancestry.com/search/collections/texasconfederatepensions/.

Biographical Directory of the American Congress, 1774–1949 (online database hosted by Ancestry.com, 1998). https://www.ancestry.com/search/collections/conbio/.

Boggs, Lilburn W. Letter to General John B. Clark, 27 October 1838. In *Document Containing the Correspondence, Orders, &c., in Relation to the Disturbances with the Mormons; and the Evidence Given before the Hon. Austin A. King, Judge of the Fifth Judicial Circuit of the State of Missouri, at the Court-House in Richmond, in a Criminal Court of Inquiry, Begun November 12, 1838, on the Trial of Joseph*

Smith, Jr., and Others, for High Treason and Other Crimes against the State, General Assembly of Missouri. Fayette, MO: *Boon's Lick Democrat* office, 1841.

California State Roster, 1911 Government and Military Records (online database hosted by Ancestry.com). Compiled by Debra Graden. Provo, UT: Generations Network, 2002. https://www.ancestry.com/search/collections/castro1911/.

Commission Records, Illinois State Militia, 1835–1844 (typescript). Compiled by Lyman Platt. Family History Library. The Church of Jesus Christ of Latter-day Saints. Salt Lake City.

Deseret (State). Constitution of the State of Deseret, with the Journal of the Convention Which Formed It and the Proceedings of the Legislature Consequent Thereon. CHL.

Illinois, Compiled Marriages, 1851–1900 (online database hosted by Ancestry .com, 2005). https://www.ancestry.com/search/collections/illinoismarriages_ga/.

Iowa State Census Collection, 1836–1925 (online database hosted by Ancestry .com, 2007). https://www.ancestry.com/search/collections/iastatecen/.

Nauvoo, Illinois Tax Index, 1842 (online database hosted by Ancestry.com, 1999). Compiled by Lyman Platt. https://www.ancestry.com/search/collections/nauvoo iltax/.

Salt Lake County, Utah Civil and Criminal Case Files, 1852–1887 (online database hosted by Ancestry.com, 2003). https://www.ancestry.com/search/collections /utslccriminal/.

State of Illinois. Illinois, Public Land Purchase Records, 1813–1909 (online database hosted by Ancestry.com, 1999). https://www.ancestry.com/search /collections/lantrac/.

Territory of Utah. Legislative Assembly Rosters, 1851–1894. Division of Archives and Records Service. Department of Administrative Resources, State of Utah. https://archives.utah.gov/research/guides/legislative-assembly-rosters.pdf.

United States, Bureau of Land Management. Wisconsin, Homestead and Cash Entry Patents, Pre-1908 (online database hosted by Ancestry.com, 1997). https:// www.ancestry.com/search/collections/wi/.

United States, General Land Office Records, 1776–2015 (online database hosted by Ancestry.com, 2008).

United States Library of Congress, Legislative Reference Service. "The Presidential Election Campaign of 1844 and the Role of Joseph Smith as Candidate." Washington, DC: US Library of Congress, 1941.

Utah, Compiled Census and Census Substitutes Index, 1850–1890 (online database hosted by Ancestry.com, 1999). https://www.ancestry.com/search/collections/utcen/.

Utah Historical Records Survey. "County Government of the Provisional State of Deseret." Historical Records Survey, Division of Women's and Professional Projects, Works Progress Administration, 1937.

LEGAL DOCUMENTS

Chase, Isaac. Isaac Chase Deeds, 1828–1846. CHL.

Land Claims in Mississippi Territory, 1789–1834 (online database hosted by Ancestry.com, 2002). https://www.ancestry.com/search/collections/earlysettlers miss/. Original publication: Lowrie, Walter, ed. *Early Settlers of Mississippi as Taken from Land Claims in the Mississippi Territory: American State Papers.* Washington, DC: Duff Green, 1834.

NEWSPAPERS

Alton Telegraph, Alton, IL

Buffalo Courier, Buffalo, NY

California Star, San Francisco, CA

Daily Missouri Republican, St. Louis, MO

Deseret News, Salt Lake City, UT

Evening and Morning Star, Independence, MO

Frontier Guardian, Kanesville, IA

Gospel Reflector, Philadelphia, PA

Jeffersonian Republican, Jefferson, MO

Latter-day Saints' Messenger and Advocate, Pittsburgh, PA

Latter-day Saints' Millennial Star, Manchester, England

Nauvoo Expositor, Nauvoo, IL

Nauvoo Neighbor, Nauvoo, IL

New York Herald, New York City, NY

New York Times, New York City, NY

Niles National Register, Washington, DC

Ogden Standard, Ogden, UT

Pittsburgh Morning Post, Pittsburgh, PA

The Politician, Belleville, IL

The Prophet, New York City, NY

Saints' Herald, Plano, IL

Salt Lake Tribune, Salt Lake City, UT

Sangamo Journal, Sangamo, IL

St. Louis Luminary, St. Louis, MO

Times and Seasons, Nauvoo, IL

Voree Gospel Herald, Voree, WI

Warsaw Signal, Warsaw, IL

Wayne Sentinel, Wayne, NY

Zion's Reveille, Voree, WI

ELECTRONIC MATERIALS

Bancroft, Hubert Howe. *The Works of Hubert Howe Bancroft* (online database hosted by Ancestry.com, 2003). https://www.ancestry.com/search/collections/bancroftshist-1884/. Originally printed in thirty-nine volumes. San Francisco, CA: A. L. Bancroft, 1882–88.

Bates, William H. *Souvenir of Early and Notable Events in the History of the North West Territory, Illinois and Tazewell County* (online database hosted by Ancestry.com, 2004). https://www.ancestry.com/search/collections/genealogy-glh46544092/. Original publication: Pekin, IL: W. H. Bates, 1916.

Black, Susan Easton. Latter-day Saint Vital Records II Database. BYUSC.

College of Life Sciences, Brigham Young University. "Winter Quarters." Winter Quarters Project. http://winterquarters.byu.edu.

Early Latter-day Saints: A Mormon Pioneer Database. Historical Pioneer Research Group. http://earlylds.com.

History of Cincinnati, Ohio: With Illustrations and Biographical Sketches (online database hosted by Ancestry.com, 2005). https://www.ancestry.com/search /collections/genealogy-glh28364506/. Original publication compiled by Henry A. Ford and Kate B. Ford. Los Angeles: Williams, 1881.

History of Jefferson County, Iowa: A Record of Settlement, Organization, Progress and Achievement (online database hosted by Ancestry.com, 2003). Original publication: Chicago: S. J. Clarke, 1912–14.

IAGenWeb Project. "First Families of Jefferson County." Jefferson County, Illinois, Online. Published 4 November 2007. http://iagenweb.org/jefferson/First _Families.html.

Overland Travel Database. The Church of Jesus Christ of Latter-day Saints. https:// history.lds.org/overlandtravels.

Pioneer Immigrants to Utah Territory (online database hosted by Ancestry.com, 2001). https://www.ancestry.com/search/collections/suppionbind/.

Sons of the Utah Pioneers—Ancestor Histories, Presented by Members of the East Mill Creek Chapter (online database hosted by Ancestry.com, 2001). https:// www.ancestry.com/search/collections/suppionfact/.

Strangite database. http://strangite.com.

Tales of a Triumphant People: A History of Salt Lake County, Utah, 1847–1900 (online database hosted by Ancestry.com, 2005). https://www.ancestry.com /search/collections/genealogy-glh42044148/. Original publication: Daughters of Utah Pioneers. Salt Lake City: Stevens and Wallis Press, 1947.

Utah, Our Pioneer Heritage (online database, Ancestry.com, 1998). https://www .ancestry.com/search/collections/oph/. Original publication: International Society of the Daughters of Utah Pioneers. *Our Pioneer Heritage*. Salt Lake City: Infobases, 1996.

BIOGRAPHICAL MATERIALS

PUBLISHED WORKS

Anderson, Devery S., and Gary James Bergera, eds. *Joseph Smith's Quorum of the Anointed, 1842–45: A Documentary History.* Salt Lake City: Signature Books, 2005.

———. *The Nauvoo Endowment Companies, 1845–1846: A Documentary History.* Salt Lake City: Signature Books, 2005.

Benson, Ezra Taft. "Ezra Taft Benson, I: An Autobiography." *Juvenile Instructor,* May 1945, 213–18.

Bitton, Davis. *Guide to Mormon Diaries and Autobiographies.* Provo, UT: Brigham Young University Press, 1971.

Bingham, Stephen D. *Early History of Michigan, with Biographies of State Officers, Members of Congress, Judges and Legislators.* Lansing, MI: Thorp and Godfrey, state printers, 1888.

Black, Harvey Bischoff, ed. *LDS Seventies: Early Seventies.* BYUSC.

Boyle, Henry G. "The Savior's Promise to Believers." *Juvenile Instructor* 17 (June 1882): 180–81.

Brown, Benjamin. *Testimonies for the Truth: A Record of Manifestations of the Power of God, Miraculous and Providential, Witnessed in the Travels and Experience of Benjamin Brown, High Priest in the Church of Jesus Christ of Latter-day Saints, Pastor of the London, Reading, Kent and Essex Conferences.* Liverpool: S. W. Richards, 1853.

Brown, Lisle. *Nauvoo Sealings, Adoptions, and Anointings: A Comprehensive Register of Persons Receiving LDS Temple Ordinances, 1841–1846.* Salt Lake City: Signature Books, 2006.

Browning, John, and Curt Gentry. *John M. Browning, American Gunmaker: An Illustrated Biography of the Man and His Guns.* Garden City, NY: Doubleday, 1964.

Burns, Enoch. "Biographical Sketch." Miscellaneous Mormon Diaries, vol. 16. BYUSC.

"Buzzard, P. H." Polk County 1880 Saylor Township Biographies, Polk County, Iowa. http://ftp.rootsweb.com/pub/usgenweb/ia/polk/bios/plktwpbio9.txt.

Candland, David. *A Transcription of the Journal of David Candland (1819–1902) from the Years 1841 to 1902 Concerning His Conversion to the Mormon Church.* Lewisburg, PA: D. K. Candland, 1967.

Carter, Kate, comp. *Heart Throbs of the West.* 12 vols. Salt Lake City: Daughters of Utah Pioneers, 1947.

Duke Family Organization, eds. *Journal of Jonathan Oldham Duke.* N.p.: Duke Family Organization, 1970. CHL.

Duke, Jonathan O. Jonathan O. Duke Reminiscences and Diary, June 1850–July 1857. CHL.

Duncan, Chapman. "Biography of Chapman Duncan, 1812–1900." Americana Collection. BYUSC.

Egan, Howard. *Pioneering the West, 1846 to 1878: Major Howard Egan's Diary.* Edited by William Monroe Egan. Richmond, UT: Howard R. Egan Estate, 1917.

Farr, Aaron F. Aaron F. Farr Journal, 1852–1854. Manuscript Collection. BYUSC.

Gregg, Thomas. *History of Hancock County, Illinois: Together with an Outline History of the State, and a Digest of State Laws.* Chicago: C. C. Chapman, 1880.

Gudde, Erwin G. *Bigler's Chronicle of the West: The Conquest of California, Discovery of Gold, and Mormon Settlement as Reflected in Henry William Bigler's Diaries.* Berkeley and Los Angeles, CA: University of California Press, 1962.

Hardy, John. *History of the Trials of Elder John Hardy.* Boston: Conway, 1844.

Hatch, JoAnn F. *Willing Hands: A Biography of Lorenzo Hill Hatch, 1826–1910.* Pinedale, AZ: Kymera, 1996. http://www.b13family.com/html/journal-lorenzo _hatch.htm#_ftn58.

"History of Henry Bailey Jacobs." Oa Jacobs Cannon Collection of Biographical Papers, circa 1980. CHL.

Hogan, Mervin Booth. *The Vital Statistics of Nauvoo Lodge.* Des Moines, IA: Research Lodge No. 2, 1976. CHL.

Horner, James M. "Adventures of a Pioneer." *Improvement Era* 7 (1904): 214.

Jackman, Levi. "A Short Sketch of the Life of Levi Jackman." Twentieth Century Western and Mormon Manuscripts. BYUSC.

Jenson, Andrew. *Latter-day Saint Biographical Encyclopedia.* Salt Lake City: Andrew Jenson History, 1901.

Johnson, Joel Hills. *Voice from the Mountains, Being a Testimony of the Truth of the Gospel of Jesus Christ, as Revealed by the Lord to Joseph Smith Jr.* Salt Lake City: Juvenile Instructor, 1881.

Kimball, Heber C. *On the Potter's Wheel: The Diaries of Heber C. Kimball.* Edited by Stanley B. Kimball. Salt Lake City: Signature Books, 1987.

Lee, John D. *A Mormon Chronicle: The Diaries of John D. Lee, 1848–1876.* Edited by Juanita Brooks. San Marino, CA: Huntington Library, 1955.

———. *Mormonism Unveiled: Or, The Life and Confessions of the Late Mormon Bishop John D. Lee.* St. Louis, MO: Bryan, Brand and Company, 1877.

Lisonbee, Janet. *Obituaries and Life Sketches of the Early Saints Who Lived and Died in the Kirtland, Ohio Area.* Self-published, 2003.

Little, James Amasa. "Biography of William Rufus Rogers Stowell (1893–ca. 1950)." CHL.

Littlefield, Lyman Omer. *Reminiscences of Latter-day Saints: Giving an Account of Much Individual Suffering Endured for Religious Conscience.* Logan, UT: Utah Journal, 1888.

Mecham, Leonidas De Von. *Tolman Family Book of Remembrance and Genealogy with Allied Lines.* N.p.: printed by the author, 1952.

Meynell, J. B. *A Few Incidents of Travel in England Connected with the Immutable Principles of Truth, Called the Gospel of Jesus Christ.* Boston: John Gooch, 1845.

Miller, George. *Correspondence of Bishop George Miller with the Northern Islander, From His First Acquaintance with Mormonism up to Near the Close of His Life.* Burlington, WI: Wingfield Watson, 1916.

Polk, James K. *James K. Polk: The Diary of a President, 1845–1849.* Edited by Allan Nevins. Reprint Services Corp., 1929.

Pratt, Parley P. *Autobiography of Parley P. Pratt.* Edited by Parley P. Pratt Jr. Salt Lake City: Deseret Book, 1985.

Quincy, Josiah. *Figures of the Past from the Leaves of Old Journals.* 3rd ed. Boston: Roberts Brothers, 1883.

Sly, James Calvin. Journal. Edited by Jeffrey M. Sly. Unpublished journal, 2003. CHL.

Stout, Hosea. *On the Mormon Frontier: The Diary of Hosea Stout, 1844–1861*. Edited by Juanita Brooks. 2 vols. Salt Lake City: University of Utah Press, 1964.

Tullidge, Edward W. *History of Salt Lake City*. Salt Lake City: Star Printing Co., 1886.

———. *Tullidge's Histories*. Vol. 2. *Containing the History of All the Northern, Eastern and Western Counties of Utah; Also the Counties of Southern Idaho*. Salt Lake City: Juvenile Instructor, 1889.

Wilkerson, Ben. "Lewis Robbins" (biography). https://www.familysearch.org/photos/artifacts/20959224?p=16741486&returnLabel=Beri%20Lewis%20Robbins%20.

Woodbury, Angus Cannon. *History of the Jeremiah Woodbury Family*. Burley, ID: Reminder Press, 1958.

Woodruff, Wilford. *Wilford Woodruff, Fourth President of the Church of Jesus Christ of Latter-day Saints: History of His Life and Labors as Recorded in His Daily Journals*. Edited by Matthias F. Cowley. Salt Lake City: Deseret News, 1909.

———. *Wilford Woodruff's Journal of 1833–1898*. Vol. 2, *1 January 1841–31 December 1845*. Edited by Scott G. Kenney. Midvale, UT: Signature Books, 1983.

———. *Wilford Woodruff's Journal of 1833–1898*. Vol. 4, *1 January 1846–31 December 1850*. Edited by Scott G. Kenney. Midvale, UT: Signature Books, 1983.

Youngberg, Florence C., ed. *Conquerors of the West: Stalwart Mormon Pioneers*. 2 vols. Salt Lake City: Agreka Books, 1999.

UNPUBLISHED WORKS

Austad, Thomas R. "The Life of Nathaniel Leavitt (son of Nathaniel Leavitt and Deborah Delano)." Unpublished biography. http://leavittfamilies.org/family_history/Library/Docs/H_Nathaniel%20Leavitt%20Jr.htm.

Christopherson, Ressman, comp. "History of Lindsay Anderson Brady." In *The Lindsay Anderson Brady Book*, last modified 2000. Electronic edition. https://www.familysearch.org/service/records/storage/das-mem/patron/v2/TH-201-37108-2-91/dist.txt?ctx=ArtCtxPublic.

Correspondence F, Foutz Article, and McCaslin Frost History, 1968–1969. Nauvoo Restoration, Inc. Corporate Files, 1839–1992. CHL.

"Enoch Reese: Builder, Mason, Politician, Church Leader, Explorer, Blacksmith, Businessman, Banker, Settler, Freighter, Missionary." Unpublished biography. http://mormontrails.org/Pioneer%20SLC/GSLC/Property%20Owners/Biographies/Reese,%20Enoch.docx.

Gardner, Maurice. "Daniel and Lorena Gardner: History and Genealogy, 1773–1997." Unpublished biography. https://moobbq.com/aaqvkv/daniel_and_lorena_gardner_history_and_genealogy_1773_1997.pdf.

Hansen, Stanley D. "Story of Charles Henry Bassett." Unpublished biography, last modified 2007. CHL.

"A History and Genealogy of John Chapman Duncan and Teresa Ann Ferrell, Their Ancestors and Descendants." Compiled by Ivan Perry, Archie Perry, and Rolland Perry. CHL.

Hubbard family. "A Biography of Charles Wesley Hubbard." Unpublished biography, 1956. CHL.

Jennings, Annie McArthur. "History of Duncan and Susan McArthur." Unpublished biography, 1990. CHL.

McDonough, Lynee W. "Chauncey Walker West." Unpublished biography, n.d. Copy in author's possession.

Morrell, Eldon P., and Irene V. Deeben, comps. "Ancestry and Descendants of Chapman Duncan" (1991). Americana Collection. BYUSC.

Paxton, Robert C. "Short History of John S. Fullmer" (2007). http://trees.ancestry.com/pt/ViewStory.aspx?tid=1298896&pid=-1956607911&did=447113fc-a200-46a4-bf5c-930cb28ff5d5&src=search.

Rogers, Leo Richie. "Biographical Sketch of David White Rogers, circa 1981." CHL.

Slater, Regina R. "A Short Sketch of the Life of My Grandfather: Samuel Whitney Richards." CHL.

Standley, George Burton, comp. "History of Freeman Upson [father-in-law of Arteus Greer]." Unpublished biography, 8 November 1931. Copy in author's possession.

Stewart, Amelia Spencer. Histories of Daniel Spencer, circa 1931. CHL.

Sudweeks, Earl Max. "Biography of David and Mary Savage" (1991). CHL.

Thomas, William. "Historical Sketch and Genealogy of the Thomas Families, 1888–1895." CHL.

SECONDARY

MONOGRAPHS

Abzug, Robert. *Cosmos Crumbling: American Reform and the Religious Imagination*. New York: Oxford University Press, 1994.

Allen, James B., and Glen M. Leonard. *The Story of the Latter-Day Saints*. Salt Lake City: Deseret Book, 1976.

Anderson, Nels. *Desert Saints: The Mormon Frontier in Utah*. Chicago: University of Chicago Press, 1942.

Andrus, Hyrum L. *Joseph Smith and World Government*. Salt Lake City: Hawkes Publishing, 1972.

Arrington, Leonard J. *Great Basin Kingdom: Economic History of the Latter-day Saints, 1830–1900*. Lincoln: University of Nebraska Press, 1966.

———. *From Quaker to Latter-day Saint: Bishop Edwin D. Woolley*. Salt Lake City: Deseret Book, 1976.

Backman, Milton V., Jr. *The Heavens Resound: A History of the Latter-day Saints in Ohio, 1830–1838*. Salt Lake City: Deseret Book, 1983.

Baker, LeGrand L. *Murder of the Mormon Prophet: Political Prelude to the Death of Joseph Smith*. Salt Lake City: Eborn Books, 2006.

Barrett, Ivan J. *Joseph Smith and the Restoration: A History of the LDS Church to 1846*. Provo, UT: Brigham Young University Press, 1973.

Berrett, William Edwin. *The Restored Church: A Brief History of the Growth and Doctrines of The Church of Jesus Christ of Latter-day Saints*. Salt Lake City: Deseret Book, 1961.

Bigler, David L. *The Forgotten Kingdom: The Mormon Theocracy in the American West, 1847–1896*. Logan: Utah State University Press, 1998.

Bitton, Davis. *The Martyrdom Remembered: A One-Hundred-Fifty-Year Perspective on the Assassination of Joseph Smith*. Salt Lake City: Aspen Books, 1994.

———. *The Redoubtable John Pack: Pioneer, Proselyter, Patriarch.* Salt Lake City: John Pack Family Association, 1982.

Black, Susan Easton. *Who's Who in the Doctrine and Covenants.* Salt Lake City: Bookcraft, 1997.

Boller, Paul F., Jr. *Presidential Campaigns.* New York: Oxford University Press, 1984.

Brock, William R. *Parties and Political Conscience: American Dilemmas, 1840–1850.* Millwood, NY: KTO Press, 1979.

Brodie, Fawn M. *No Man Knows My History: The Life of Joseph Smith.* New York: Vintage Books, 1945.

Brooke, John L. *"The Refiner's Fire": The Making of Mormon Cosmology, 1644–1844.* New York: Cambridge University Press, 1994.

Bushman, Richard Lyman. *Joseph Smith: Rough Stone Rolling.* New York: Vintage Books, 2005.

Byrne, Gary C., and Paul Marx. *The Great American Convention: A Political History of Presidential Elections.* Palo Alto, CA: Pacific Books, 1976.

Campbell, Eugene E. *Establishing Zion: The Mormon Church in the American West, 1847–1869.* Salt Lake City: Signature Books, 1988.

Carter, Kate, comp. *Treasures of Pioneer History.* Vol. 3. Salt Lake City: Daughters of Utah Pioneers, 1954.

Carwardine, Richard J. *Evangelicals and Politics in Antebellum America.* New Haven, CT: Yale University Press, 1993.

Church History in the Fulness of Times Student Manual. 2nd ed. Salt Lake City: Church Educational System, The Church of Jesus Christ of Latter-day Saints, 2003.

Cohn, Norman. *The Pursuit of the Millennium: Revolutionary Millenarians and Mystical Anarchists of the Middle Ages.* Rev. ed. New York: Oxford University Press, 1970.

A Collection of Sacred Hymns, for the Church of the Latter Day Saints (1835). Compiled by Emma Smith. Kirtland, OH: F. G. Williams and Co., 1835. CHL.

Compton, Todd. *In Sacred Loneliness: The Plural Wives of Joseph Smith.* Salt Lake City: Signature Books, 1997.

Cook, Lyndon W. *Revelations of the Prophet Joseph Smith*. Salt Lake City: Deseret Book, 1985.

Cook, Lyndon W., and Donald Q. Cannon, eds. *Far West Record: Minutes of the Church of Jesus Christ of Latter-day Saints, 1830–44*. Salt Lake City: Deseret Book, 1983.

Cook, Lyndon W., and Milton V. Backman, eds. *Kirtland Elders' Quorum Record, 1836–1841*. Provo, UT: Grandin Book, 1985.

Cooley, Brigham, and Everett L. Young. *Diary of Brigham Young, 1857*. Salt Lake City: Tanner Trust Fund, University of Utah Press, 1980.

Cornog, Evan and Richard Whelan. *Hats in the Ring: An Illustrated History of American Presidential Campaigns*. New York: Random House, 2000.

Crawley, Peter. *A Descriptive Bibliography of the Mormon Church*, vol. 1. Provo, UT: Religious Studies Center, Brigham Young University, 1997.

Cross, Whitney. *The Burned-Over District: The Social and Intellectual History of Enthusiastic Religion in Western New York, 1800–1850*. Ithaca, NY: Cornell University Press, 1950.

Davidson, Karen Lynn, David J. Whittaker, Mark Ashurst-McGee, and Richard L. Jensen, eds. *Histories, Volume 1: Joseph Smith Histories, 1832–1844*. Vol. 1 of the Histories series of *The Joseph Smith Papers*. Edited by Dean C. Jessee, Ronald K. Esplin, and Richard Lyman Bushman. Salt Lake City: Church Historian's Press, 2012.

Daynes, Kathryn M. *More Wives Than One: Transition of the Mormon Marriage System, 1840–1910*. Urbana: University of Illinois Press, 2008.

Doyle, Don Harrison. *The Social Order of a Frontier Community: Jacksonville, Illinois, 1825–70*. Urbana: University of Illinois Press, 1978.

Durham, G. Homer. *Joseph Smith, Prophet-Statesman: Readings in American Political Thought*. Salt Lake City: Bookcraft, 1944.

Elliott, Norma L. *A Biographical Sketch of Jefferson Hunt*. N.p.: Karen LaDuke, 1983.

Esshom, Frank. *Pioneers and Prominent Men of Utah*. 2 vols. Salt Lake City: Utah Pioneers Book, 1913.

Faragher, John. *Sugar Creek: Life on the Illinois Prairie*. New Haven, CT: Yale University Press, 1986.

Faulring, Scott. *An American Prophet's Record: The Diaries and Journals of Joseph Smith*. Salt Lake City: Signature Books, 1989.

Field, Homer H., and Joseph R. Reed. *History of Pottawattamie County, Iowa*. Chicago: S. J. Clarke, 1907.

Fitzpatrick, Doyle C. *The King Strang Story: A Vindication of James J. Strang, the Beaver Island Mormon King*. Lansing, MI: National Heritage, 1970.

Flake, Kathleen. *The Politics of American Religious Identity: The Seating of Senator Reed Smoot, Mormon Apostle*. Chapel Hill: University of North Carolina Press, 2004.

Flanders, Robert Bruce. *Nauvoo: Kingdom on the Mississippi*. Urbana: University of Illinois Press, 1965.

Ford, Thomas. *A History of Illinois: From Its Commencement as a State in 1818 to 1847*. Urbana: University of Illinois Press, 1854.

Godfrey, Kenneth. *The Importance of the Temple in Understanding the Latter-day Saint Nauvoo Experience*. Logan: Utah State University Press, 2001.

Godfrey, Matthew C., Spencer W. McBride, Alex D. Smith, and Christopher James Blythe, eds. *Documents, Volume 7: September 1839–January 1841*. Vol. 7 of the Documents series of *The Joseph Smith Papers*. Edited by Ronald K. Esplin, Matthew J. Grow, and Matthew C. Godfrey. Salt Lake City: Church Historian's Press, 2018.

Gooch, John. *Death of the Prophets Joseph and Hyrum Smith, Who Were Murdered While in Prison at Carthage, on the 27th Day of June, A.D. 1844: Compiled and Printed for our Venerable Brother in Christ, Freeman Nickerson*. Boston: Printed by John Gooch, Minot's Building Spring Lane, corner Devonshire Street, 1844.

Grant, Carter E. *The Kingdom of God Restored*. Salt Lake City: Deseret Book, 1955.

Gregory, Tom. *History of Sonoma County, California: With Biographical Sketches of the Leading Men and Women of the County, Who Have Been Identified With Its Growth and Development from the Early Days to the Present Time*. Los Angeles: Historic Record, 1911.

Hale, Heber Quincy. *Bishop Jonathan H. Hale of Nauvoo, His Life and Ministry: Including Brief Biographies of Aroet L. Hale, Alma H. Hale, Rachel Hale Hoagland, Solomon H. Hale.* Salt Lake City: n.p., 1938.

Hand, H. Wells, ed. *1808–1908 Centennial History of the Town of Nunda.* Rochester, NY: Rochester Herald Press, 1908.

Hansen, Klaus. *Quest for Empire: The Political Kingdom of God and the Council of Fifty in Mormon History.* Lincoln: University of Nebraska Press, 1974.

Hardinge, Emma. *Modern American Spiritualism: A Twenty Years' Record of the Communion between Earth and the World of the Spirits.* New York: printed by the author, 1870.

Hartshorn, Leon R., Dennis A. Wright, and Craig J. Ostler, eds. *The Doctrine and Covenants, a Book of Answers: The 25th Annual Sidney B. Sperry Symposium.* Salt Lake City: Deseret Book, 1996.

Hatch, Nathan O. *The Democratization of American Christianity.* New Haven, CT: Yale University Press, 1989.

Havel, James T. *U.S. Presidential Candidates and the Elections: A Biographical and Historical Guide.* New York: Macmillan Library Reference USA, 1996.

Hedges, Andrew H., Alex D. Smith, and Richard Lloyd Anderson, eds. *Journals, Volume 2: December 1841–April 1843.* Vol. 2 of the Journals series of *The Joseph Smith Papers.* Edited by Dean C. Jessee, Ronald K. Esplin, and Richard Lyman Bushman. Salt Lake City: Church Historian's Press, 2011.

Hill, Marvin S. *Quest for Refuge: The Mormon Flight from American Pluralism.* Salt Lake City: Signature Books, 1989.

Historical Department Journal History of the Church, 1896–July 2001. CHL.

Hyde, John. *Mormonism: Its Leaders and Designs.* New York: W. P. Fetridge, 1857.

Jackson, Richard H. *The Mormon Role in the Settlement of the West.* Provo, UT: Brigham Young University Press, 1978.

Jenson, Andrew. *Encyclopedic History of the Church of Jesus Christ of Latter-day Saints.* Salt Lake City: Deseret News, 1941.

———. *The Historical Record.* 5 vols. Salt Lake City: Deseret News Co., 1886.

Jessee, Dean C., Mark Ashurst-McGee, and Richard L. Jensen, eds. *Journals, Volume 1: 1832–1839.* Vol. 1 of the Journals series of *The Joseph Smith Papers.*

Edited by Dean C. Jessee, Ronald K. Esplin, and Richard Lyman Bushman. Salt Lake City: Church Historian's Press, 2008.

Johnson, Clark V., ed. *Mormon Redress Petitions: Documents of the 1833–1838 Missouri Conflict*. Provo, UT: Religious Studies Center, Brigham Young University, 1992.

Journal of Discourses. 26 vols. London: Latter-day Saints' Book Depot, 1854–86.

Kling, David W. *A Field of Divine Wonders: The New Divinity and Village Revivals in Northwestern Connecticut, 1792–1822*. University Park: Pennsylvania State University Press, 1993.

Launius, Roger D., and Linda Thatcher, eds. *Differing Visions: Dissenters in Mormon History*. Urbana: University of Illinois Press, 1998.

Launius, Roger D. *Joseph Smith III: Pragmatic Prophet*. Urbana: University of Illinois Press, 1995.

Larson, Gustive Olof. *Prelude to the Kingdom: Mormon Desert Conquest, a Chapter in American Cooperative Existence*. Francestown, NH: Marshall Jones, 1947.

Leonard, Glen. *Nauvoo: A Place of Peace, a People of Promise*. Salt Lake City: Deseret Book, 2002.

Little, James A. *Jacob Hamblin, a Narrative of His Personal Experience, as a Frontiersman, Missionary to the Indians and Explorer: Disclosing Interpositions of Providence, Severe Privations, Perilous Situations, and Remarkable Escapes*. Salt Lake City: Deseret News, 1909.

Littlefield, Lyman Omer. *The Martyrs: A Sketch of the Lives and a Full Account of the Martyrdom of Joseph and Hyrum Smith*. Salt Lake City: Juvenile Instructor Office, 1882.

Ludlow, Daniel H., ed. *Encyclopedia of Mormonism*. 4 vols. New York: Macmillan, 1992.

Lyman, Edward L. *San Bernardino: The Rise and Fall of a California Community*. Salt Lake City, UT: Signature Books, 1996.

Martin, Stuart. *The Mystery of Mormonism*. New York: E. P. Dutton, 1920.

Matthews, Robert J. *"A Plainer Translation": Joseph Smith's Translation of the Bible; A History and Commentary*. Provo, UT: Brigham Young University Press, 1975.

May, Dean L. *Three Frontiers: Family, Land, and Society in the American West, 1850–1900*. New York: Cambridge University Press, 1994.

———. *Utah: A People's History*. Salt Lake City: University of Utah Press, 2002.

McBride, Spencer. *When Joseph Smith Ran for President: The Politics of American Religious Inequality* (tentative title). New York: Oxford University Press, forthcoming.

McKiernan, F. Mark, and Roger D. Launius, eds. *An Early Latter Day Saint History: The Book of John Whitmer, Kept by Commandment*. Independence, MO: Herald Publishing House, 1980.

Melville, Keith J. *Conflict and Compromise: The Mormons in Mid-Nineteenth-Century American Politics*. Provo, UT: Brigham Young University Printing Service, 1974.

Minute Book 1, [ca. 3 December 1832–30 November 1837]. The Joseph Smith Papers. https://www.josephsmithpapers.org/paper-summary/minute-book-1.

Minute Book 2, [ca. June 1838], [ca. October 1842], [ca. June 1844]. The Joseph Smith Papers. https://www.josephsmithpapers.org/paper-summary/minute-book-2.

Morgan, Dale. *The State of Deseret*. Logan: Utah State University Press, 1987.

Mulder, William, and A. Russell Mortensen, eds. *Among the Mormons: Historic Accounts by Contemporary Observers*. Lincoln: University of Nebraska Press, 1958.

Nelson, Lowry. *The Mormon Village: A Pattern and Technique of Land Settlement*. Salt Lake City: University of Utah Press, 1952.

Newell, Linda King. *Mormon Enigma: Emma Hale Smith*. Urbana: University of Illinois Press, 1994.

Oaks, Dallin H., and Marvin S. Hill. *Carthage Conspiracy: The Trial of the Accused Assassins of Joseph Smith*. Urbana: University of Illinois Press, 1975.

O'Dea, Thomas F. *The Mormons*. Chicago: University of Chicago Press, 1978.

Park, Benjamin. *The Kingdom of Nauvoo: A Story of Mormon Politics, Plural Marriage, and Power in Nineteenth-Century America*. W. W. Norton/Liveright, forthcoming.

Prince, Gregory A. *Power from on High: The Development of Mormon Priesthood*. Salt Lake City: Signature Books, 1995.

Quaife, Milo Milton. *The Kingdom of Saint James: A Narrative of the Mormons.* Whitefish, MT: Kessinger Publishing, 2004.

Quinn, D. Michael. *The Mormon Hierarchy: Origins of Power.* Midvale, UT: Signature Books, 1994.

———. *The Mormon Hierarchy: Extensions of Power.* Midvale, UT: Signature Books, 1997.

Remini, Robert V. *Joseph Smith.* New York: Viking, 2002.

Roberts, B. H. *A Comprehensive History of the Church of Jesus Christ of Latter-day Saints.* 6 vols. Provo, UT: Brigham Young University Press, 1965.

———. *The Missouri Persecutions.* Salt Lake City: Bookcraft, 1965.

———. *The Rise and Fall of Nauvoo.* Salt Lake City: Deseret News, 1900.

Rogers, Brent. *Unpopular Sovereignty: Mormons and the Federal Management of Early Utah Territory.* Lincoln: University of Nebraska Press, 2017.

Rogers, Jedediah S. *The Council of Fifty: A Documentary History.* Midvale, UT: Signature Books, 2014.

Rust, Val. *Radical Origins: Early Mormon Converts and Their Colonial Ancestors.* Urbana: University of Illinois Press, 2004.

Saffell, David, and Richard Remy. *The Encyclopedia of U.S. Presidential Elections.* New York: Franklin Watts, 2004.

Schlesinger, Arthur, and Fred L. Israel. *History of Presidential Elections, 1789–1968.* New York: Chelsea House, 1971.

Scott, Thomas. *The Pursuit of the White House: A Handbook of Presidential Election Statistics and History.* New York: Greenwood Press, 1987.

Shade, William, Ballard C. Campbell, and Craig R. Coenen. *American Presidential Campaigns and Elections.* Armonk, NY: Sharpe Reference, 2003.

Shafer, Ronald G. *The Carnival Campaign: How the Rollicking 1840 Campaign of "Tippecanoe and Tyler Too" Changed Presidential Elections Forever.* Chicago: Review Press, 2016.

Smith, Heman. *History of the Reorganized Church of Jesus Christ of Latter Day Saints.* Vols. 1–4. Independence, MO: Church Press, 1969.

Smith, Joseph. Joseph Smith, History, 1838–1856. Volume A-1 (23 December 1805–30 August 1834). The Joseph Smith Papers. https://www.josephsmithpapers.org/paper-summary/history-1838-1856-volume-a-1-23-december-1805-30-august-1834/1.

———. *History of the Church of Jesus Christ of Latter-day Saints.* Edited by B. H. Roberts. 7 vols. Salt Lake City: Deseret News, 1902.

Smith, Joseph F. *Gospel Doctrine: Sermons and Writings of President Joseph F. Smith.* Salt Lake City: Deseret Book, 1986.

Smith, Joseph Fielding. *Blood Atonement and the Origin of Plural Marriage.* Independence, MO: Press of Zion's Printing and Publishing Co., 1905.

Snow, Eliza Roxey. *Biography and Family Record of Lorenzo Snow.* Salt Lake City: Deseret News, Printers, 1884.

Southwick, Leslie. *Presidential Also-rans and Running Mates, 1788–1996.* Jefferson, NC: McFarland, 1998.

Speek, Vickie Cleverley. *"God Has Made Us a Kingdom": James Strang and the Midwest Mormons.* Salt Lake City: Signature Books, 2006.

Stringham, Ida Watt. *England's First "Mormon" Convert: The Biography of George Darling Watt.* Salt Lake City: David J. Ellison, 1958.

Talbot, Wilburn D. *Acts of the Modern Apostles.* Springville, UT: Cedar Fort, 1985.

Tanner, Rev. George C. *William Tanner, Sr. of South Kingstown, Rhode Island and His Descendants in Four Parts.* Faribault, MN: printed by the author, 1910.

Tanner, George S. *John Tanner and His Family: A History-Biography of John Tanner of Lake George, New York.* Salt Lake City: John Tanner Family Association, 1974. CHL.

Taylor, Mark H., comp. and ed. *Witness to the Martyrdom: John Taylor's Personal Account of the Last Days of the Prophet Joseph Smith.* Salt Lake City: Deseret Book, 1999.

Tuttle, Hudson, and James Martin Peebles. *The Year-Book of Spiritualism for 1871.* Boston: William White, 1871.

Underwood, Grant. *The Millenarian World of Early Mormonism.* Urbana: University of Illinois Press, 1993.

Unruh, John D., Jr. *The Plains Across: The Overland Emigrants and the Trans-Mississippi West, 1840–60*. Urbana: University of Illinois Press, 1993.

Van Noord, Roger. *Assassination of a Michigan King: The Life of James Jesse Strang*. Ann Arbor: University of Michigan Press, 1997.

Van Wagoner, Richard S. *Mormon Polygamy: A History*. Midvale, UT: Signature Books, 1989.

———. *Sidney Rigdon: A Portrait of Religious Excess*. Midvale, UT: Signature Books, 1994.

Walker, Ronald, Richard E. Turley Jr., and Glen M. Leonard. *Massacre at Mountain Meadows*. New York: Oxford University Press, 2008.

Warrum, Noble, ed. *Utah Since Statehood*. 4 vols. Salt Lake City: S. J. Clarke, 1919.

Watson, Harry L. *Liberty and Power: The Politics of Jacksonian America*. New York: Hill and Wang, 1990.

Whitney, Orson F. *History of Utah*. 4 vols. Salt Lake City: George Q. Cannon and Sons, 1892.

Wicks, Robert S., and Fred R. Foister. *Junius and Joseph: Presidential Politics and the Assassination of the First Mormon Prophet*. Logan: Utah State University Publications, 2005.

Writers' Program of the Work Projects Administration in the State of Michigan, comp. *Michigan: A Guide to the Wolverine State*. New York: Oxford University Press, 1941.

Young, Joseph. *History of the Organization of the Seventies*. Salt Lake City: Deseret News, 1878.

ARTICLES, ACADEMIC PAPERS, AND CHAPTERS

Allen, Bruce. "Academy Tennessee Branch." *Amateur Mormon Historian* (blog), 27 April 2015. http://amateurmormonhistorian.blogspot.com/2015/04/academy-tennessee-branch.html.

Allen, James B. "Ecclesiastical Influence on Local Government in the Territory of Utah." *Arizona and the West* 8, no. 1 (Spring 1966): 35–48.

Anderson, Margo J., ed. *Encyclopedia of the US Census.* Washington, DC: Congressional Quarterly Press, 2000.

Arrington, Leonard J. "The John Tanner Family." *Ensign*, March 1979.

Backman, Milton V., Jr. "Establish a House of Prayer, a House of God: The Kirtland Temple." In *The Prophet Joseph: Essays on the Life and Mission of Joseph Smith*, edited by Larry C. Porter and Susan Easton Black, 208–25. Salt Lake City: Deseret Book, 1988.

Bates, Irene M. "William Smith, 1811–93: Problematic Patriarch." *Dialogue: A Journal of Mormon Thought* 16, no. 2 (Summer 1983): 11–23.

Beecher, Dale F. "Colonizer of the West." In *Lion of the Lord: Essays on the Life and Service of Brigham Young*, edited by Susan Easton Black and Larry C. Porter. Salt Lake City: Deseret Book, 1995.

Bennett, Richard. "'Has the Lord Turned Bankrupt?' The Attempted Sale of the Nauvoo Temple, 1846–1850." *Journal of the Illinois State Historical Society* 95, no. 3 (Autumn 2002): 235–63. https://www.jstor.org/stable/40193435.

Bergera, Gary James. "Identifying the Earliest Mormon Polygamists, 1841–44." *Dialogue: A Journal of Mormon Thought* 38, no. 3 (Fall 2005): 1–74.

Bitton, Davis. "Mormons in Texas: The Ill-Fated Lyman Wight Colony, 1844–1858." *Arizona and the West* 11, no. 1 (Spring 1969): 5–26.

———. "A Re-evaluation of the 'Turner Thesis and Mormon Beginnings . . .'" *Utah Historical Quarterly* 34, no. 4 (Fall 1996): 326–33.

Black, Susan Easton. "How Large Was the Population of Nauvoo?" *BYU Studies* 35, no. 2 (Spring 1995): 91–94.

———. "The Pivotal Role of John Taylor in the Political Campaign of Joseph Smith." In *Champion of Liberty: John Taylor*, edited by Mary Jane Woodger, 21–44. Provo, UT: Religious Studies Center, Brigham Young University, 2009.

Bringhurst, Newell G. "Charles B. Thompson and the Issues of Slavery and Race." *Journal of Mormon History* 8 (1981): 37–47. https://www.jstor.org/stable/23285871.

———. "Elijah Abel and the Changing Status of Blacks within Mormonism." In *Neither White nor Black: Mormon Scholars Confront the Race Issue in a*

Universal Church, edited by Lester E. Bush Jr. and Armand L. Mauss, 131–49. Midvale, UT: Signature Books, 1984.

Buerger, David John. "'The Fulness of the Priesthood': The Second Anointing in Latter-day Saint Theology and Practice." *Dialogue: A Journal of Mormon Thought* 16, no. 1 (Spring 1983): 10–44.

Campbell, Eugene Edward. "The Mormon Gold Mining Mission of 1849." *BYU Studies* 1, no. 2, and 2, no. 1 (Autumn 1959–Winter 1960): 19–31. https://www .jstor.org/stable/43041704.

Carol, Mary. "Weakley County's Connection to the Ill-Fated Donner Party of 1846–47: Murphy Family of Weakley County–Part of Donner Party." http:// sites.rootsweb.com/~tnweakle/MurphySarah.htm.

Christensen, Craig H. "The Separation of Ecclesiastical and Civil Court Jurisdiction in Early LDS Church History" (typescript). Paper for Comparative Church and State Seminar. J. Reuben Clark Law School, Brigham Young University, 1985.

Christy, Howard A. "Weather, Disaster, and Responsibility: An Essay on the Willie and Martin Handcart Story." *BYU Studies* 37, no. 1 (1997): 6–74.

Cook, Lyndon W. "William Law, Nauvoo Dissenter." *BYU Studies* 22, no. 1 (1982): 47–72.

Crawley, Peter L., and Richard L. Anderson. "The Political and Social Realities of Zion's Camp." *BYU Studies* 14, no. 4 (Summer 1974): 406–20.

Daynes, Kathryn. "Mormon Polygamy: Belief and Practice in Nauvoo." In *Kingdom on the Mississippi Revisited: Nauvoo in Mormon History*, edited by Roger D. Launius and John E. Hallwas, 130–46. Urbana: University of Illinois Press, 1996.

Dennis, Ronald D. "Dan Jones, Welshman: Taking the Gospel Home." *Ensign*, April 1987.

Derr, Jill Mulvay. "The Lion and the Lioness: Brigham Young and Eliza R. Snow." *BYU Studies* 40, no. 2 (2001): 54–101.

Dredge, C. Paul. "Dispute Settlement in the Mormon Community: The Operation of Ecclesiastical Courts in Utah." In *Access to Justice, Volume IV: The Anthropological Perspective*, edited by Klaus-Friedrich Koch, 193–214. Milan, Italy: Sijthoff and Noordhoff, 1979.

"Early Black Mormons." *Mormon Heretic* (blog). Published 9 March 2009. https://mormonheretic.org/2009/03/09/early-black-mormons/.

Ehat, Andrew F. "'It Seems Like Heaven Began on Earth': Joseph Smith and the Constitution of the Kingdom of God." *BYU Studies* 20, no. 3 (Spring 1980): 253–79.

Esplin, Ronald K. "'A Place Prepared': Joseph, Brigham, and the Quest for Promised Refuge in the West." In *Window of Faith: Latter-day Saint Perspectives on World History*, edited by Roy A. Prete, 71–97. Provo, UT: Religious Studies Center, Brigham Young University, 2005.

———. *The "Council of Fifty" in History and Theology—An Inquiry into the Role of the Government of God in the Last Days*. Americana Collection. BYUSC.

———. "The Significance of Nauvoo for Latter-day Saints." In *Kingdom on the Mississippi Revisited: Nauvoo in Mormon History*, edited by Roger D. Launius and John E. Hallwas, 19–38. Urbana: University of Illinois Press, 1996.

Flanders, Robert Bruce. "The Kingdom of God in Illinois: Politics in Utopia." In *Kingdom on the Mississippi Revisited: Nauvoo in Mormon History*, edited by Roger D. Launius and John E. Hallwas, 147–159. Urbana: University of Illinois Press, 1996.

Faulring, Scott. "The Return of Oliver Cowdery." In *The Disciple as Witness: Essays on Latter-day Saint History and Doctrine in Honor of Richard Lloyd Anderson*, edited by Stephen D. Ricks, Donald W. Parry, and Andrew H. Hedges, 117–73. Provo, UT: FARMS, 2000.

Gaunt, LaRene Porter. "Edward Hunter: Generous Pioneer, Presiding Bishop." *Ensign*, July 2004.

Gentry, Jeffrey S. "Joseph Smith—Religious Prophet and Secular Politician." BYU Student Paper, 1994. Americana Collection. BYUSC.

Gentry, Leland Homer. "The Danite Band of 1838." *BYU Studies* 14, no. 4 (Summer 1974): 421–50.

Godfrey, Kenneth. "Crime and Punishment in Mormon Nauvoo, 1839–1846." *BYU Studies* 32, no. 1 (1992): 195–228.

———. "Joseph Smith and the Masons." *Journal of the Illinois Historical Society* 64, no. 1 (Spring 1971): 79–90.

Hampshire, Annette P. "Nauvoo Politics." *Encyclopedia of Mormonism*. New York: Macmillan, 1992.

Harper, Howard K., Steven C. Harper, and David P. Harper. "Van Wagoner's *Sidney Rigdon: A Portrait of Biographical Excess*." *FARMS Review of Books* 14, no. 1 (2002): 261–74.

Hartley, William G. "From Men to Boys: LDS Aaronic Priesthood Offices, 1829–1996." *Journal of Mormon History* 22, no. 1 (Spring 1996): 81–136.

———. "Missouri's 1838 Extermination Order and the Mormons' Forced Removal to Illinois." *Mormon Historical Studies* 2, no. 1 (Spring 2001): 5–27.

IAGenWeb Project. "Boyer Township: 1868 History of Harrison County." http://iagenweb.org/harrison/twp/twpboyer.htm.

Ingals, Ephraim. "Autobiography of Dr. Ephraim Ingals." *Journal of the Illinois State Historical Society* 28 (1936): 279–308.

"An Introduction to the Mormon Participation in the Civil War." *Juvenile Instructor* (blog), 17 March 2009. https://juvenileinstructor.org/an-introduction-to-the-mormon-particpation-in-the-civil-war/.

Jack, Ronald Collett. *Utah Territorial Politics: 1847–1876*. Salt Lake City: Department of Political Science, University of Utah, 1970.

Johnson, Janiece L. "'The Scriptures Is a Fulfilling': Sally Parker's Weave." *BYU Studies* 44, no. 2 (2005): 111–22. https://scholarsarchive.byu.edu/byusq/vol44/iss2/9.

"Jonathan Browning, Mormon Gunsmith." Muzzle Blasts Online. Published August/September 1997. https://www.muzzleblasts.com/archives/vol2no4/articles/mbo24-2.shtml.

Kimball, James L., Jr. "The Nauvoo Charter: A Reinterpretation." *Journal of the Illinois State Historical Society* 54 (Spring 1971): 66–78.

Lyman, E. Leo. "Larger than Texas: Proposals to Combine California and Mormon Deseret as One State." *California History* 80, no. 1 (Spring 2001): 18–33.

Mason, Patrick Q. "God and the People: Theodemocracy in Nineteenth-Century Mormonism." *Journal of Church and State* 53, no. 3 (Summer 2011): 349–75. https://doi.org/10.1093/jcs/csq135.

Matthews, Robert J. "The Restoration of All Things: What the Doctrine and Covenants Says." In *The Heavens Are Open: The 1992 Sperry Symposium on the Doctrine and Covenants and Church History*, compiled by Byron R. Merrill, 68–91. Salt Lake City: Deseret Book, 1993.

Mayo, Martha, and Connell O'Donovan. "Members and Missionaries of the Lowell, Massachusetts Branch of The Church of Jesus Christ of Latter-day Saints, 1835–1860." https://history.churchofjesuschrist.org/overlandtravel/sources/30072/mayo-martha-and-o-donovan-connell-members-and-missionaries-of-the-lowell-massachusetts-branch-of-the-church-of-jesus-christ-of-latter-day-saints-1835-1860.

McBride, Spencer W. "The Council of Fifty and Joseph Smith's Presidential Ambitions." In *The Council of Fifty: What the Records Reveal about Mormon History*, edited by Matthew J. Grow and R. Eric Smith, 21–30. Provo, UT: Religious Studies Center, Brigham Young University, 2017.

Oaks, Dallin H., and Joseph I. Bentley. "Joseph Smith and Legal Process: In the Wake of the Steamboat *Nauvoo*." *BYU Studies* 19, no. 2 (Winter 1979): 167–99. https://www.jstor.org/stable/43040808.

O'Donovan, Connell. "'I Would Confine Them to Their Own Species': LDS Historical Rhetoric and Praxis Regarding Marriage between Whites and Blacks." Published 28 March 2009. http://www.connellodonovan.com/black_white_marriage.html.

———. "'Let This Be a Warning to All Niggers': The Life and Murder of Thomas Coleman in Theocratic Utah." Unpublished paper, last modified June 2008. Microsoft Word file. Copy in author's possession.

Parkin, Max H. "Joseph Smith and the United Firm: The Growth and Decline of the Church's First Master Plan of Business and Finance, Ohio and Missouri, 1832–34." *BYU Studies* 46, no. 3 (2007): 5–66. https://scholarsarchive.byu.edu/byusq/vol46/iss3/1.

Peterson, Paul H. "The Mormon Reformation of 1856–1857: The Rhetoric and the Reality." *Journal of Mormon History* 15 (1989): 59–87.

Petty, James W. "A Walk Down Parley Street." *Ensign*, August 2003.

Platt, Lyman D., comp. "Early Branches of The Church of Jesus Christ of Latter-day Saints, 1830–1850." Mormon Historic Sites Foundation, 1991. http://mormon historicsites.org/wp-content/uploads/2013/05/NJ3_Platt.pdf.

Poll, Richard. "Joseph Smith's Presidential Platform." *Dialogue: A Journal of Mormon Thought* 3, no. 3 (Autumn 1968): 17–36.

Porter, Larry C. "The Restoration of the Aaronic and Melchizedek Priesthoods." *Ensign*, December 1996.

Quinn, D. Michael. "The Council of Fifty and Its Members, 1844–1945." *BYU Studies* 20, no. 2 (Winter 1980): 163–97.

———. "Joseph Smith's Experience of a Methodist 'Camp-Meeting' in 1820." *Dialogue: A Journal of Mormon Thought*. Dialogue e-paper no. 3, 12 July 2006. Copy in author's possession.

———. "The Mormon Succession Crisis of 1844." *BYU Studies* 16, no. 2 (Winter 1976): 187–233.

Reeve, W. Paul. *Religion of a Different Color: Race and the Mormon Struggle for Whiteness*. New York: Oxford University Press, 2015.

Ridge, Martin. "Mormon 'Deliverance' and the Closing of the Frontier." In *The American West: The Reader*, edited by Walter Nugent and Martin Ridge. Indianapolis: Indiana University Press, 1999.

Riggs, Michael S. "'His Word Was as Good as His Note': The Impact of Justus Morse's Mormonism(s) on His Families." *John Whitmer Historical Association Journal* 17 (1997): 49–80.

Robertson, Margaret C. "The Campaign and the Kingdom: The Activities of the Electioneers in Joseph Smith's Presidential Campaign." *BYU Studies* 39, no. 3 (2000): 147–80.

"Salt Lake's Original Nineteen LDS Wards." *An Enduring Legacy* (online database hosted by Ancestry.com).

Shumway, Craig Leland. "Social Variables of Ecclesiastical Leadership." Master's thesis, Department of Sociology, Marriott Library, University of Utah, 1972.

Smith, George D. "Nauvoo Roots of Mormon Polygamy, 1841–46: A Preliminary Demographic Report." *Dialogue: A Journal of Mormon Thought* 34, no. 1/2 (Spring/Summer 2001): 123–58.

Smith, Joseph. "Letterbook 2" (1839–ca. summer 1843). The Joseph Smith Papers. https://www.josephsmithpapers.org/paper-summary/letterbook-2/1.

Stake, Mark L., and LaJean P. Carruth. "John Taylor's June 27, 1854, Account of the Martyrdom." *BYU Studies* 50, no. 3 (2011): 47–49.

Thompson, Margaret C., ed. *Presidential Elections since 1789*. Washington, DC: Congressional Quarterly, 1987.

"The Trail Ran East from Council Bluffs: Mormons Who Made It So Far, Then Left for Wisconsin and Michigan." Paper prepared for the annual meeting of the Mormon History Association, Omaha, NE, 23 May 1997. http://www.strangite.org/Bluffs.htm.

Van Orden, Bruce. "William W. Phelps's Service in Nauvoo as Joseph Smith's Political Clerk." *BYU Studies* 32, nos. 1 and 2 (1992): 81–94. https://scholarsarchive.byu.edu/byusq/vol32/iss1/9.

Wahlquist, Wayne L. "Population Growth in the Mormon Core Area: 1847–90." In *The Mormon Role in the Settlement of the West*, edited by Richard H. Jackson, 107–34. Provo, UT: Brigham Young University Press, 1978.

Walker, Jeffrey N. "Mormon Land Rights in Caldwell and Daviess Counties and the Mormon Conflict of 1838: New Findings and New Understandings." *BYU Studies* 47, no. 1 (2008): 4–55. https://scholarsarchive.byu.edu/byusq/vol47/iss1/1.

Walker, Ronald W. "'A Banner Is Unfurled': Mormonism's Ensign Peak." *Dialogue: A Journal of Mormon Thought* 26, no. 4 (1993): 71–91.

Ward, Maurine Carr. "A Partial List of Church Members Living in Nauvoo." *The Nauvoo Journal* 4 (1992): 15–69.

Watson, Elden J. "The Nauvoo Tabernacle." *BYU Studies* 19, no. 3 (Spring 1979): 416–21.

Watt, Ronald G. "Sailing 'The Old Ship Zion': The Life of George D. Watt." *BYU Studies* 18, no. 1 (Fall 1977): 48–65.

Whitsitt, William H. "Sidney Rigdon: The Real Founder of Mormonism." Unpublished manuscript. Library of Congress. http://sidneyrigdon.com/wht/1891WhtB.htm.

Whittaker, David J. "East of Nauvoo: Benjamin Winchester and the Early Mormon Church." *Journal of Mormon History* 21, no. 2 (Fall 1995): 31–83. https://digital commons.usu.edu/mormonhistory/vol21/iss2/1.

Widtsoe, John Andreas. "Questions Concerning Priesthood, 1941." CHL.

Winkler, Phillip. "A Mormon in Tennessee: Presenting the Life of Colonel Solomon Copeland." Presentation at Dyersburg State Community College, Dyersburg, TN, n.d.

DISSERTATIONS AND THESES

Andrus, Hyrum L. "World Government as Envisioned in the Latter-day Saint 'City of Zion.'" Master's thesis, Brigham Young University, 1952.

Bailey, Raymond T. "Emma Hale: Wife of the Prophet Joseph Smith." Master's thesis, Brigham Young University, 1952.

Baumgarten, James N. "The Role and Function of the Seventies in LDS Church History." Master's thesis, Brigham Young University, 1960.

Clegg, Dennis A. "Levi Ward Hancock, Pioneer, Soldier, Political and Religious Leader of Early Utah." Master's thesis, Brigham Young University, 1966.

Colvin, Don F. "A Historical Study of the Mormon Temple at Nauvoo, Illinois." Master's thesis, Brigham Young University, 1962.

Drake, J. Raman. "Howard Egan, Frontiersman, Pioneer and Pony Express Rider." Master's thesis, Brigham Young University, 1956.

Eddy, Majorie E. "The Precepts of Zion and Joseph Smith's City of Zion Plan: Major Influences for the Planning of Nauvoo." Master's thesis, Brigham Young University, 1999.

Ehat, Andrew F. "Joseph Smith's Introduction of Temple Ordinances and the 1844 Mormon Succession Question." Master's thesis, Brigham Young University, 1982.

Gentry, Leland Homer. "A History of the Latter-day Saints in Northern Missouri from 1836–1839." PhD diss., Brigham Young University, 1965.

Hansen, Klaus. "The Theory and Practice of the Political Kingdom of God in Mormon History, 1829–1890." Master's thesis, Brigham Young University, 1959.

Hawkes, John Douglas. "A History of The Church of Jesus Christ of Latter-day Saints in Australia to 1900." Master's thesis, Brigham Young University, 1965.

Jack, Ronald Collett. "Political Participation in Utah before the Formation of Political Parties, 1847–1869." Master's thesis, University of Utah, 1967.

Jensen, Robin Scott. "Gleaning the Harvest: Strangite Missionary Work, 1846–1850." Master's thesis, Brigham Young University, 2005.

Jensen, Therald N. "Mormon Theory of Church and State." PhD diss., University of Chicago, 1938.

Kilts, Clair T. "A History of the Federal and Territorial Court Conflicts in Utah, 1851–1874." Master's thesis, Brigham Young University, 1959.

Lawson, John. "A Study of the History of the Office of High Priest." Master's thesis, Brigham Young University, 2006.

Marrot, Robert L. "History and Functions of the Aaronic Priesthood and the Offices of Priest, Teacher, and Deacon in the Church of Jesus Christ of Latter-day Saints, 1829 to 1844." Master's thesis, Brigham Young University, 1976.

Olsen, Steven L. "The Mormon Ideology of Place: Cosmic Symbolism of the City of Zion, 1830–1846." PhD diss., University of Chicago, 1985.

Page, Albert R. "Orson Hyde and the Carson Valley Mission." Master's thesis, Brigham Young University, 1970.

Peterson, John A. "Warren Stone Snow, a Man in between: The Biography of a Mormon Defender." Master's thesis, Brigham Young University, 1985.

Quinn, D. Michael. "Organizational Development and Social Origins of the Mormon Hierarchy, 1832–1932: A Prosopographical Study." Master's thesis, University of Utah, 1973.

Shipps, Jan. "The Mormons in Politics: The First Hundred Years." PhD diss., University of Colorado, 1965.

Shumway, Craig Leland. "Social Variables of Ecclesiastical Leadership." Thesis, University of Utah, 1972.

Travis, Marilyn Reed. "Social Stratification and the Dissolution of the City of Zion in Salt Lake City." PhD diss., University of Utah, 1994.

Warner, Edward Allen. "Mormon Theodemocracy: Theocratic and Democratic Elements in Early Latter-day Saint History, 1827–1846." PhD diss., University of Iowa, 1973.

INDEX

The letter *t* following a page number denotes a table.

Fillmore, Millard, 217
First Presidency, 7
flag of Deseret, 201–7, 224n16
Flanigan, James H., 59, 61–62, 115,
    160, 218
Fleming, Joseph, 236
Fleming, Josiah W., 234
Folsom, Abby, 137
Ford, Thomas, 21, 148, 149, 150–51,
    166n8
Foster, Charles, 146
Foster, Lucian R., 102, 182
Foster, Robert D., 91–93, 100, 146
frontier, American, 291–93, 296–97. *See
    also* Deseret; exodus
Fuller, Hannah, 172
Fuller, Thomas E., 172
Fullmer, David, 40, 61, 118, 122–23,
    160, 212, 243
Fullmer, John S., 69, 149, 151
"fullness of the priesthood," 22–23

G

Gardner, Daniel, 246
Gates, Jacob, 64, 65
gathering of Saints, 4–5, 16–17, 27n60, 88
*General Joseph Smith's Views of the
    Powers and Policies of the Gov-
    ernment of the United States*, 31,
    36–39, 40–41, 53n21, 82, 120,
    121, 125–26
Glines, James H., 62, 74, 117, 128, 297n8
God, government of, 17–21
Goforth, William G., 67, 81, 100–103
Gold Rush, 193
Goodyear, Miles, 208
government of God, 17–21
Grant, Jedediah M., 69, 74, 155, 202–3,
    227, 231–32, 241–43
Great Basin Kingdom. *See* Deseret
Great Flood, 139n10

Green, Harvey, 122–23
Greene, John P., 34, 98
Greig, James, 59, 179
Grierson, John W., 180, 267
Groves, Elisha, 226n51, 258
Guinard, Julius, 67
Gurley, Zenos H., 179, 243–44

H

Haight, Isaac, 263, 264
Hale, Johnathan H., 190
Hallet, Clark, 190
Hamblin, Jacob, 63, 133, 160–61, 175,
    265–66, 278n23
Hampton, Jonathan, 77
Hancock, Levi W., 74, 154, 192
Hancock, Mosiah, 154
Hanks, Sidney A., 234
Harding, Dwight, 133
Harding, Ralph, 133
Harris, Martin, 181
Harrison, William Henry, 16, 27n55,
    80, 81
Hatch, Jeremiah (nephew), 196n6
Hatch, Jeremiah (uncle), 172, 196n6
Hatch, Lorenzo H., 133, 172–73
Hawn's Mill massacre, 14, 77
healings, 69
Heath, Samuel, 183
Hedrickite movement, 245
Herriman, Henry, 74
Heywood, Jonathan L., 33, 78, 79
Hickerson, George W., 193, 232–33
Hickey, Lorenzo D., 182
Higbee, Chauncey L., 100, 146
Higbee, Francis M., 100, 146
Higginbotham, Louisa, 267–68
Higginbotham, Simon, 268
Higginbotham, William E., 267–68
"High on the Mountain Top," 201, 205
"History of Joseph Smith," xii–xiii

Hodges, Amos, 189
Hoge, Joseph, 21–22
Holbrook, Joseph, 118, 125, 189, 193, 242
Hollister, David S., 61, 96, 129, 135, 138, 181
Holmes, Milton, 62, 126
Holt, James, 116–17, 158–60
home missionary program, 241–43
Horner, John, 138–39, 194, 233–34
Hubbard, Charles W., 269–70
Hunt, Daniel D., 117
Hunt, Jefferson, 192, 193, 237–38, 258
Hunter, Edward
    on assassination of Joseph and Hyrum Smith, 153–54
    background of, 67
    as Council of Fifty member, 283
    devotion of, to Joseph Smith, 70
    experience of, as electioneer missionary, 128–29
    lives law of consecration, 73
    political involvement of, 78
    and Salt Lake Temple construction, 232
Hyde, Orson, 46, 62, 99–100, 104, 130
Hyde, William, 117, 163, 172–73, 175, 191

I

Illinois. *See also* Nauvoo, Illinois
    electioneer missionaries in, 120
    occupational distribution in Jacksonville, 75–76
    Saints driven from, 164
Illinois State Convention, 101–3
Ingals, Ephraim, 101
Iowa, evacuation of Saints from western, 231
Iron Mission, 237, 239, 258

J

Jackman, Levi, 12, 63, 117, 134
Jacksonville, Illinois, occupational distribution in, 75–76
Jacob, Norton
    called as electioneer missionary, 61, 63
    on exodus, 194
    experience of, as electioneer missionary, 122–23
    plural marriage practiced by, 271
    reaction to assassination of Joseph and Hyrum, 155
    receives temple ordinances, 187
    and Strang's bid for church leadership, 181
    on US government, 207
Jeffersonian Democracy, 97, 102–3, 138
Johnson, Aaron, 258
Johnson, Joel H., 67, 161, 201, 205
Johnson, Richard M., 33
Johnstun, Jesse, 75, 77
Jonas, Abraham, 146
Jones, Dan, 73, 149, 150, 233
Jones, John, Jr., 160, 189
Jones, John, Sr., 189
Jones, Nathaniel V., 234
Judah, David, 245

K

Kanab, 273
Kane, Thomas L., 191, 210, 261, 262–63
Kelting, Joseph A., 236
Keyser, Guy M., 117, 193
Killmer, Jonas (Jonah), 85n30
Kimball, Heber C., 2, 51, 60, 62, 63–64, 143
King, Thomas, 59
kingdom of God
    establishment of, 45–46
    political, 17–21

introduces temple ceremonies, 18–19
as nation's best hope, 89–93
and Nauvoo government, 16
nominates political candidates, 19–20
opposition to, 21, 100, 133–34
and organization of The Church of Jesus Christ of Latter-day Saints, 3
on presidential candidacy, 42–43
presidential nomination of, 31–32
and priesthood restoration, 7
prophesies concerning Andrew
Lamoreaux, 233
prophesies concerning exodus, 171
speaks at April 1844 conference,
48–49
and standard of freedom, 202
successor of, 173, 175–84
vision for theodemocracy, xiv,
17–21, 97
visited by influential politicians,
100–101
Smith, Joseph, III, 244–45
Smith, Joseph F., 304
Smith, Moses, 61, 122–23, 155, 180, 181
Smith, William
creates Society for the Diffusion of
Truth, 105–6
departure of, 109
endowment of, 98
experience of, as electioneer missionary, 130–31
instructs electioneer missionaries, 97
as Joseph's successor, 177, 182–83
as newspaper editor, 93
Smoot, Abraham O.
and assassination of Joseph and
Hyrum Smith, 156, 171–72
career arc of, 299–302, 305
as Council of Fifty member, 283
and emigration of Saints, 236

experience of, as electioneer missionary, 125–26
leadership positions of, 301
persecution experienced by, 135–36
and Utah War, 261
wealth of, 301–2
Smoot, Reed, xii–xiii, 299, 302–4
Snow, Eliza, 5–6, 77, 91
Snow, Erastus
called as apostle, 211–12
and colonizing missions, 239
and emigration of Saints, 237
enters Great Salt Lake Valley, 194
experience of, as electioneer missionary, 62, 127
on Joseph's appointment as king, 90
missionary efforts of, 218
previous missions of, 66
and standard of freedom, 202
Snow, James C., 64, 74
Snow, Lorenzo
called as apostle, 211–12
departure of, 114
experience of, as electioneer missionary, 5–6, 121–22
missionary efforts of, 218, 219, 234
as personification of electioneer
cadre, 290–97
as presiding authority at Winter
Quarters, 190
reaction to assassination of Joseph
and Hyrum, 164
and Reed Smoot's Senate election, 304
vision of, 69
Snow, Willard, 212, 235, 236
Snyder, George G., 193
Snyder, Jane, 269
Society for the Diffusion of Truth, 105
Society Islands, 234
South, electioneer missionaries in,
124–26, 300

Young, Brigham (*continued*)
 and calling of electioneer missionaries, 50–51, 57, 62
 and Civil War, 266
 and colonizing missions, 237, 239, 273
 and Deseret flag, 201–2
 establishes emigration parties, 193–94
 and evacuation of Saints from western Iowa, 231–32
 and excommunication of Strangite
  missionaries, 180
 and expulsion from Nauvoo, 187–89
 and gathering of Saints to Deseret, 231
 on government, 259
 as governor of Deseret, 217
 as Joseph's successor, 173, 175–77, 205
 leads Saints in Salt Lake Valley,
  195–96
 and Mormon Battalion, 191, 192
 and Mormon Reformation, 241–43
 on need for constitution, 90–91
 on optimism in Nauvoo, 105, 113
 and Pioneer Day celebrations, 204
 and plans for Joseph's presidency, 38
 rebukes Franklin D. Richards and
  Daniel Spencer, 228–29

 reconstitutes Council of Fifty, 283
 and statehood for Deseret, 210
 and Utah War, 260, 261, 263
 vision of, for Deseret, 220
Young, John, 232
Young, Joseph, 77, 134–35
Young, Phineas H., 40, 242–43

Z

Zion. *See also* Deseret
 America as, 49
 economic, 9–10
 electioneer missionaries and building of, 176–77
 Latter-day Saint doctrine concerning, 4–5
 Nauvoo as, 15–17
 in Ohio and Missouri, 5–12
 political, 10–12, 17–21
 religious, 7–9
 social, 9
Zion's Boards of Trade, 283–84
Zion's Camp, 11, 246–47
Zion's Cooperative Mercantile Institu-
 tions (ZCMI), 283